Dear Tom -

Merry Christmas and a happy 1999 - you are a dear friend -

My love -

Nita

John M. Harbert III

Marching to the Beat of a Different Drummer

Portrait by Everett Raymond Kinstler

JOHN M. HARBERT III

Marching to the Beat of a Different Drummer

LEAH RAWLS ATKINS

Tarva House
Birmingham
1999

Printed in the United States of America

Design and production by Bob and Faith Nance

Library of Congress Cataloging-in-Publication Data

Atkins, Leah Rawls.
John M. Harbert III : marching to the beat of a different drummer / Leah Rawls Atkins.
p. cm.
Includes bibliographical references and index.
ISBN 0-9666546-0-9 (hc.)
1. Harbert, John M. 2. Harbert Corporation—History. 3. Businessmen—United States—Biography. 4. Construction industry—United States—History. I. Title.
HD9715.U52H333 1999
338.7'624'092—dc21
[B] 98-40007
CIP

To Wita Harbert,
who lived this life with John
and without whose commitment
this book could never have been written,

and to John and Wita's children,
Jay, Raymond, and Margie,
and their grandchildren
who have such a goodly heritage,

and to all those men and women
who are or once were part of the
extended family
of
The Harbert Corporation

*"Problems create opportunities.
Winners solve problems."*

March 7, 1995

CONTENTS

Portrait by William Draper

PREFACE

Marguerite Jones Harbert, called Wita since childhood, is the person responsible for having John Harbert's biography researched and written. Married to John for almost forty-four years and bereaved by John's sudden death on March 31, 1995, following a severe attack of pancreatitis, she spent much time thinking about their life together. As the months went by, Wita gained new perspectives and became more and more aware of John's unusual gifts and the truly remarkable life they shared. For years she had kept diaries, scrapbooks of photographs, correspondence, and journals during their travels. She knew that the Harbert Corporation had an extensive archive, in-house publications, numerous clipping files and scrapbooks, and an unpublished history of the corporation written by Charlotte Gafford in the late 1980s. John had given dozens of speeches and printed many of them. She recognized that one day John Harbert would be the subject of a biography, and she became determined to see that one would be written during her lifetime. Wita had no interest in re-creating a mythical John but wanted a true portrait of this man she felt was so extraordinary.

Wita spent hours in long conversations with me about John and their life together. These visits stretched over almost two years. She answered hundreds of my questions and when she did not know the answer, she suggested someone who would. She gave me lists of people to consult, allowed me to read her journals, provided photographs and clippings, explained things, and listened to me read paragraphs soon after they were written to make sure the material was accurate. When I struggled with interpretations, she talked the issues through with me, and when I was seeking just the right word to express something, she helped me find it. She entertained me in Highlands, North Carolina, at Pinebloom, and in Birmingham. Being familiar with the places John loved most was helpful to me in writing about his life. I am grateful for her hospitality.

Wita is a strong and determined woman in her own right. Her oldest child suffered developmental problems, and in a time when medicine gave scant attention and society offered little or no support to parents with such dilemmas, she worked alone with determination to see that he would have the best life possible and would learn to take care of his daily responsibilities. She spent tremendous amounts of time working with him and finding the right schools for him to attend. All the time she cared for two other children and managed John's life outside his work, making sure that his clothes were perfect, that his favorite foods were served at her table, and that hundreds of other tasks wives routinely do for their husbands were accomplished on time. During her long years of marriage, she found herself at odds with John over various matters, and she often struggled to maintain her own sense of self. Friends commented about what a good team they were and appreciated her role in the marriage. Her children, relatives, and close friends recognized that a weaker woman might have been lost in a relationship with John. Without her enthusiastic involvement in the research and writing, this work could not possibly have been attempted.

To write about the life of John Harbert without writing a history of the Harbert Corporation would be impossible. Yet inherent difficulties occur in dealing with sensitive business history and financial matters that are so recent they might be ongoing. There are problems in treating events in which so many living people took part and have their own distinct memories of "how it was," memories that differ from others who were there or from the contemporary record. Harbert Construction Corporation, later reorganized as the Harbert Corporation, has always been privately held and has never been required to release the annual reports and information demanded of businesses whose stock is publicly traded. John Harbert protected the privacy of his financial dealings, yet he gave numerous interviews and the company distributed hundreds of press releases. Harbert contracts, sales, and acquisitions are the subjects of dozens of articles in newspapers and business journals.

Aware of the problems and challenges such a biographical study presented, John and Wita's son Raymond, who followed his father as Chief Executive Officer of the Harbert Corporation, nonetheless supported the effort, as did their other two children, Jay and Margie, who were very encouraging and supplied information not available elsewhere. I am grateful to them for sharing their memories and giving me the benefit of their insights into their father's life. Wita's sister, Acky McGriff, and her family; John's brother, Bill Harbert, and his wife, Joy, and their daughter, Ann Harbert Moulton; John's first cousin, Virginia Gorin Daday; Ed Dixon, Ted Randolph, Wayne Peake, Tom Bradford, Jack Bowen, Boone Pickens, and Hall Thompson all shared insights.

Dozens of John's other friends talked to me, answered questions, and shared their best "John Harbert story." Their names are in the endnotes. I am grateful to all for their interest and assistance with this project, especially to Rex Barrington. Numerous times I was stopped on the street or cornered at social functions by someone who wanted to share with me a story about John. The one story most often remembered was that John started his company with money he won gambling on the ship coming home from World War II. Memory plays tricks on all of us and frequently stories and recollections differed. A concerted effort was made to verify oral and published information with internal records and other sources.

The Harbert Corporation officers and employees could not have been more helpful. Sandi Falkenhagen, who served as John's assistant for twenty-two years, was an especially valuable resource in identifying files for my use, while Bill McWhorter, records manager for Harbert, retrieved dozens of file boxes for me. Will Brooke, Charlie Miller, Tricia Mandt, Carole Shafer, Margaret Russo, Brenda Harris, Shirley Henson, and Kay Lucas clarified dates or issues, shared stories, or assisted me in some way. Sharon Juett and Debra Radigan were always able to find me for messages. Charlotte Gafford's manuscript history of the Harbert Corporation and her typed interviews were valuable sources.

Neville Palmer, Louise Hall, and Will Rudolph made be feel welcome when I was working at the Harbert homes. They took great interest in this manuscript and shared with me their recollections of "Mr. Harbert." There are many more who helped, and I express my appreciation to all those whose names appear in the text or notes and to those who talked to me but for one reason or another I did not quote or cite. Photographic credits are listed elsewhere. Many of John and Wita's visitors took pictures at Pinebloom during their visits and sent copies to Wita. Sometimes it was not possible to determine the photographers of photographs in the Pinebloom Collection.

Norwood Kerr retrieved materials for me at the Alabama Department of Archives and History from the Governors' Papers, the ABC Board files, and the Commission on Higher Education. Jim Baggett and Don Vesey at the Department of Archives and Manuscripts at the Birmingham Public Library helped me locate Harbert materials in the Hill Ferguson Collection and the Young Women's Christian Association records. Bryding Adams sent me information from the YWCA, and Gail Trechsel and Margaret Livingston helped me locate materials at the Birmingham Museum of Art. Jim Vickrey wrote me about his friendship with John when Jim was president of the University of Montevallo, and Neal Berte sent me information about John's involvement on the Board of Trustees of Birmingham-Southern College.

I appreciate the help of colleagues and friends at Auburn University: Fred Hudson, Joe Judkins, and Bill Walker gave me an understanding of the AU civil engineering department when John was a student; Bill Muse, Betty DeMent, George Atkins, Buck Bradberry, Wayne Shell, and Jim Marion all worked with John on various projects and shared their information and memories with me; historians Larry Gerber and Steve McFarland shared their special expertise on President Jimmy Carter's administration and the Middle East, clarified points, gave me materials, and suggested books I might read; Wayne Flynt shared his understanding and bibliography of Kentucky coal mining; finance professor John Jahera lent me books from his personal library and sent me a bibliography so I might better understand the 1980s stock market; John Fletcher confirmed for me the semesters/quarters when John was actually enrolled at Alabama Polytechnic Institute (Auburn University's former designation); librarians at the Auburn University Library (who were mostly working in the new addition that the Harbert Corporation built) were most helpful, especially Beverly Powers, who searched through Auburn presidential papers and other AU archival materials seeking Harbert information, and Dave Rosenblatt, Peter Brannon, Dale Foster, and Joyce Hicks; Pat Wingfield checked records at the president's office, and Jeff Etheridge searched AU photographic files for pictures of John; and Jay Lamar, my friend and former colleague at the Center for the Arts and Humanities, read behind me to catch my errors and took a special interest in this project. I am grateful to Beverly Denbow for her usual very careful editing.

I first met John Harbert many years ago at an Auburn University function, and in the late 1970s and early 1980s I served on the Jefferson County Committee of the Auburn Generations capital fund drive under his leadership. My husband, George, as an Auburn University development officer, spent more time with John than I did and will forever remember his visits to his office and to Pinebloom and fishing with John on Long Pond. John Harbert stories were shared at our dinner table long before this project was proposed. I met Wita casually at Auburn when the John M. Harbert III engineering building was dedicated, but our first conversation was during the Nineteenth Century Club history project in 1994. Regrettably, I never had the opportunity to know either of them well until this venture. I am grateful to Wita for her friendship and for the opportunity to come to know such a remarkable man.

INTRODUCTION

JOHN M. HARBERT III

"marching to the beat of a different drummer"

John Murdoch Harbert III was a man who literally altered the face of the land all over the world and by his work changed and improved the way people lived their lives. He created jobs for thousands, built interstate highways and bridges, constructed dams and created lakes, brought water and natural gas to towns through his pipelines, created new communities, built skyscrapers, and developed new ways to create energy. He changed the way coal was retrieved in Kentucky. He was called a true builder in every sense of the word, a man with an awesome combination of energy and intelligence and with a strong physique and a powerful heart. Those who knew him have described him as having supreme confidence, tenacity, and brilliance marked by practicality and "street smarts." He was, his friend Hall Thompson said, "a straight-arrow guy."[1]

Born in Greenville, Mississippi, in 1921, Harbert moved to Birmingham, Alabama, when he was a child. Except for a few years in Gulfport, Mississippi, where he graduated from high school, a short stay in Seattle, Washington, and the time he spent in college at Auburn and in the U.S. Army during World War II, John lived his entire life in the Birmingham area. The city benefited most from his professional accomplishments and his philanthropy.

John has been called many things: a maverick, a genius, a self-made millionaire, a workaholic, a mythmaker, a gambling risk-taker, a lucky man, and a great prevaricator who never told a lie. Often it appeared as though he made quick decisions or acted on the spur of the moment when in reality he more often investigated, read widely, gathered data, and carefully thought out and planned his every move. He rose every day at five o'clock, and he believed that the harder he worked, the luckier he got, but he was never a detail person. An unfailing optimist, he was healthy, lived moderately, and was physically tough and mentally strong as well as innovative, creative, impatient, and aggressive. He had enormous energy and a compelling vitality. He was an excellent negotiator and could relate to all people. He also had charisma.

John was careful with his money when he spent it, invested it, or gave it away, but when he lost bundles of it, he never looked back and mourned. Although he gave away millions of dollars during his lifetime—to universities, medical foundations, civic projects, and charities—he occasionally promised more than he could deliver. The cyclical nature of his business and a variable economy sometimes offered doses of reality for his willing heart and his exuberant commitments. On one occasion he resorted to a bank loan to meet a pledge obligation.

John fits comfortably into Birmingham's history, which is replete with speculating entrepreneurs and determined engineers. In fact, the city was founded in 1871 by southerners who staked their fortunes on the potential worth of industrial minerals in the hills of north Alabama and on an anticipated real estate boom from land development where two railroads then under construction, the Alabama and Chattanooga and the South and North, would cross. Birmingham was founded in an old cornfield belonging to Benjamin F. Worthington and Drayton Nabers, John's wife's great-grandfathers. The initial capital for the city's development came from native sources, but the growth of the "Magic City" was fueled by money imported by dreamers and speculators who came from the North and the South and from Europe to seek their fortunes. These new capitalists were intent upon exploiting the iron ore, coal, and limestone of the Birmingham mineral district and building a New South economy based upon mines, mills, and industry.

The most colorful early speculator in the mineral district was Henry Fairchild DeBardeleben. In Birmingham, DeBardeleben parlayed his wife's inheritance from the Daniel Pratt gin works into a fortune, which he lost at least twice and then won back. DeBardeleben swaggered across the district, founding companies and towns, digging coal mines, fostering mergers, selling out, buying back, and dropping immortal quotes as he went. He once said that "there's nothing like taking a wild piece of land all rock and woods—ground not fit to feed a goat on—and turning it into a settlement of men and women; bringing railroads in, making payrolls, starting things to going; nothing like boring a hillside through and turning over a mountain!"[2] John Harbert could have said the same. Although John's quiet personality contrasts sharply with DeBardeleben's style, it is not amiss to compare the impact John made upon Birmingham and Alabama with that of DeBardeleben. And John, too, had imagination and a flair for the dramatic, was a dreamer and a zealous man impatient with mediocrity and slowness. Time was to him "perhaps of all the dimensions of our daily life ... the most difficult to deal with" because "there never seems to be enough of it, and we cannot manufacture more."[3]

John might also be compared to Erskine Ramsay, a fellow engineer and another giant of Birmingham's early industrial history. The Scotsman's biographer notes that Ramsay "was forever looking ahead, and far ahead, to see what other men failed to even guess. Once he saw the future, based upon the signs of his own times, he acted quickly and with daring."[4] It is fitting that in 1976, WYDE radio awarded John its Erskine Ramsay Award, presented "to honor those who have contributed the most toward making Birmingham a better place to live."[5] As much as Ramsay gave to Birmingham and Alabama, and as successful a businessman as he was, he falls far behind John Harbert.

John would probably have found the comparison with DeBardeleben and Ramsay amusing. His formative years in Birmingham were spent in the city and in a modest home on Bonita Drive near the boundary of Homewood and Mountain Brook, an affluent suburban community where wealthy families from old Birmingham money—including DeBardelebens, Bowrons, Woodwards, Shooks, and Irelands—mixed easily with new capitalists. John attended elementary school at Shades Cahaba and Mountain Brook in the Jefferson County school system. His parents were not from Birmingham, and the fact that he grew up with old Birmingham money but was not part of it may have increased his drive to succeed. His father was a native of

Memphis, Tennessee, a descendant of pioneer Tennessee stock and a graduate engineer from Washington State University. While in the West, he met and married Mae Hamilton Schooling of Palouse, Washington. John's family lived frugally because his father's construction company occasionally went through hard times and often suffered cash flow problems, and during the Great Depression years there was never enough money. Yet the Harberts were not poor, despite son John's later emphasis upon his humble origins.

The Harbert name is indelibly impressed upon Birmingham and Alabama: the AmSouth/Harbert Plaza is the tallest skyscraper in downtown Birmingham; the John M. Harbert III building is the most modern engineering facility on the Auburn University campus; John's wife, the former Marguerite "Wita" Jones, has a state-of-the-art classroom building named for her on the campus of her alma mater, Birmingham-Southern College; a writing center at the University of Montevallo is named for John; 150 different groups meet annually for lunch at the Harbert Center on Fourth Avenue in Birmingham; and Interstate 459 is named the John M. Harbert III Freeway.

John built a company and a corporate family of talented and creative people who were hard working and undaunted at any task. John encouraged them, and together they had the confidence to tackle anything. The bow-legged "H" logo of the Harbert Corporation has been seen all over the world—from the islands of the Caribbean to Central America, from the jungles of South America to Thailand, and from the Israeli Negev Desert to Abu Dhabi in the United Arab Emirates. Harbert has constructed bridges, dams, roads, interstate highways, shopping malls, hotels, skyscrapers, air bases, power plants, desalinization facilities, and sewer, gas, and water systems. John Harbert developed raw land into communities such as Riverchase in north Shelby County and brought new life to Kentucky coal mining districts. He had the vision to pipe natural gas to Florida and the courage to tackle cutting through Red Mountain in the heart of Birmingham, threading the freeway forty-five feet below the foundations of two high-rise apartment buildings. All the while John brought jobs to Alabama, pumped money into the local economy, and proudly carried the names of his hometown and his state around the world.

How a young man survived some of the toughest infantry fighting of World War II, took an Alabama Polytechnic Institute (Auburn University) civil engineering degree, mixed it with hard work, a disciplined life, a flair for taking risks, and a heap of good luck, and turned it into the first and for many years the only Alabama listing in *Forbes* Four Hundred is a story worth telling.

Wita likes to call her husband a maverick. He once said of himself: "When everybody goes that way, I go this way."[6] Wita believed John was always marching to the beat of a different drummer and often kept his own counsel. One of John's favorite quotations, one he kept on his desk and had framed and hanging on the wall of his and Wita's Highlands, North Carolina, home, was from Henry David Thoreau: "If a man does not keep pace with his companions, perhaps it is because he hears a different drummer. Let him step to the music which he hears, however measured or far away." The beat that John Harbert heard may have been different from the one his contemporaries followed, but it was certainly not measured: a faster tempo kept him far ahead of the pack.

John was able to develop an incredible loyalty in people who worked for him. He demanded dedication, hard work, and, above all, competence. He was beloved by close friends and associates, respected and admired by many, including strangers who never knew him. He was no doubt feared by some and disliked by others. He did have enemies, but they rarely revealed themselves openly. Some were clearly jealous of his successes.

John certainly offended and alienated at least a few people during his lifetime. He was involved in the world of business, where profit was the bottom line, and he often had to make hard business decisions that adversely affected the lives of others, although he maintained patience almost to a fault with employees who made mistakes and lost his money.

If the saying "a hero with clay feet" means that great figures are also finally human, it is true that John had his faults. He has been described as egocentric, and he was concerned with his own welfare and that of his family and the Harbert Corporation, which was his life. But he never possessed an exaggerated feeling of self-importance, and he could adjust to the most rugged physical discomforts. He had a temper, and he was frequently opinionated. He enjoyed control, and he understood power and was not shy about using it when something mattered to him.

Although his public philanthropy is well known, the true character of the man can be found in those many acts of generosity that are private and have gone unreported. Stories abound of his kindnesses to strangers and to workers, who were surprised by his modesty. He had "an instinctive sense about getting along with people. He knew how to relate to people—to people of all positions in life," and he treated everyone with deep respect.[7] He was a verbal man who was at his best when he was dealing with people face to face. Sometimes he was referred to as "The Man" or "Big John," not because he was so tall, but because he strode across the plain of life with large steps. He often dominated the scene before him, and he could galvanize a room by his mere presence.

John Harbert had a sense of history. He read biographies and history, and he was mindful that the use of the Harbert name had commercial significance and would be a legacy. He had a flair for public relations and recognized the market value of a highly visible name. In the early years of his corporation, he was by necessity tightfisted and fiscally restrained, but a number of his long-time top employees were made millionaires by his personal successes and many of his fieldworkers and staff people have enjoyed a more comfortable retirement because of his corporation's profit-sharing plan. The vast majority of those who knew him admired and liked him, and many who were closely associated with him loved him dearly.

It has not always been easy for Wita to be the wife of John, nor Jay, Raymond, and Margie to be his children. Despite the fact that they enjoyed a truly exciting life, material security, and the comfort of knowing they were loved, their husband and father frequently missed important milestones in their lives. There were many times after the children became young adults when John realized that part of the price of his success was not sharing enough of his children's childhoods. John worked long hours and was often away from home, frequently out of the country. He expected the same toughness in his family that he demanded of himself and his employees. When he accepted the Cornerstone Award of the Associated Builders and Contractors of Alabama on November 4, 1994, only five months before he died, John Harbert listed among "the kind of people who have made my career in construction so rewarding" his family, "who forgave the missed births and birthdays and offered love and support in return."[8]

Over the course of his lifetime, John was invited to give many speeches—to civic clubs, business associations, and students. He often talked about his life and the history of his company. John gave an address to the Newcomen Society in North America in 1982. In the title of that speech he used a saying he was fond of quoting when talking about the evolution of his company—that the history of the Harbert Corporation was one of "continuous beginnings."[9] The same could be said of his own life.

1

FAMILY AND GROWING UP

"not half the man my father was"

John M. Harbert III, through his father, is descended from English and Scottish colonists who were involved in the eighteenth-century westward movement from the seaboard South. His ancestors came from Virginia to North Carolina and then moved over the Appalachian Mountains to settle Tennessee. They were pioneers who fought Native Americans, carved farms from the wilderness, and founded towns that became cities.[1] Two of his great-great-grandfathers were living in Tennessee before 1800. One ancestor was Captain John Robertson, who married Elizabeth Williamson in Wilson County, Tennessee, on March 9, 1809.[2] One of John's great-grandmothers was descended from Colonel John Ramsey, a North Carolina Revolutionary War soldier who settled in Tennessee after the war and entered a claim for 5,000 acres on the lower Chickasaw bluff on the Mississippi River, land that later became part of the city of Memphis.[3]

The Harberts originated in Virginia from ancestor William Herbert, who emigrated to America from Wales with his three small sons. His Virginia and Revolutionary War records spell his name variously as Herbert and Harbert. He was one of the Virginia militiamen who marched over the mountains during the winter of 1773-74 and engaged the Shawnee Indians in desperate fighting to claim the land south of the Ohio River for Virginia. William and his son Thomas were Revolutionary soldiers who provided horses for the troops commanded by the Marquis de Lafayette.[4] Both died in August 1776, perhaps in battle. Another of William's sons, named William, who was born March 9, 1733, had a son he named for his brother Thomas. He was born June 25, 1773, in what is now Wythe County, Virginia. His son, John, was born in Virginia on February 22, 1797, and moved west, first to North Carolina, and was living there briefly in the early part of the nineteenth century. The 1810 census lists one William Harbert and three John Harberts in North Carolina, but by the 1820 census there is only one, and John and William Harbert are now in Madison County, Tennessee.[5] John Harbert married Narcissa Cherry on July 4, 1827, and they established a plantation near Denmark, Tennessee. Here their son Daniel Cherry Harbert was born April 11, 1828.[6]

Daniel Cherry Harbert married the daughter of William Murdoch Murchison, who was a member of the North Carolina legislature in 1830.[7] Murchison moved his family to Madison County, Tennessee, in the 1830s, and his daughter, Frances (Fannie) Estelle Murchison, married young Harbert on January 15, 1851. They named their son John for Daniel's father and gave him the middle name of Murdoch from Fannie's father. The first John Murdoch Harbert was born March 15, 1857, in Denmark, Tennessee, which is northeast of Memphis. Before the Civil War, his grandparents, John and Narcissa Cherry Harbert, moved to Shelby County. The old Harbert estate was in the Belvedere section of Memphis and provided the name for the city's modern Harbert Avenue. The homestead once stood where number 1786 Harbert Avenue was located in the 1990s.[8]

John Murdoch Harbert spent his childhood in Memphis during the Civil War, and his marriage on October 29, 1884, to Dorthea "Dolly" (sometimes spelled Dollie) Cash (1863-94), daughter of Memphis merchant Francis Marion Cash, joined two old Tennessee families. In 1870 Cash's business establishment was located at Madison and Front Streets.[9] The marriage produced the second John Murdoch Harbert, who was born in Memphis on September 14, 1887. By the time the child was six years old, both his parents were dead from tuberculosis. This may explain why he later elected to use the Roman numeral II at the end of his name rather than Junior, but his niece Virginia Daday remembers that he did not like being called "Junior."[10] In later years when he signed his name he always abbreviated his first name, Jno. Young Harbert and his older sister, Bessie, were sent to live in Memphis with their maternal grandmother, Elizabeth Drake Cash Hamilton; their mother's two unmarried sisters, Imogene Cash and

John M. Harbert (far right) grew up in his grandmother's house on Poplar Street in Memphis, Tennessee. In a photograph taken about 1899, he plays here with his cousins, Charles R. Cash and George Reed, and his sister, Bessie.

Elizabeth Cash, also lived in the homestead on Poplar Street. Later both aunts married, and the two orphaned Harbert children were included in their busy household. Harbert told his sons about a childhood that was not particularly happy.[11]

As soon as he graduated from high school, young Harbert left his aunts' home and headed west. He went, according to his son John, "for food and freedom from the two aunts."[12] In 1905 Harbert took a job with the Great Northern Railroad, built by Canadian-American James J. Hill and his incomparable chief engineer, John F. Stevens. Stevens became a legend in western railroad history for his survey of the Great Northern line and for his engineering accomplishments. The main line was completed from Duluth to Seattle by 1893; however, Hill's master plan called for an artery system of spur railroads, and it was on the construction of these lines that Harbert labored as "chainman, rodman, topographer, and draftsman."[13] Perhaps Harbert once met Stevens; surely he heard stories about his engineering feats. This experience may have instilled in Harbert a love for engineering and helped to make him the meticulous engineer he became. The work on the railroad was exciting and dangerous, and the terrain through Indian country varied from snowcapped mountains to sweeping plains. When the survey crews reached Pullman, Washington, in January 1906, Harbert was laid off for the winter. A kindly railroad supervisor suggested that he enter Washington State University at Pullman and complete his education.[14]

Harbert worked his way through WSU, holding various jobs, some with the Great Northern Railroad. He relished his university experiences, especially Latin and Greek classes. In 1910 he earned a civil engineering degree and took a position as the principal assistant engineer of the LCI Company in Clarkston, Washington, doing hydroelectric, irrigation, and water supply work. Harbert returned to the South in 1911, and for the next year he lived in Memphis doing private engineering for waterworks and sewer projects. He then secured a job with the Yazoo County Drainage District in Mississippi, and in 1912 he joined Jacob Stein as a junior partner. Operating under the name Stein and Harbert Engineers, the two men specialized in Mississippi River Delta drainage, municipal engineering, and levee and highway construction.[15]

While he was a student at Washington State University, Harbert met and courted Mae Hamilton Schooling, a native of Spokane, Washington, and the daughter of James Hamilton and Eva Lebold Hamilton. The Harbert family never knew anything about Hamilton, but Mae shared stories with her grandchildren of a childhood in Alaska. She told about dogsledding, and she had small pieces of jewelry that she said were made of gold from her father's mine.[16] However, when Mae was about five years old, her mother brought her home to Washington. What happened to Mae's father is a mystery, but it is generally assumed that he remained in Alaska. Eva remarried, to a man named Schooling, and young Mae took his last name. The Schoolings had a 160-acre wheat farm in Palouse, not far from Pullman, where Harbert was in school at Washington State. Mae attended college in California but never finished because she and John M. Harbert II were married in Seattle, October 7, 1914. Following the honeymoon the groom left his bride in Seattle for a short time when he returned South, but Mae joined him in Indianola, Mississippi, sometime after November 1.

Harbert's partnership with Jacob Stein was short-lived, for Stein died at Camp Beauregard during the severe World War I influenza epidemic.[17] Harbert adopted the new company name of John M. Harbert Engineering Company and continued in business paving streets and working on sewers, drainage, waterworks, and highways. In his first year he grossed less than $1,500, but for

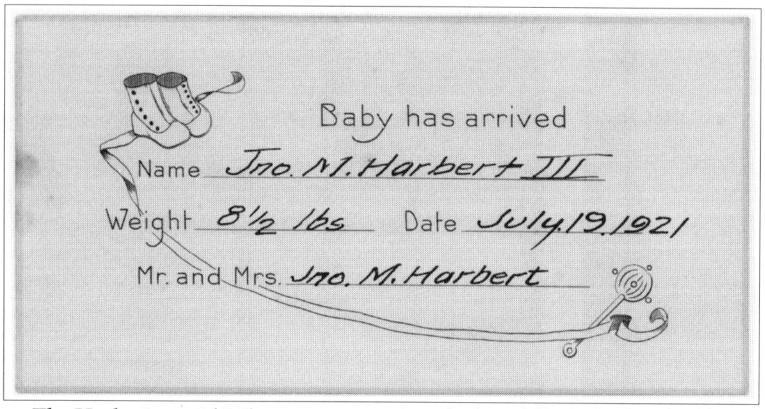

The Harberts sent birth announcement cards from Mississippi to family and friends after the arrival of their first baby. Mr. Harbert always abbreviated his first name.

a young engineer in those days this was a respectable figure. John and Mae's first child, a son they named John M. Harbert III, was born on July 19, 1921, in Greenville. The proud father wired Mae's mother that the baby boy weighed eight and a half pounds and mother and baby were "doing fine."[18] The baby was probably born in a hospital because he was not born in Indianola where his twin siblings, Billy and Betty, were born two years later.

When John was a baby, his father had trouble with his workers on one of the Harbert jobs. Threats were made against Harbert and his family. Many nights when her husband was gone, Mae sat rocking John with a shotgun across the arms of her chair.[19] Hearing this story may have influenced her son, for in later years John worked hard to maintain good labor relations with his employees, and he always tried to operate with nonunion labor.

In 1924 Harbert secured street paving contracts in the new community of Mountain Brook near Birmingham, Alabama. He moved the Harbert family from Mississippi to a house at 2123 Avenue E in Ensley. By the next year Harbert Engineering Company was operating from offices in the Farley Building on Third Avenue and Twentieth Street. Charles J. Cargile, a young civil engineering graduate of the University of Alabama, joined the firm, and the Harbert family moved to a larger house on Fifth Avenue South.[20] By 1927 the Harberts were living at 200 Bonita Drive in the Hollywood section of Homewood. This was the house where John spent his growing-up years and the one he most identified as his childhood home.

On October 25, 1929, just four days before Black Monday when the New York stock market crashed and the Great Depression began, Harbert joined in a partnership with Cargile, and the two engineers incorporated as Harbert and Cargile Construction Company. From his own Harbert Engineering Company, Harbert transferred assets that included two cars, a Ransome paver, a finishing machine, a Caterpillar tractor, and other road construction and paving equipment.[21]

John remembered his father's partner, Cargile, as "an extremely engaging man" who was "a friend to everyone and everybody" and who gave his time "to anyone who asked for it." John believed that his father and Cargile had a "perfect partnership." In the late 1980s John wrote:

> As a young man—I began to see the many attempts by individuals with selfish interests to cause dissension between Mr. Cargile and my father for one reason or another—Many times I saw people try to come between them—to divide them, but their common bond, for better or worse, fought it off—and this has always impressed me even today when I realize the need for strength for individuals with common goals to fight together and not get divided and dispersed over minor disagreements—particularly those espoused by third parties with selfish interests.[22]

Mae Schooling Harbert with her new baby, John M. Harbert III, in Greenville, Mississippi.

John's father shows off the third John Murdoch Harbert for the camera.

John, and his siblings, twins Betty and Billy, with their grandmother, Eva Lebold Hamilton Schooling, on one of her visits to Birmingham.

Despite the depression, Harbert and Cargile incorporated an investment company in 1930 and a realty company in 1931 but dissolved them both by 1932.[23]

In 1927 John entered elementary school at Shades Cahaba, which was part of the Jefferson County school system. When the Mountain Brook Grammar School was being constructed the next year, he transferred there and attended second grade in a makeshift classroom over Gilchrist's Drug Store because the new school building was not ready for occupancy when the school term began in the fall of 1928.[24] The Harbert family attended Shades Valley Presbyterian Church and joined in community activities. John was "an inquisitive youngster who tried to get into everything," his mother remembered.[25] Neighbors on Bonita Drive recalled young John as hard working and ambitious, a polite little boy with nice manners. He sold magazines, and when he was barely big enough to see over his bicycle basket, he had a paper route for the afternoon *Birmingham Post*. John remembered that "in those days the paper sold for twelve cents, of which the newsboy got six cents and the *Post* got six. It was the best damn business experience a 12- or 13-year-old could have." During the depression, John recalled, one of his most "vivid experiences was learning how to collect money from housewives who really didn't have twelve cents at the end of the week." He often cleared $5 a week and recollected that "there was nobody my age who had $5 a week. I was rich."[26]

John remembered another job he had during the depression, and in the mid-1960s he suggested that he "had been headed for construction since the age of twelve, when I carried buckets of water down a hot country road to thirsty highway construction crews."[27] These workers may well have been his father's road crew working on the streets of Mountain Brook. When he was older John worked weekends at a Homewood gasoline station near his home. He was small for his age, wore glasses, and was very shy, and years later he confessed that he was "often the target of jokes and ridicule from older and larger classmates," an experience that made him particularly sensitive to children who suffered the same plight.[28]

John's mother provided a large Sunday lunch, which she prepared herself, and it usually included a standing rib roast cooked rare. At Christmastime a tall tree covered with decorations stood in the living room, and on Christmas morning the family gathered for a large breakfast. Presents were opened after they finished eating.[29] Because of the depression the three Harbert children learned to entertain themselves in ways that did not require money. John recalls "going skinny-dipping in the creek that runs through the Birmingham Zoo," and it was near the creek that during a rock-throwing incident a strange boy threw a rock that hit Betty in the head. Afterward she suffered episodes of seizures. John enjoyed hunting rabbits and squirrels in the wooded areas south of Homewood and Mountain Brook, remembering that in the 1930s Mountain Brook "was considered to be out in the boondocks."[30] He enjoyed fishing in Lake Purdy and held a fishing permit from the Birmingham Water Works.

The 1929 depression hit construction firms especially hard. Although cash flow was always a problem and money was tight and Harbert and Cargile struggled, they did not go under. However, in 1932 the Harbert family drove to Seattle to live for a while with Mae's mother. It may well have been on this trip that the family story of John going up the mountain originated. Mrs. Harbert loved to tell about the time when the boys were "acting up" in the car, and after Mr. Harbert repeatedly corrected John, he told him that if he "did that one more time" he would stop the car and put him on the side of the road. John repeated his misbehavior, and his father stopped the car and said: "Son, get out." John did. They had stopped beside a mountain, and, when out of the car, John immediately started climbing it. Despite his mother's pleading with him to come back, he kept on going. John came down only after it was dark. No one seems to recall what consequences he suffered.[31]

During the next year the entire Harbert family lived in Seattle with Mae's mother, whom the boys called "Coonie." They enjoyed their grandmother's house, located on Beach Drive on the water at Alki Point. During that year, John's father remodeled Coonie's house, added on to a bedroom, and rebuilt the kitchen. Puget Sound had a fifteen-foot tide in front of the house, and the outgoing tide left three hundred feet of rocky beach. John and his brother, Billy, dug oysters and clams.

They built a raft, played in the water, and walked the shoreline looking for bottles. John attended sixth grade in Seattle, and Billy and Betty were in fourth grade. Betty maintained a perfect attendance for the school year 1932-33, and John was awarded a Safety Patrol Merit Medal.[32] While the Harberts lived with Mrs. Schooling, the family also visited the Palouse farm. The farm produced an abundance of green peas in addition to wheat, and both at the farm and in Seattle, the family ate a lot of pea soup.[33] At some point Mr. Harbert left the family in Seattle and returned to Birmingham, and family stories relate that he slept in his office to save expenses.[34]

Sometime in 1934 the family returned to Alabama, and John's father was employed as a superintendent on a Works Progress Administration road-building project south of Mobile. The family lived for a while in Coden.[35] But by 1935 the Harberts were back in Birmingham in their house on Bonita Drive, and John was once again at Shades Cahaba. Beyond school and working, John's major activity was Boy Scout Troop 53, an outstanding troop led by Winnie Currie. The troop met once a week at the Mountain Brook Grammar School, and the Bonita neighborhood scouts would be driven to the meeting by Claude Shill's father, who lived a few doors away from the Harberts. Wayne Peake recalls that the first time he met John was when the scouts were all piling into Mr. Shill's car and the smaller ones were told to sit on the laps of the bigger boys. John turned to Wayne and said, "I'm little now, but I'm going to grow."[36] He did, and by the time they were adults John was several inches taller than Wayne.

In those depression years John "had little else in the way of entertainment," and the Friday night scout meetings "were the highlight of the week."[37] John was an avid reader of *Boy's Life* magazine, once succumbing to an advertisement that promised he could "be the life of the party" by learning to play the guitar. He purchased a ten-dollar guitar and took weekly lessons at fifty cents a lesson; but he gave up music when his teacher told him "he could no longer accept" his money because he "had no musical ability and would never be able to play the guitar."[38]

John once thought he might enjoy being a taxidermist. When he was thirteen years old he tried to earn his taxidermy badge and ordered on credit a ten-dollar taxidermy kit from an Omaha company. He tried to skin and mount a crow but ended up covered with lice and creating a thing that "looked like a fat, black duck." Meanwhile, his ten-dollar account was running interest, and he was being "threatened by bill collectors, telephone calls, legal-sounding letters." Afraid to tell his parents, John went to Mr. Cargile, who "managed to straighten things out" for him.[39]

Although John never completed his music or earned his scout taxidermy badge, he did qualify for Eagle Scout rank. As an adult he appreciated the wide variety of experiences he had in the scouting program.[40] John became an Eagle Scout on the night of April 30, 1937, at a Birmingham Council Court of Honor at the Edgewood Baptist Church (later named Dawson Baptist Church). John and his friend Wayne Peake were both awarded Eagle Scout rank, and on the same night Troop 53 broke all previous records by attaining 6,270 points at the Court of Honor.[41] Ten days later James E. West, chief scout executive, congratulated John on his achievement. Writing from scout headquarters in Washington, D.C., West urged John to continue his education in college, become a leader of his community, and take advantage of all the opportunities that his country offered.[42] John would do just that.

Years later John wrote that "I have never known a man who said that he was sorry he stayed in Scouting long enough to earn his Eagle rank, but I have met many who express regret that they failed to achieve this, the highest rank." Despite wanting "to quit a thousand times," he was always proud that he stayed the course. He never forgot his

Members of Birmingham's Jamboree Troop 15 paused during the first National Boy Scout Jamboree in Washington, D.C., in 1937. First row: Jack Smith, Fred Harrison, Bill Levy, Howard Fuldenwider, Douglas Shook, Ed Ebbert. Second Row: John M. Harbert III, Mercer Doty, Whit Terrell, Dan Donald, John Wilson, Roderick Garth, Eugene Edwards, Thomas Wood, Bill Leighton. Third Row: John A. Reynolds, Billy Thuss, the Honorable Luther Patrick (member of Congress representing Jefferson County), Scoutmaster Jack F. Broda, Griff Harsh, John Orr, Edwin Ellis, George Bentley (from Clinton, Louisiana). Fourth Row: Richard Deadman, Wayne Peake, Gray Buck, Charles Guy, Clifford Beasley, Talmage Amberson, Donald Brewer, Rudolph Shannon.

scouting lessons. Knowledge of the constellations he memorized for his astronomy badge helped him find his way back to the American lines when he was lost once on a cold winter night behind German lines in World War II. All his life John took pleasure and pride in being able to identify trees and plants in the woods and "almost every bird around" from its "flight pattern or the sound of its song." Scouting, John acknowledged, taught him perseverance, how to become a leader, and the necessity of setting goals. It helped him to "be successful on the road of life" and gave him "the confidence that I could be somebody, some day."[43]

During the summer of 1937 John was part of the first National Boy Scout Jamboree, which was held in Washington, D.C. He and the Birmingham scouts rode a train to the capital. John's father had supplied John with a Western Union card, which allowed him to wire home collect. From June 30 to July 9, John was one of the 26,223 scouts and leaders who camped along the Mall close to the Washington Monument. Four hundred scouts came from foreign countries, and scouts representing every U.S. state created villages with specially designed and constructed entrances and gateways that reflected the individual state's history or geographical region. Organization was based upon the troop and patrol system. John and the Alabama scouts were camped by the Potomac River in the theater area. Each night "giant camp fire programs" were held with singing, skits, and speeches, and during the day the scouts visited historical sites in the capital. Many celebrities and government officials, even President Franklin D. Roosevelt, spoke to the boys.[44] More than five decades later John reflected on his youthful experiences after returning from a visit to the 1989 scout jamboree. He observed that in his scouting days "we were more dressed up. We had to wear our uniforms—short pants and knee stockings." Despite the differences, he confessed that he would "always be a Scout at heart."[45]

When the Great Depression began in 1929, John was only eight years old, and the hard times his family suffered had a lasting effect upon his life. He had an understanding of how much his father had sacrificed in order to keep his business going during difficult times, and John came to appreciate what a very fine and highly professional engineer his father was.[46] In later years John frequently said: "I'm not half the man my father was."[47] John recalled that "financially, my father had nothing, but he gave me something much more important ... a good name. He taught me something that I will never forget ... that the three most important ingredients a man can possess are integrity, responsibility, and credibility."[48]

By 1935 John was a student at Phillips High School and Billy and Betty were students at Mountain Brook Grammar School.[49] At Phillips, John enrolled in the arts and science school to prepare for college, but he selected a typing class in the business school, which was not part of the college-bound curriculum. When John was discovered, he was removed from the class. Later he recalled that "the powers to be in Phillips at that time didn't think it proper for an Arts student to burden himself with practical courses such as typing. ... Phillips believed in two years of Latin, two of French, a couple of Spanish, and other similar courses that belonged to the so-called Arts—a system whereby you studied a little about a lot and consequently learned nothing about everything." John "finally learned" typing at Gulfport (Mississippi) High School, "where a more practical program of education was practiced." In a typewritten letter to his father from Fort Sheridan in February 1944, John wrote that "typing by the touch system is something that I will never regret learning."[50]

While at Phillips High School, John pledged Chi Sigma Chi high school fraternity. He participated in fraternity activities but usually showed up for the socials without a date. He was known as the "perennial stag." This status came in handy once for his sister, who had a date with Claude Shill for the Chi Sigma Chi leadout. Betty had a new dress and was excited about the dance, but Claude's appendix ruptured. Mrs. Harbert convinced John, who had no date, to escort his sister to the dance. Mrs. Harbert then called all the neighborhood teens and made them promise to "make sure John doesn't leave Betty on the middle of the dance floor." John was popular with the younger teens because when he received his driver's license he was willing to drive them where they needed to go.[51]

During the depression the Harberts were unable to pay the mortgage on their house on Bonita Drive and the Home Owners Loan Corporation foreclosed. They left their furniture, renting it to the people who moved into the house, and after John finished his junior year at Phillips High School, the family moved to Pass Christian, Mississippi.[52] Harbert and Cargile was building a bridge from Henderson Point to Bay Saint Louis. John was too young to labor on the construction site, but he worked at a small restaurant, which served food to the construction crews on the bridge.

Once Mr. Cargile sent John with a flatbed truck to pick up a load of plywood. Either the wood was improperly loaded or John was driving too fast, for the four-by-eight sheets slid off the truck bed and blocked traffic "for three hours while young John, red hair wet with sweat, reloaded the plywood by himself." For three weeks John worked for Mr. Cargile as "a reinforcing steel-rod tier at thirty cents an hour" until his father found out and fired him, telling his son to go out and find his own job.[53]

Living on the Gulf of Mexico had advantages. There was always swimming, and John often told stories about shooting ducks on the way to school.[54] The Harbert boys had a rowboat and a sailboat and would pluck oysters from the bay and catch fish to sell for spending money. John's experiences at Gulfport High School were positive ones, mainly because of his English teacher, Margaret Evans, who "really inspired" him to do better. More than thirty years later John recalled that Mrs. Evans was "the only teacher I had who inspired me to do anything more than what was basically required to pass."[55] After three decades he traced her to Jackson, Mississippi, where she had retired and was living with her sister. Mrs. Evans recognized John from his photographs, the face of the teenage boy she had once taught, just "grown strong and wise—and `bigger'!"[56] John recalled that Mrs. Evans had encouraged him "to do and be all" he could be. She wrote that in young John she had seen a "willingness ... earnestness ... appreciative listening ability... [and a] sweetness of spirit." Sometimes, she penned, "I detected a bit of dreaminess, but somehow I never suspected you of frivolous things—rather that you were dreaming of great things in far-away places." And, she added, "so you were!"[57]

That first summer on the gulf coast, Mrs. Harbert invited a group of her children's friends from Bonita Drive to visit the family at Pass Christian and "to stay in her little brown house" located near the highway and a short walk across the sand to the beach. Mak and Wayne Peake, Fay Belt, Claude Shill, and Top Miller were there. Wayne recalls that a large black man named Tapoc took him and John "in his flat-bottomed skiff out and around the inlet off Bay St. Louis" where "he netted shrimp, and we filled up a wash tub" before the shear pin on the outboard motor broke.[58]

During the summer of 1939 the Harberts had moved to Gulfport, and Barbara Howell joined the group. The kids sailed a catboat up and down the Mississippi Sound, went swimming and shrimping, and sunbathed. Top Miller stepped on an oyster bed and cut his feet. Mrs. Harbert escorted the group to New Orleans, gave them a tour of the French Quarter, and showed them the field where Andrew Jackson defeated the British in 1815. She took the teenagers to an old restaurant to eat soft-shell crabs. It was a delightful summer experience with memories to last a lifetime for young people about to have their lives caught up in a world war.[59]

2

AUBURN ENGINEERING

"with fair grades"

In the summer of 1939 Harbert and Cargile Construction Company was completing its job at Henderson Point, Mississippi. John was a recent high school graduate and, as he once told the story, had plans to work as a deckhand on a small freighter scheduled to leave Gulfport, Mississippi, in mid-September with a cargo of cattle headed for Brussels, Belgium. An ocean voyage to Europe would be an adventure for a young man who loved excitement and had not yet determined his course in life. The ship would return to the Mississippi port with a load of cement. However, before these plans materialized, Adolph Hitler's German army invaded Poland and the ship's manifest was changed to ammunition and TNT—not a safe way for an eighteen-year-old to head into a war zone. John now had no job and no plans, and his friends had all left for college.[1]

Earlier in the summer John had received a letter from Wayne Peake, his Boy Scout buddy and childhood friend in Birmingham. Wayne was going to the Alabama Polytechnic Institute at Auburn to study engineering. He asked if John would join him. Years later John recalled that the choice of Auburn and engineering was his own, for "My father never gave me any advice, and if I asked for it, he told me to make my own decision."[2] So "with nothing more appealing available and completely on the spur of the moment, I packed a suitcase and hitchhiked to Auburn, where I enrolled a little late in the freshman engineering class."[3] Although John may have been influenced to study engineering by his friend, his work experience in the construction industry and his father's example probably weighed more heavily.[4] He recalled in 1986 that he "chose civil engineering because it was broad-based in its appeal, and closer to the essence of engineering than the other disciplines."[5] At the time John entered API the official title of the department was Civil Engineering and Highway Construction.

Wayne and two other Birmingham boys, Sumner Nesbitt and Vaughn Pope, were living at 254 South Gay Street. They had rented a "sleeping room" in a large old house owned by Professor and Mrs. L. M. Ware, who lived next door. Ware was the head of the API horticulture department, and Mrs. Ware handled the business arrangements with the boys. When John arrived in Auburn, he moved in with his three friends from Phillips High School days. The boys had two double-decker iron-spring beds on a sleeping porch and four desks in a study room in the middle of the house. Although John often joked about coming to college with his belongings in a "cardboard suitcase," his roommates recalled that he came as well fitted-out with starched clothes as they were. John and his roommates visited around town, eating at such famous boardinghouses as the Green House, known for its cornbread and buttermilk biscuits, and at Mrs. Gertrude Lane's, where the fried chicken was particularly good.[6]

In October 1939, soon after they arrived on the API campus, John and his roommate Wayne Peake posed for a photograph on the campus wearing their ROTC caps and some of their uniforms.

The house on Gay Street was conveniently located no more than two blocks from Samford Hall, if you followed the sidewalk, but a dirt path, a short-cut behind the Wares' garden, went between the New Fraternity Row houses that faced South College Street. The boys walked by the Delta Sigma Phi house several times a day and were impressed with its grandeur. One of John's roommates, Sumner Nesbitt, had already pledged Delta Sig, so it is not surprising that the fraternity, which called itself the "hub of New Fraternity Row," soon "hot-boxed" John and Wayne into pledging. John's father was a Sigma Nu, and John's decision to join another fraternity was one more example of his independence. The boys stayed with Mrs. Ware for one semester and then moved into the fraternity house.[7]

As John began his first classes in the API civil engineering curriculum, radio flashes announced daily the successes of the German army. The complete capitulation of Poland came quickly. There was divided opinion on campus about what this loss would mean to America. Some isolationists believed that the Atlantic Ocean would protect the United States. But API dean George Petrie, who held forth in Langdon Hall one evening a week discussing current events and the world situation to an audience of students and townspeople, was convinced that the United States would eventually be pulled into the war. There is no doubt that the academic motivation of all the young men at Auburn was affected by the war in Europe. Because API was the land-grant college of Alabama, its Reserve Officers' Training Corps (ROTC) program was compulsory for all male freshmen and sophomore students. Boys wore gray-caped uniforms every Tuesday and Thursday and drilled twice a week. They attended classes in military theory and tactics. The instructors, all career military men, made clear to their API students that their mission was to train Auburn boys to serve as officers in the regular army should the need arise.

Years later John wrote that at Auburn he was

"interested in a wide variety of non-academic activities" and that he "studied just enough to pass most courses." As a student he felt that "taking a course was like jumping a fence ... I exerted just enough effort to barely clear it. I saw no reason to leave any blue sky between me and the top rail, so long as I got over the fence." He confessed that his grade point average was not that "of a serious scholar" and admitted that he was "a C student, a poor C student."[8] With hindsight and maturity, he later faulted himself for not taking his studies more seriously. He recalled that he "had the typical sophomoric engineering student's attitude toward the required English courses," believing that an engineer did not need English 101 and 102.[9] John "rebelled" against "the academic setting" because "things went too slowly; so much seemed like a waste of time. I was not interested in making good grades; I was interested in getting out of school." He acknowledged that he did well "in subjects and with professors I liked and poorly if the reverse were true."[10] At Auburn John made good use of his ability to type, and he was grateful for the course at Gulfport High School. He "made spending money typing themes and theses—made better grades on my own work when I typed it."[11]

Auburn was an exciting place outside the classroom, too. There were special events, such as the ODK Cake Race and Sadie Hawkins Day, and parties, proms, and balls, where visiting top bands or the Auburn Knights belted out jazz and played the slow popular rhythms of the day. In 1990 John reminisced that during his days at Auburn students did not use drugs and consumed only a little alcohol. Although a pint of good bourbon or Barcardi rum from the state store cost just 85 cents, few students had the money to spend. There was no parking problem, because there were no cars on campus. He recalled that "we all had grown up through the Depression, and the austerity of that period profoundly affected us. Nevertheless, for the life of me, I cannot recall a single person who considered himself deprived."[12]

Men outnumbered women on the Auburn campus, and dates were hard to come by. In the fall of 1939 when John entered API, there were 3,765 students, only 643 of them female.[13] It was some time before John knew any girls well enough to date. In 1980, when he reminisced about his days in Auburn, he shared a story of how several of the "wilder" Delta Sig upperclassmen played a joke on him, getting him a blind date for a big dance, probably the Military Ball, with an Opelika girl who was pregnant. Although none of his friends remembers the incident and it has the ring of apocrypha, John recalled that he was naive and she was "attractive enough, even though I thought she was a little plump." At the dance he was puzzled by the way "everybody was looking at us, smiling and winking and whispering." When a friend finally pointed out to John that his date was pregnant, John's reaction was typical. He determined not to allow the culprits to have "a big laugh at my expense—not to mention hers—and I wasn't about to give them that enjoyment. Somehow she and I survived the evening, and I chalked up the experience as one more lesson in the ways of the world."[14]

As a fraternity pledge he marched in the Wreck Tech Pajama Parade, went to pep rallies, and took blind dates to pledge swaps. John attended campus football games and at least once piled into a car with five fraternity brothers and drove to Atlanta for the Auburn–Georgia Tech game. Two boys checked into the Biltmore Hotel, but all six stayed in the room. After the game one of the group partied too much and was picked up by the Atlanta police when he failed to show his draft card. The student, along with several other Auburn boys, was taken to the Atlanta tank. He called John, who was now back at the hotel, and asked him to post bail. John had no money, so he put on his ROTC cap and collected contributions from friends and strangers until he had the seventeen-dollar fine to free his friend from jail.[15]

Fraternity brothers remembered that John was always finding a way to earn money and that he was willing to work hard to make it. Fred Hopton-Jones recalled that while he and other fraternity brothers were glad for the breaks between semesters and planned rest and recreation, John would locate a job as soon as college classes were in recess. On at least one occasion he worked for Algernon Blair on the construction of the Coosa River Ordnance Plant near Talladega, which Blair was building in joint venture with Sullivan, Long and Hagerty. This plant, operated by the Brecon Loading Company, loaded explosives into bags or shells. John also worked on wartime construction projects in Childersburg associated with the Alabama Ordnance Works. In the winter of 1940, John worked as "a structural iron worker" on a plant in Tyler, Tennessee, near Chattanooga. The facility, which was to produce TNT, was being constructed by Stone and Webster of New York. Laboring in the field to John meant enjoying the excitement that went with construction, and it was better than a vacation.[16]

At the end of John's first two semesters at Auburn, his photographs in the 1940 *Glomerata*, in the freshman engineering section and on his fraternity page, show a smiling young man with a boyish thin face and glasses. His hair was smoothed down and parted on the side. John says that he was shy then, weighed only 120 pounds, and "had not done anything particularly outstanding, good or bad." When John showed a *Glomerata* freshman photograph to Margie, his sixteen-year-old daughter, she laughed at the skinny kid who looked back at her.[17] Reflecting on his college days from a distance of forty years, John commented that he did not believe "any soul has ever shown up at Auburn any greener, more naive, less sophisticated than I." At

John Harbert had his portrait taken in his API ROTC uniform. Within a few years, this young man with a thin boyish face would earn his manhood on battlefields in Europe.

the time he "thought smoking a cigarette was an original sin," and John omitted one fraternity from his possible choices "because he had seen some of the leaders smoking." To drink alcoholic beverages was "beyond" his imagination.[18] One year later John's sophomore photograph in the *Glomerata* presents a more mature young man, but still thin faced and youthful.

In August 1940, the summer following John's freshman year, he was working on a construction job, probably with Algernon Blair. His father had finished his work on the Mississippi coast, and the family decided to return to Birmingham so Billy and Betty could start their last year in high school. Mae rented a house in Birmingham on Forty-second Street South and returned to Gulfport to pack their personal items. John was home from Auburn to help with the move. With all the clothes, linens, and dishes packed and ready for a daylight departure, Betty took a batch of high school notes and love letters to a wire incinerator behind the house where the Harberts had been burning trash all day. A few minutes later John carried some trash back to the fire and found Betty unconscious and lying on her back near the incinerator. She was severely burned from the waist up; her face, arms, and hands were black. Betty had evidently had a seizure while she was standing over the fire and had fallen in. John screamed, and his father and Billy rushed to his side. Mr. Harbert cradled Betty and instantly realized she was in great pain. As he explained in a letter to his sister, "I knew at a glance she was beyond hope and prayed that she might not live even until I could get her to a hospital."[19] She was rushed to King's Daughter Hospital, but she died early the next morning on August 29, 1940.[20] Betty was buried in Memphis in the Harbert plot of Elmwood Cemetery, where three, and eventually five, generations of Harberts were buried.[21]

The Harberts returned to Gulfport and drove the packed truck and car to Birmingham. Friends retrieved the Harbert furniture from the Bonita Drive house and moved it to the rented house. Mr. Harbert wrote his sister that "so much light seems to have gone out of life—thousands of things suggest memories and haunt one—my business and domestic plans are chaotic—but one must carry on."[22] Mr. Harbert began to build a small house on some property he owned on Shades Mountain. It kept him busy and was a way for him to fight his grief. Mrs. Harbert called the house "Trebrah," which is Harbert spelled backwards.

The Harberts never really recovered from the death of their seventeen-year-old daughter. Mr. Harbert's health began to decline, and although he lived until 1964, he never had the spirit he once had. Mrs. Harbert became more protective of her sons, especially the youngest, who had lost his twin. When the United States went to war and they both were shipped overseas to the European theater, it was especially difficult for her. For John, being the first one to find his sister was especially traumatic. He pushed the scene to the back of his memories, but he never forgot it.[23]

In the spring of 1941, John was involved with Wayne Peake and another Auburn engineering student in an ROTC map-drawing assignment that was improperly carried out. What happened, who was to blame, how the affair unfolded, and just what the consequences were are still matters of dispute. In a 1994 speech John took all the blame for the affair and said he was asked to leave school; however, Wayne Peake insists that he was the guilty party, John the more innocent one, and they left school on their own accord.[24] In any case, the significant point, and the one all agree on, is that the ROTC professors refused to recommend Harbert, Peake, and another friend for advanced ROTC, thus ending their chance of obtaining commissions in the military through the API ROTC program.

John did leave school for two semesters and convinced his parents that "it was in my best

In January 1991 Jack Dunlop loaned John an original photograph of members of the Delta Sigma Phi fraternity made about 1940. John made copies and sent them to several of his fraternity brothers. He observed in a cover letter that this was the "house where we spent many hours studying diligently, perfecting the manners of true southern gentlemen, and practicing sobriety." John is sitting on the front row dressed in the white slacks.

Front row: R. L. Zachry, Charles Brown, Donald Hopton-Jones, Barna Wayne Peake, Sumner G. Nesbitt, John M. Harbert III, Robert P. Kloeti, Robert B. Hudson, James B. McCorstin. Second row: W. Dallas Benton, William B. Carroll, Robert G. Campbell, Marion K. Williams, Winfrey Boyd, Mrs. Annie Stover (housemother), Thomas R. Mitchell, Jr., Jack M. Dunlop, Albie R. Smith, Freddy Bass, James L. Caraway, Jr. Third Row: James McFarland, Elbert C. Davidson, William E. Shofner, Harold Jacobs, Malcolm E. Hannah, Roger C. Hamel, Jr., William G. Greene, Sherrill E. Embry, Thomas E. Greene, John N. McCabe. Back row: *William J. Califf, Jr., Robert A. Sawyer, Walter L. Nichols, Van B. Seelbinder, Bert Simpson, Joseph M. Sprague, John C. Arnold, Jr., Fred Hopton-Jones.*

interests to get some solid work experience."[25] He took a job in Huntsville tying steel on a construction site at the Redstone Arsenal. This work experience was valuable, but it also persuaded him that he "needed a real education."[26] John was not in school when the Japanese bombed Pearl Harbor on December 7, 1941. Although he had no possibility of a commission through the ROTC program, with America at war a civil engineering degree itself might lead to a commission. So John went back to Auburn in the fall of 1942. He later spoke of the uncertainty of the times and how difficult it was for him to concentrate on his studies when "the disruption and turmoil" of his life "escalated as the months went by. The registration for the draft, interest in volunteering for service, and constant bad news of the German Wehrmacht successes did not create the best atmosphere for college life and reflective study."[27]

In June API changed its academic calendar from a semester system to a twelve-week quarter system to enable male students to complete as many credits as possible before leaving for the military. Accelerated classes and early examinations were offered as the college pushed its students toward graduation to accommodate the nation's increasing need for well-trained officers.[28] John pressed forward with his studies. At the end of winter quarter exams in 1943, he wrote his mother that "exams are over and I passed everything—with fair grades. Wayne and I are the only ones left in the house—everybody else has moved. ... This place is really deserted—not a sound in the place. I sure hate to move, but it can't be helped." John and all the fraternity boys on campus were being moved from their fraternity houses so that female students could be housed there. The college was getting ready for the arrival of male students enrolled in the Army Specialized Training Program (ASTP) and for navy and air corps programs. Auburn had no dormitories for men and only a few dorms for women. In order to comply with military requests for dormitory space for these special military students, API moved the girls from Alumni Hall and the new quadrangle dorms to fraternity houses, thus dislocating the fraternity boys. John headed back to Mr. and Mrs. Ware's, this time to stay in their Garden Court Apartments Annex, which the Wares had recently constructed behind their two houses on Gay Street.

John's mother wrote to inquire about his schedule for the spring. He replied that he had decided to take Spanish, along with world geography, engineering economy, and sewage disposal. Two of John's close friends were fraternity brothers Don and Fred Hopton-Jones, who were from Cuba and often spoke Spanish with John around the fraternity house. John wanted to build on his high school Spanish, but he had difficulty obtaining the civil engineering department's approval of his Spanish course. He explained to his mother that he "thought about it a long time before I signed up for the course."[29] He had to justify taking the class to Professor Thomas Marvel Lowe, head of the civil engineering department, who was a graduate of the Massachusetts Institute of Technology and a taskmaster "heavily grounded in theory." Lowe believed engineers should take engineering courses.[30] John related that he told Professor Lowe that "I ought to know more than anybody else what is best for me—for this reason—I am the only person that knows all the plans and ideas of what I want to do." John had considered "everybody's advice in as many different lights as possible," but in the end he believed that he "should be able to have the best judgment as to what is the best thing for me to do." He "had a devil of a time" getting his schedule approved. He wrote his mother that "I ... talked my head off to Professor Lowe and I know I must have sounded like a Philadelphia lawyer talking to Mr. Edwards (the registrar). I finally convinced them and received their begrudged blessings, so I don't see why I can't convince you."[31]

Considering alternatives, weighing various points of view, and then making decisions with confidence and acting upon them in a decisive manner were character traits that stayed with John Harbert far beyond his college years. So did his persistence in getting what he wanted, a childhood trait that was sometimes wearing on his parents. In this letter John assured his mother that he had good reasons for his choice of Spanish. One wonders if perhaps John envisioned that after the war there would be engineering opportunities in environments where understanding and speaking Spanish might be a great advantage. Throughout his life he enjoyed using his Spanish and regretted that he was not more fluent or able to speak other languages as well.

Beyond the Spanish course, John had other differences with the philosophy of the API engineering school. John recalled later that when he was a student at API the head of civil engineering, Professor Lowe, "had little or no respect for contractors. Each year, he delivered a routine lecture to the first-year engineering students on the evils of the construction industry." He encouraged his students to enter "pure engineering" rather than pursue careers in construction. The professor "expressed concern" when John told him he planned "to find employment on a construction project" and that "one day" he wanted to have his "own contracting business." John enjoyed the outdoor life and "the thrill and excitement of building." The head of civil engineering "was aghast" that John would consider "wasting" an "Auburn engineering education by becoming a contractor."[32]

But the world was at war. With the American military on the defensive in the Pacific theater during much of 1942 and with the training camps full, by fall John realized he would soon be drafted. In a speech in 1980 during an executive-in-residence program, John recalled those bleak days in Auburn:

> We looked forward to being called to active duty. And slowly but surely, one by one, we began disappearing from the "loveliest Village of the Plains." The exodus started on a small scale in 1940 and gradually increased with each passing month until late spring of 1943, when everybody was called up except those who failed to pass the physical. I had volunteered in the fall of '42 and was ordered to report to active duty later the next spring.[33]

In September 1940, before the United States joined the war, there were 4,000 students at API; but by 1943 there were only 1,709 civilian students. Along with many of his college friends, John joined the army reserves. He completed the spring term before the army needed him, taking exams early; however, he was still five hours short and lacked the course in indeterminate structures to earn his civil engineering degree when he received orders from the U.S. Army to report to duty. On June 19, 1943, the War Department ordered all reservists from the Alabama Polytechnic Institute to various enlistment facilities. John was assigned with a large group of his API friends to report for active duty to Fort McPherson, Atlanta, Georgia, on July 5, 1943.[34]

3

THE ARMY AND WORLD WAR II

"soaking wet and muddy all day"

Three days after John reported for active duty at Fort McPherson, Georgia, he finally had time to sit down and write his parents his first army letter. He knew they were concerned about how he was getting along and how he was taking to "the army and army life." John assured them that he liked the army "better than I thought I would, but I am too much of an individual and don't appreciate being told how to handle every minute detail to the extent that is necessary to be a good soldier." John wrote that from his "observations in this place—I would say that morons would make the best soldiers." The food was excellent and abundant, and the PX (post exchange) was filled with candy and gum "and all those things that ceased to appear for the civilians some time ago." Although he was assigned to the same barracks as brother Billy and his buddies from Auburn, he was disappointed that he was not processed with the others. While his friends were being interviewed and assigned, John "scrubbed barrack floors, washed windows, cleaned out latrines, flushed sewer lines, washed beds" and was so tired that he hit the sack "every night before dark." Billy had been classified as a draftsman and was headed back to school. John had requested "combat duty with the construction engineers" and looked forward to knowing where he would go for training. He confided to his parents that "the dice—at present—are not rolling my way."[1]

By Tuesday of the next week Billy and all of the boys with whom John had come to camp had left, and he wrote his mother that he had no idea where they had been sent. He was upset because he had stood in "formation for mail call twice every day for an hour each time," and he had not "received a single letter." On Sunday John had KP, and "it was really rough work." He thought he was as "unlucky as hell" and hated "everything connected" with Fort McPherson. He did have some good news for his parents. He had scored at the top on his mental test and high on a structural iron workers' test. He was now classified "as a fluent speaker of Spanish" and "a construction foreman suitable for duty in a Spanish-speaking country." The army was "a hell of a life—and especially so since all the [Auburn] boys have gone."[2]

Five days later John wrote his mother that he had arrived at Fort McClellan, Alabama, and was assigned to Company B, Twenty-first Training Battalion. He soon discovered that Billy and the other Auburn boys were there, too, and things began to look "much brighter." The day room was nice, the officers "more reasonable," there were plenty of books and magazines to read, and everything was clean and cool. He was to receive thirteen weeks of training in basic infantry tactics. He asked his mother to send him "ten good coat hangers," some fountain-pen ink, and two history books.[3]

John wrote his mother two days later to thank her for sending his requests so quickly, and he gave her another list of items he needed. Army life had already changed. He was "busy with a scheduled program 24 hours of the day." He told his mother not to expect him and Billy home for the weekend because Birmingham "exceeds our 50-mile limit" and "we are going to be here 13 weeks & it is too early to start making mistakes or take chances."[4]

On July 25 John evaluated his first week of basic training. His endurance was good because he did not smoke, and the heat, which was plaguing the northern boys so much, was not bothering him. He was irritated by the large number of New Yorkers in his company, Yankees who he thought had "less common sense than a herd of sheep" and "haven't been anywhere but Brooklyn" but "think they know everything." John reported that the "Southern fellows are trying to teach the Northern boys our way of life." Rudeness, crude table manners, and discourtesies annoyed John the most, but he assured his parents that "we Southern boys are going to make gentlemen out of most of them—already you can see improvements in their behavior." On another matter, he wrote his parents that "you ought to see me in a gas mask with a bayoneted rifle & carrying full field pack & with my helmet on. You certainly wouldn't recognize me as being from this planet."[5]

During the time John was stationed at Fort McClellan for basic training, he frequently hitchhiked home. His leave always began on Saturday afternoon, and he had to be back on base by 11:00 P.M. Sunday. Once John brought a friend from Utah, Marden Hatch, home with him, and this may have been the weekend when John had a date with Impy Shook and asked her to find a blind date for his friend. Mary Porter Shook, known as Impy, lived next door to his parents on Shades Mountain and was a student at Birmingham-Southern College. Impy made a deal with her roommate, Wita Jones, who had a boyfriend stationed at Maxwell Field in Montgomery. If Wita would come home with Impy and go out with John's friend, she would ride the train to Montgomery with Wita on Sunday so Wita could visit her air cadet beau. Wita knew John Harbert because they had been students together at Mountain Brook Grammar School and Phillips High School. Years later Wita recalled this evening and remembered more about her blind date trying to be too amorous than she did about John Harbert. It would be three years before Wita saw John again.[6]

As the end of basic training came near, John and Billy realized they would probably be shipped in different directions. Both passed the advance tests necessary to enter the Army Specialized Training Program, but their separation was delayed when, for unknown reasons, their basic instruction was extended another four weeks. It was the middle of October before the brothers received their assignments and left Fort McClellan. Billy was sent east to ASTP at Newark College of Engineering, and John was headed for the ASTP at the University of Illinois at Champaign.[7]

John was in charge of the McClellan group during the train ride north and carried all the records of the men.[8] By chance John was on the same train with a number of boys he knew from Birmingham, including Bill Ireland. The group arrived in Champaign on October 22 after an overnight trip from Alabama. John was very impressed with the Illinois campus. To him it was a large place with "many big fraternity houses," a student building "that looks bigger than the Federal capitol," and an armory "that's big enough to hold most of Auburn." For the first time in his life, John realized "how small" his section of the country was. He was assigned a comfortable first-floor room in the Alpha Delta Phi house. He wrote his mother and asked her to please mail him his "slide rule, green calculus book, applied mechanics book, [and] all surveying books." He had already figured out that he was going to have to study hard.[9]

During his stay at the University of Illinois at Champaign, where he was enrolled in the Army Specialized Training Program (ASTP), John practiced surveying. On the back of this photograph, dated January 1944, he wrote: "Pfc. Harbert, surveyor—in business with the U.S. Army, Inc."

By the first week of November John had made a trip to Chicago and filed complaints with the army because he had not received a paycheck. He was broke and wrote his mother to send him some money "pronto." In case she could not translate his Spanish correctly, he added that it meant "hurry, I need much money right now." John was proud when he was made company commander.[10] As captain, he initiated social activities and worked with the first sergeant to arrange parties with some of the sororities. The two leaders took thirty members of the company over to the Alpha Gamma Delta house for Sunday afternoon tea. John wrote his mother that he really needed another wool uniform because "he hated to stand in front of 200 men without looking anything other than a perfect soldier." He hoped she could find some wool pants in Birmingham because they were too expensive in Chicago—$10 to $15 a pair. He needed a 29-inch waist and a 31-inch length. His shirt size was 14½-inch neck and 32-inch sleeve. He was uneasy, for classes were scheduled to begin in three days. Fun time was over. John wished his mother a happy birthday and hoped that he would be home on her next one.[11]

As John began his studies, he anticipated that they were going to be difficult for him, so as company commander he selected for his adjutant an MIT student who was good in the subjects in which he thought he was weak.[12] John was proud of his men, and at drill they were the "best looking outfit on the drill field." John spent Thanksgiving studying, foregoing a trip to Rock Island to visit his Aunt Nita and promising he would have more leave time at Christmas. The course that was giving him the most trouble was electricity. He had not taken a single course in electricity at Auburn, and to make matters worse, he was unable to obtain a textbook.[13] But John reported he was doing well in courses in military surveying, structural drafting, calculus, and applied mechanics.

As company commander, John was responsible for drilling his men. He had a sore throat from yelling his orders, but "handling 300 men is a wonderful experience," for "there is a certain amount of confidence gained in drilling troops. You have to have it or you can't put over your commands & have them obeyed without hesitation. I put the entire company through every maneuver known to the foot soldier this afternoon." He told his parents he was grateful for the excellent training he had received at Fort McClellan.[14]

On December 5, John posted a discouraged letter to his parents. He observed—and Billy concurred—that "the boys from Northern colleges were much better prepared than the boys from the Southern colleges." John questioned whether he was "cut out to be an engineer" and confessed that "the only thing I ever did like about engineering was the romance of construction." He felt there were other things he could do better than engineering and even wondered at the low pay engineers received. But he realized that "it takes something more than an introvert math genius to make a successful engineer or to make for success in any field of endeavor. A man with talents for organizing and handling other men could control all the brains & so-called geniuses in the world and have them working for his benefit."[15]

John worried about his grades and assured his parents that he was studying and was doing his best "and that is all that I can ask of myself."[16] The Harberts were concerned about John's low spirits, and in mid-December they decided to travel to Illinois to visit him and then go up to Rock Island to spend Christmas with Aunt Nita. John would join them for the holidays. He made arrangements for his parents' visit and reserved rooms for them at a hotel in Champaign. He shared the latest rumor—"that A.S.T.P. is going to fold up pronto"—which had been flying all over the campus.[17] The gossip was correct. Although by late 1943 the American army had secured North Africa and invaded Italy, the Russians had driven Hitler's troops from the Crimea and were poised to push into the Balkans and Poland; the Japanese line of aggression was slowly being pushed back, U.S. casualties were high, and front-line fatigue was extensive. Fresh troops were needed for the cross-channel invasion that the Allies were planning for the spring of 1944. In late 1943 the college courses of ASTP did not fit into the military's pressing needs. The army needed men immediately.

After the Christmas holiday John had enough time off to spend New Year's Eve in Chicago, then he was back studying for examinations. He warned his parents that if he were not retained in the program he would "be shipped immediately to some classification center" and would not receive a furlough.[18] The encouragement his parents gave him during their December visit had faded; John confessed that he had lost confidence in himself. He told his parents not to worry, for "if I get beat—I will at least have the satisfaction of knowing it took guys who were plenty on the ball to do it. The race has been a fast one & far above average."[19] Two weeks later John mailed his parents two newspaper clippings, one dated January 25, 1944, about congressional debates on ending ASTP. The House military committee determined that abolition or drastic curtailment would free 150,000 young soldiers for combat duty. By the end of the month John Harbert was out of the program, assigned to army ground forces, and awaiting word on where he would be shipped. John wrote home that he was disappointed that his career was "washed up" and that it had "more or less taken the starch out of me." He regretted not getting a furlough, writing that "I would call, but just don't feel like saying much." He told his parents not to expect to hear from him "until I get where I'm going."[20]

John was sent to Fort Sheridan, Illinois, and was soon back drilling again with all the "damn foolishness that goes on." He had gone "from a private room with bath to a flop house in one jump." The place was full of "misfits and worn-out old sergeants of all grades." John was living in a garage converted to a barracks for 900 men who were sleeping in double-decker beds "jammed right together." There appeared, he wrote, "no reason for being here—no aim in each day's work."[21] He was able to obtain a furlough, but not long enough to go anywhere except Chicago, where he took a room at the Palmer House, ate a Chinese dinner, and saw the show *Good Night Ladies*. He wanted some money from home because, if he could make it back to Chicago the next week, he had a Saturday night date.[22] John was able to return, and he took his date dancing at the Black Hawk, the city's finest nightclub. The evening cost him "a fortune"—twenty dollars.[23]

In early February scarlet fever broke out at Fort Sheridan. The soldiers were marched to the dispensary for a throat examination, and the line of men stretched "three blocks up the road." John's throat was fine, and he assured his parents that he did not "even have a cold." John had taken a scarlet fever shot in 1939 that may have given him some protection.[24] But the army was concerned enough that the medical corps placed the fort on quarantine. The idea of being confined to the converted garage, what John referred to as "the flop house," was not a pleasant thought. During his long hours in the barracks, John entertained some of the men with card tricks and was assigned several days of KP duty.[25] By the sixth day of the quarantine the men were settling down, but not John.[26] The extra time allowed him to write longer letters home and to expound on the shoddy construction work on his barracks. Although he appreciated that time was an important factor in putting up the buildings quickly when the war began, in the case of one error John thought it was "just dumbness on the part of the workmen." As he explained to his father:

> In this building we have about twelve wash basins and eight toilets for six-hundred and forty-six men. The hot water faucets in the wash basins have always run cold water—no matter what time you get up. We have had to shave in water that is just above zero—it comes from Lake Michigan. I had always figured that there was never any hot water because men nearer the latrine than I am would get there first and use up any hot water that might have been in the tank. Well, the other day a former ASTP man was using the toilet and flushed it without getting up—he was scalded somewhat in the process of the flushing. He, being an ASTP man and somewhat more intelligent than the general run of the mill here, investigated and discovered that the hot water system was connected up with the toilets. All this time and probably long before the ASTP showed up here, the men have been shaving and washing in the cold water—the toilets have been flushed and probably thoroughly sterilized by the hot water. Fifteen minutes' work this morning by a couple of plumbers reversed the situation, and we have all the scalding water we can handle.[27]

John went on that he was particularly upset because H. V. Kaultenborn had just announced the discontinuance of ASTP on his nightly radio broadcast. John knew that "all the boys we left behind" in ASTP would be pouring into army camps soon. If he had not been quarantined for the scarlet fever, he would "probably have a couple weeks' jump on them." John was also angry because the officers were not quarantined but "come and go anytime they feel like it. I've yet to find out how bars make a man immune to disease." John told his parents that rumors were flying around the fort that as soon as the quarantine was lifted his group would be shipped out immediately for "five weeks training camp and then to a POE [port of embarkation] for immediate shipment across the high seas." John also bragged to his father that he had parlayed a fifty-cent stake into twenty-five dollars.[28]

Mrs. Harbert sent John a large box of food to help him cope with the quarantine, and it arrived just in time, for within a few days John was on a troop train headed west. The long train attracted attention in the small towns it passed through, and John wrote his mother that "with each turn of the wheel, I'm getting further and further away from home." He was outside Little Rock, Arkansas, when he explained to her how the boys would just throw letters out the windows of the train and someone would pick them up and mail them.[29] John sent a postcard to his mother from San Antonio, Texas, writing that he was glad to be back in the South where it was warm.[30] At a stop in Texas several hundred boys from ASTP at Texas A & M University boarded the train. John immediately found an old Auburn classmate, John Risen Jones of Huntsville, among the group. The two would stay together in the same division and regiment throughout the war, and their mothers would become close friends, sharing news from the front through correspondence and telephone calls but never meeting.[31]

On February 28, 1944, John posted a USO card to his mother. He wrote that the train had passed through Yuma, Arizona, and he saw "row after row of tents sitting on the desert" and was "glad we didn't stop at Yuma." He thought he was going to California and might be stationed within 200 miles of Los Angeles. John was enjoying speaking Spanish with Mexicans he met in towns the train passed through and wanted his Spanish books. While his New York comrades "resent this country and can't see anything here," John had "enjoyed the trip immensely."[32] The pleasure was not to be long-lived. When the train arrived at Indio, California, at 1:30 in the afternoon, it was met by a convoy of trucks that transported the soldiers four hours to the northeast. Then the young men hiked into the desert.[33] On February 28 John explained to his parents: "At the present I'm in the middle of nowhere—just below the Mohave Desert—just south of Death Valley in the Grand Desert. We are in a circle of mountains—very rugged looking from here. Past this circle of mountains there is another ring of mountains that are snow-covered."[34]

John was uneasy, for his living conditions were getting "progressively worse." He wrote that "the old barn (at Fort Sheridan), in light of what I see here, was indeed a castle of luxury." John thought he was at the lowest ebb, and "it can't get any lower." The previous night he had slept in a tent on a cot under three blankets, and it was "too cold to do much sleeping. The place is known as a Base Camp for the 104th Division (that's my outfit). But don't let that term fool you. If this is the Base Camp, I know I never want to see the advance camp."[35]

The 104th Division to which John had been assigned was organized in 1921 as a reserve infantry division composed of personnel from the western states and with headquarters in Utah. In 1924 the division adopted an insignia with the head of a gray timberwolf on a balsam green background, and the division became known as the Timberwolf Division. On September 15, 1942, at Camp Adair, Oregon, the 104th was activated. During the fall and winter of 1942-43, soldiers poured into Camp Adair from Officer Candidate Schools and enlistment centers across the United States in order to bring the division up to full strength. After extensive training and maneuvers in the Oregon mountains, Major General Terry de la Mesa Allen, who had commanded the Fighting First Division in the invasion of Sicily, assumed command on October 15, 1943. There was little doubt that the 104th was being trained for the Allied invasion of Europe. On November 7, the 104th moved to Camp Hyder, on the California-Arizona border, and launched into brutal maneuvers on the desert and in the mountains. General Allen preached that "discipline, technique, physical toughness, and a belief in your units are essential" for a successful combat division.[36] Later that month the division moved to Camp Horn and began thirteen weeks of desert training.

In March 1944, at Camp Granite, California, Private First Class Harbert posed before his pup tent with his sergeant. Although John wrote home that the night view of candles and bonfires and daylight scenery were beautiful, the training and maneuvers were tough.

The men of the 104th had been through five hard months in the field when the two Alabama college students arrived in the California desert to join them. The two Johns were assigned to the 414th Regiment, but they were in different companies; however, they remained close friends throughout the war. John explained that "at present the 104th is fighting the 80th Division in the mountains around here. We can hear the firing and see the planes. This mock war is over on the 4th of March and the Division returns here for a weekend of rest. The 104th is a crack division and is winning every mock engagement." Although the soldiers had been on maneuvers and in the desert so long that "some of them have gone crazy," the division was "well trained" and "ready to be shipped overseas." John wrote that "Overnight things took on a different set of values. Money is just so much paper. Water and food have untold values. All water is hauled in by truck in 5-gallon containers. We stand in line to get our daily quart of water. ...There are no lights in this whole valley—so we have to go to bed when the sun goes down. The box of food you sent me while I was at Sheridan has become a box of gold."[37]

John soon found out that the division had been successful in attacking the Palen Pass, something that had never before been accomplished in a training maneuver. John was assigned to Company K. Within a few days of his arrival, the division moved to Camp Granite, California, where John found the scenery "very beautiful." He wrote that "we are sleeping in pup tents now and it is very pretty to look over the countryside and see thousands of little tents with candles burning in each one—bonfires blazing." However, the night operations, training in weapon proficiency, reconnaissance, combat exercises, battle drills, and rapid movements over rugged terrain made John understand General Allen's motto for the Timberwolves GET SMART AND GET TOUGH, and his principle of "Find 'em, fix 'em, fight 'em."[38]

The California camp was still in the desert and was little different from Camps Hyder and Horn except that the wind blew more violently.[39] The day after John arrived, the army moved the camp about five miles down the valley, and John spent the day pitching tents. He wrote his mother by candlelight that the nights were cold and the days hot. He had been given a physical examination, and when the doctor asked him if he had anything to complain about, John replied he wanted "some electricity for my radio and more comforts of home." The doctor laughed. John had not "heard a word" about anything since he left Fort Sheridan. "I haven't seen a newspaper or read anything about the war since I've been here," he wrote.[40]

The division, out on maneuvers when John arrived, began to drift into camp in groups and was all accounted for by March 5. The return of the division caused a remarkable improvement in living conditions. John reported that "a PX moved in last night [with] candy, gum, ice cream, writing paper, soap & so forth." The GIs saw Rosalind Russell in *What a Woman*; the screen was the back of a truck, and "the desert sand doubled for seats."[41] John wrote that "Life here in the desert is not at all to my liking, but I can't do much to alter the situation. There is nothing here but sand and desert waste—the sun broils you during the day and you freeze at night—the wind blows continuously at velocities of twenty or thirty miles per hour, blasting sand into the food, water, and against exposed parts of the body. With the elements doing their part it doesn't take long to look weather beaten & leathery."[42]

On March 10 John was part of a dawn forced-march to the base of Mount Palen, a distance of about twenty-five miles. The men rested a few hours and then after dark began the climb up the mountain in order to reach their target at 3 A.M. The force they were trying to "dislodge" had numerical superiority, but the element of surprise attack in the dark was on their side. The mountain was "about 4,500 feet high," and John did not "relish the climb at all." Rumors were that the division was getting ready to move out, and the artillerymen were "preparing their big guns for transportation." He was writing by candlelight, the wind was blowing his "tent around like it was tissue paper," and he had all his gear "rolled and ready to go early in the morning. My rifle and bayonet are polished to the nth degree, and I have the rifle in bed with me to keep sand from blowing in the chamber."[43]

After the attack up the mountain and a quick weekend in Los Angeles, John returned to camp to find a full sandstorm blowing. The wind was roaring fifty miles an hour, equipment was being destroyed, canvas was ripping, truck tarps were being torn off, and the men had retreated to the shelter of their tents. But being inside was little better, for sand filled their shoes even there. John finally pulled a blanket over his head and tried to sleep. He knew that on March 19 the division was being sent to Camp Carson, Colorado, where he expected to be stationed for several weeks.

John wrote home on March 21 that "the last week in the desert was terrible—sandstorms all the time." One night the "storm started while we were at a picture show—I was about 30 feet from the screen ... at times [the sand] blotted out the screen and finally clogged the projector—so we didn't see all of the show. I had to walk backwards getting back to my tent. Just crawled in the tent and covered up with blankets and overcoat to get out of the sand. ... All night long shelter halves, clothes, etc. flew past." In the morning eight inches of sand covered everything, and John had to "dig around looking" for his bayonet and books. He told his mother that "it was useless to try to eat, so we packed our equipment and loaded in trucks and rode 20 miles to a railroad siding." John stayed there "in the wind and sand" until 1:30 in the afternoon when he and the division boarded troop trains headed for Camp Carson, which was located just east of Pike's Peak and seven miles from Colorado Springs.[44]

At Camp Carson John began five weeks of intensive training designed for the thousands of new soldiers who were arriving daily. John thought the camp "excellent compared to what we have had the last month." He was happy to be back in civilization with "electric lights, running water, a PX across the way, show down the street, eating in a mess hall." Although he hoped to get a furlough home, the best he could manage was a trip to Colorado Springs, where he "ate a big $3.00 steak dinner with caviar as a beginning."[45] John found it difficult to make friends in his company because its members "have been together for some twenty months and have formed tight cliques," making it hard "for us new men to get anywhere." He thought that most of the men in the company were "not overly bright," "country boys" with "very little education."[46] Yet the company was "singled out" by General Terry Allen as the "outstanding company in the division" on the last maneuvers. John believed that the company came out on top because of a "bull dog tenacity to survive on top of a mountain without food, in the rain, and without any relief—and probably some luck, too." He told his father that the company "climbed up an almost impossible cliff and attacked Palen Pass from the rear."[47] Three days later John wrote his mother. He had heard from a friend at Fort Sheridan that a few days after he left Illinois for Arizona "the garage that we were staying in had burned down and that two sergeants had burned to death." John commented that he was "glad we got away from that place as I would hate to lose all my clothes, etc."[48]

John disclosed that he had filled out an OCS application and given it to his company commander before leaving California; however, he had little hope he would be tapped for the officer training program. He then confided to his father how difficult it was to know that he was

> better qualified to be a company commander than the men around me that I see trying to do the job. I am so confident that I could do the job, and do it better than it's being done by a lot of COs, that I itch for an opportunity to prove that I can do it. I think that with my experience working under different types of bosses—working men myself—watching men's reactions to different types of leaders and with a small knowledge of human psychology that it is a damn shame that I don't get a chance to prove that I can do it. It is for this reason, more than anything else, that I care to be an officer. Here I am—an *assistant* BAR [Browning automatic rifle] man in a rifle company—with all the education that I'm supposed to have and with the experience that I have—that's the best I can do in the army—an assistant BAR man—a job any moron could hold down with credit to himself. My years in college and working experience, as far as the army is concerned, are worth nothing. I really will be glad to get out of the army and get in a position where I'm not tied down by red tape and the narrow set-up found in the army.[49]

During the next weeks John endured extreme cold, exhaustion, and two hours of bayonet training each day. He trained with a mortar squad and was "soaking wet and muddy all day." He suffered from a cough, cold, and sore throat that he could not shake. The high altitude made breathing difficult, and snow was still on the ground although it was late April. Because the Timberwolves made a specialty of night attacks and fighting in the dark, almost every

While he was stationed in Colorado, John found time to take in the sights, including Cheyenne Mountain.

night he had infiltration courses to run and night problems to solve.

But occasionally John was able to obtain a weekend pass. He and John Risen Jones would go into Manitou Springs, visit the Cave of the Winds and William's Canyon, rent horses and ride into the mountains, or eat at Antlers Hotel. Sometimes they would visit Colorado Springs and have dinner at the English Village or the Indian Grill. They also discovered that the local Episcopal church served home-cooked lunch after Sunday services and had a card room where bridge games were played in the afternoons. The church even had nice ladies who arranged dates for the visiting servicemen. John occasionally went into Denver to visit his father's sister, Bess, and her husband, Frank Gorin, their daughter, Virginia, and her husband, Ed Daday. John and Ed went fishing several times, and Aunt Bess tried to initiate a romance between John and a neighbor's daughter, named Eleanor but called Ellie.[50]

In early April the 104th Division was restricted to barracks. There was loud booing when General Allen addressed the 6,000 men who had arrived as replacements for the division. John wrote that "something was said about his [General Allen's] success with the 1st Division (he lost 87 percent of that division in North Africa) and those words weren't received so well." Because of the restriction John was forced to break a bridge date.[51] He was resigned that a transfer was impossible and that he could not move up in the army. Although his test scores put him in the highest category, he explained to his mother what he was up against: "In the business or competitive world—where things are figured on a dollar-and-cents value, it's not so hard for the man with the most ability to forge ahead of those with lesser abilities. However, in the army, things are vastly different. I can't explain the difference now but will certainly do so when and if I get home." John wrote that "since PFC [private first class] seems to be tops" he intended "to keep what privileges I have and to stay out of trouble—if that is possible."[52]

The entire 104th Division was furloughed in two-week intervals from May 1 through June. John kept waiting his turn. On May 25 he wrote his mother that he had "attended to all necessary legal matters that had to be done before going overseas. It seems that we may go before long as everything and everybody are rapidly being prepared for that move. I made my last will and testament, making you and Dad the sole beneficiaries in case of my death. I also signed papers making you the executrix and giving you power of attorney on all property that I have." John was concerned about keeping a clear title to a piece of property in Washington State that he had inherited from his mother's father jointly with Billy and several cousins. The ranch was leased to nearby farmers and was referred to in the family as "the 80th." John also explained that he had signed away his pay in war bonds paid to his mother and that "this leaves me no spending money—I haven't worked out that angle yet," he confessed. John related that the division had "been working unusually hard for the past few weeks—day and night—sometimes going 48 hours without sleep. We have been told that we have thirty days to complete all requirements for overseas movement." He assured his mother that his furlough time was nearing, that he would leave for Alabama within a few days, but he would be given no notice.[53]

John left Camp Carson for Birmingham sometime after he mailed this letter on May 25, and he was back in Colorado in mid-June; therefore, he was at home on June 6 when radio news flashed from Europe that the Allied forces had invaded France at Normandy. The 104th Division had missed D-Day but would be critically needed as fresh troops for the push into the Low Countries and Germany. From Colorado on June 14, John confided to his parents that he was "missing the life at home," was "more disgruntled than ever with the Army," and worried that he would be "caught in an army of occupation." General Allen, the 104th Division commander, had been called to Washington. John had no idea what that meant.[54]

Three days later John confided in a letter to a Harbert neighbor and family friend, Mrs. James K. Shook, Impy's mother, that he was "in hot water" because he had written a letter critical of the captain of his company. It seems that during the 104th Division parade for Infantry Day on June 15 some of the company "talked" while standing at attention "all morning in the hot sun with full equipment." There "were 15,000 men" on the field, and the company was in the rear; however, the captain chewed out his men and demanded that any soldier who "leaned on his rifle, removed his helmet, talked, etc., to step forward. He gave us ten seconds to do so. Practically every man stepped forward." The captain overreacted and threatened "a court martial or the 104th article of war." That night John typed up a letter critical of his captain and defending the honest men who had admitted not standing at attention during the duration of the review. John posted the anonymous editorial on the company bulletin board. The men read it and approved, but the captain was incensed when he saw it. John was accused of writing the letter and was called before four officers—three against him and one for him. He refused to lie. He was questioned for two hours but had no idea what the outcome would be. But he was not worried. "I know," he wrote, "I can out talk all four of the officers, and if I can get over being mad, I might even enjoy the court martial proceedings." He asked Mrs. Shook not to tell his mother because she would worry.[55]

John Risen Jones wrote John a long letter about this affair, congratulating him on having "the courage and fortitude that make a man." Jones was pleased that the Catholic chaplain, Father Edmund J. Murray, stood up for

John was shifted from company to company within the 414th Regiment of the 104th Division and sometimes was assigned to two companies at the same time, a situation he liked because it gave him free time without direct supervision.

John and helped smooth over the situation. The officers decided to transfer John to the headquarters company, and Jones thought John had "a much better break being transferred to battalion headquarters."[56] A month later the army demoted John to buck private, and he told his mother to "address all mail as Pvt. henceforth. I believe that's where I started."[57] This was not the last time John Harbert was in trouble with the army nor the last time Father Murray came to his rescue. John enjoyed telling about the time he had a conflict with an officer after he refused to take the prophylactic that the officer handed him as he left the base on a pass. The officer explained that it was army policy and that John had to take it. John said he was going to the library and did not want it, and he threw it back to the officer. John was accused of assaulting an officer, but Father Murray again was able to mediate the charges for John.[58]

Throughout July the soldiers in the 104th Division watched the news from Europe with great interest while they readied themselves to move. John wrote that "we are turning in our OD [olive drab] blouses tomorrow—it doesn't seem like they are going to leave us anything to wear. A lot of our equipment is being packed up and transported."[59] John sent Billy a letter on July 5 saying that he believed the division would receive orders soon but he was worried whether they would "get there in time to see much action." Training had been completed, and there were "no more night problems, just enough to keep us busy in the daytime." He liked the headquarters company and thought the boys were "better." He told Billy about the snow still in the mountains, the cool nights, the beautiful "white and clear" streams. He was, he said, "going to come back out here and spend some time doing nothing but looking." He confided that he "had managed to do okay this month—have already spent a good sum and sent $100 or so bucks home to bolster my bank account."[60] John's stories in later years about all the money he won shooting craps in the army are substantiated by numerous references in his war letters to winning money. John Risen Jones recalled that John was fascinated with "craps and the whole concept of number theory" and that "if there was a crap game John was there."[61]

John wrote Billy about spending a weekend at the Broadmoor Hotel in Denver. In the lobby, he saw Brigadier General Bryant E. Moore, the second in command of his division. John was never intimidated by rank, and he initiated a long conversation with the general. John told the Guadalcanal veteran that he needed "to drop around and spend a little time talking informally to the boys while they were training." A week later the general came by to visit John's company. John was "sure surprised" when General Moore "showed up at our place," but he got a good laugh when he saw "all our lieutenants blow up and run around like they had dysentery." John could never understand "why a star on a man's shoulder should make him something to fear. Maybe the lieutenants feel that they might have something to lose—whereas I haven't anything to lose. I'm standing on rock bottom and can't fall far."[62]

In the last weeks of July and the first weeks of August John spent time with Ellie, the girl from Denver, and took leave whenever he could. He and John Risen drove Ellie and her sister around in Ellie's Ford convertible. They went up to Cripple Creek, a deserted mining camp, had dinner at the Broadmoor, and danced. The evening cost the two Johns "$25 to get out of the place, but it was worth it." Sunday the four "drove all over the country with the top down, had breakfast at the Antlers Coffee Shop and dinner at the Swiss Chalet." They drove to the Helen Hunt Falls, "climbed up the stairs to the Seven Falls—threw pebbles at the rainbow trout in the lake." John told his mother he might like to stay in Colorado and live there "if it were possible to earn a living." At the very least he intended to "come back out here for a vacation after the war." He did not "know of a better place."[63] It was a wistful letter from a young man who realized he soon would be leaving his country for a battlefield a long way from home.

On July 29 all long-distance telephone calls from the base were restricted, but John was able to make one more trip to Denver and call his parents. On August 12 he wrote that he had been assigned to Company F in addition to the headquarters company and commented that "[add] a few more companies to my roster and I will have toured the 414th pretty well." John thought his "new split in command" would be "pretty nice for me. Nobody knows just where I am. I have more freedom of action."[64] One "vivid memory" that John Risen has about John Harbert during the war was that he "was moved between companies often."[65]

On August 10 the advance party left Camp Carson. In the next few days the entire 104th Division loaded onto twenty-four trains and headed east by different routes to Camp Kilmer, New Jersey, where each man was processed for overseas shipment. John wrote his parents that the trip across the country was "enjoyable" but "a very dirty one," for they "rode, as with most troop trains, with the windows open." Within an hour soot covered everyone's faces. John was comfortable, there was plenty of good food, and he was staying busy. He doubted if he would be able to write as much as he had in the past, but his parents should not worry. He cautioned that now his letters would be censored, and he explained how this would be done. In fact, this very letter was censored: John had described the mess hall and evidently had given the approximate number of men the army fed there in a day; the number part had been cut out from his letter.[66]

The soldiers were given passes to visit New York City, and John made contact with a Bonita Drive neighbor, Fay Belt, who was a nursing student at Cornell University's medical center on the East River. Fay later recalled how bleak those days were. She was the only person in New York whom many of her classmates knew, and she was often the last one from home to see many of the Birmingham boys before they were shipped to Europe. On this or another occasion, she remembered asking John what he was going to do when he completed college. He assured her he was not going into the construction business. He had seen how difficult being a contractor had been on his father. Construction was too risky, he said, and too much depended upon the weather.[67]

On August 24 the entire division gathered for a final religious service in the United States. On August 25 and 26 the division boarded coaches for the ride to New York Harbor. John's 414th Regiment was assigned to the USS *George Washington*, a converted ocean liner that in its earlier life had taken President Woodrow Wilson to Europe for the Versailles negotiations at the end of World War I.[68] Fifty-six ships were in the convoy. In addition to the troop transports, there were battleships, aircraft carriers, freighters, and destroyer escorts. The voyage passed quickly as John spent time in French classes, doing calisthenics, and being drilled in the care of weapons, air-raid practices, and gas-mask demonstrations. He was also in a few crap games.

Rumors flew around the ship regarding just where the division was going. On the morning of September 7, John woke up in Cherbourg Harbor. This was the first American convoy to sail directly from the United States to France following the Normandy invasion. A few weeks after the *George Washington* unloaded John and the rest of its troops and moved back into the English Channel, the ship was sunk by a German U-boat.[69]

Normandy was rainy, cold, and dreary. Mines were still a danger, and the devastation of war surrounded the young Americans who were bivouacked around the little village of Ste.-Mère-Église. They were in the apple-orchard region of Normandy where hedgerows, which had presented so many problems for the D-Day forces, enclosed the fields. Bodies were still being discovered and identified. As talented as the 104th Division was, responding to the immediate need of the American and British forces was something the division was not specifically trained to do. The Allied armies pushing toward Paris needed supplies. General George Patton's Third Army, which had arrived in France in July, was rapidly moving south and east to encircle Paris, meet the British troops to the north, and cut off the German army's retreat. Patton's advance was hampered only by the speed with which gasoline, food, and ammunition could reach his troops. A large part of the 104th Division was moved to Barneville and divided into twelve truck companies. For four weeks 2,500 Timberwolves "helped roll the famous Red Ball Express," hauling food, ammunition, gasoline, and supplies to Patton and other troops driving back the Germans all along the front lines.[70]

By the first week of October the men of the 104th were fully equipped for combat and on October 15 began to move by rail and coach to the front line. John's 414th Regiment went by train, riding in dilapidated "40 and 8" freight cars, so called because they would hold forty men or eight cattle. On October 16, the 104th Division was attached to the Canadian First Army as part of I British Corps in Vilvorde, Belgium.[71] Spirits were high in the division, and morale was good. During this time the Germans sent hundreds of buzz bombs over the troops. The 104th's immediate order was to throw the Germans back north of the Maas River estuary.[72] A supply port closer to the Allied lines was desperately needed, and although the British controlled the city of Antwerp, Germans occupied the area north of the city and the approach to the harbor. The heavy German guns had to be removed to secure the port for Allied shipping. The land was flat and marshy with fields that were intersected by deep water-filled ditches. On October 22, the 104th was thrown into combat for the first time, and on that night, the 414th Regiment began a night attack along the Wuestwezel-Breda Highway.[73] According to General Terry Allen's guidelines for night attacks, the plan had to be simple, surprise was essential, and the assault should be directed at the flanks of the enemy where mines and booby traps are not commonly found. The men of the 414th moved quietly into position and were successful in their assault. The soldiers had been trained well.[74] By October 26 the 104th Division had "taken Zundert, gaining control of the Breda-Roosendaal Road and overrunning the Vaart Canal defenses."[75]

In early November the 104th was transferred to the VII Corps of the First U.S. Army, but the 414th remained engaged in Holland.[76] John wrote to his Aunt Bess on November 19 and told her his division had been "out of France for some time—went through Belgium & Holland—saw a little combat there & finally got into Germany." Aunt Bess offered to send him some toys to give to the children, and John responded that it would be fine "for the kids in France, Belgium, or Holland, but here [in Germany] we don't give them a thing but dirty looks. It is against the rules to even talk to any German civilians. I used to get a big kick out of giving candy, gum, etc., to the children of Belgium & France—they were regular beggars—but I gave them all my candy & gum rations." Aunt Bess must have written about Eleanor, for John explained that although she was "a nice girl" and she "certainly seems to think a lot of me," he was not seriously interested. He explained: "I kinda hate that in a way—as I don't think I'll get back to Colorado for a hell of a long time. She seems to think that I will." John told his aunt that his relationship with Eleanor was really a small problem "compared to the big ones at hand—suppose time will solve it—if anything will."[77]

The 104th continued its night attacks in the drive to the Roer River. On November 25 near Weissweiler, John's company (now Company K), along with Company L, was surrounded by Germans; however, the regiment was able to break through and rescue them. At about this time, or perhaps earlier, as John Risen Jones tells it, "John came up with one of his ideas—the use of a compass-like attachment to a mortar that would allow the mortar tube to be separated from its very heavy base for `raiding' purposes." John was given permission to try his idea, and he was assigned to several foray groups to experiment. However, he was "never able to prevent the casing from going too deep into the ground for salvage purposes."

Jones recalled that John was very creative and had a reputation as an innovator who could figure out how to get things done. He also remembered that John was in trouble with the army on a regular basis. Once John complained when the regimental mail truck broke down and the officers opted for the shipment of whiskey instead of mail on the one truck still in operation.[78] By December 1, fresh German troops were being thrown against the 104th lines and fighting intensified. At some point during this drive John received a shrapnel wound in his leg and was sent to Paris to recuperate.[79]

On December 16-17, the 104th Division was informed that Germans were infiltrating Allied lines wearing American uniforms. Enemy troops who spoke excellent English were using American equipment and were causing havoc with ground traffic. Germans were parachuting behind the American and British lines, and there were strong probes by German patrols all across Allied lines. These activities were part of the advance maneuvers of the German army's winter Ardennes offensive, which became known as the Battle of the Bulge. Field Marshal Gerd von Rundstedt, who commanded German troops in the west, was merely a "figurehead" for the offensive campaign. Hitler himself had planned the move and was personally directing it from Berlin. Launched on December 16, the German army drove forward, catching the Americans by surprise and dividing the Allied armies and even surrounding American troops occupying Bastogne. The 104th Division was occupying an area to the north of the main German attack but was ordered into defensive positions from Merken south to Düren along the Roer River. The division was engaged in vigorous patrols, looking for enemy parachutists and resisting penetrations by enemy ground troops.[80] On the fortieth anniversary of the Battle of the Bulge, John joined 160 Birmingham veterans of the battle who had gathered to share their experiences. He recalled the tremendous bombardment he heard when the attacks began and remembered thinking that "it was our own troops attacking."[81]

The Battle of the Bulge waged on as American soldiers sought to find quiet time to celebrate Christmas. The 104th discovered Christmas decorations by "searching deserted German homes," and the men decorated Christmas trees. Chaplains rode Jeeps along the front line and conducted services despite the heavy snow and freezing temperatures. John spent Christmas Eve huddled with his staff sergeant in a small chicken coop just outside Birgel. John remembered that "It snowed during the night, and Christmas morning was clear with the sun shining for the first time in weeks."[82] By December 31 the German offensive ran out of gas and was stopped short of the Meuse River, and on January 8 Hitler approved the withdrawal of his troops.

After the first of the year the 104th Division intensified its night operations and pushed across the Roer River in assault boats. They took Düren and crossed the Erft Canal.[83] After Associated Press reporter Don Whitehead visited with the 104th Division in February

1945, he reported that it was a "tough, disciplined outfit which has made a specialty of night fighting." Whitehead noted that it requires "well-trained, disciplined, aggressive troops to fight successfully in darkness—troops with a lot of confidence in themselves, and that is what [Major General Terry] Allen has achieved with his new command." The AP correspondent reported that in the drive from Aachen to the Roer River "the Timberwolves made every major assault during dark and captured many difficult objectives" and with "amazingly light losses."[84] Long after the war, John sent a letter to his friend Wayne Peake, writing that "if World War II didn't teach me anything else, it taught me the value of life. I watched and sat with friends who were mortally wounded and knew they didn't have any hope of living, yet they fought until their very last breath was drawn."[85]

On February 20, 1945, John was on a night patrol with eight men near Düren. In 1994, speaking to a Boy Scout banquet, he recalled the evening of fifty years before:

> None of us was more than 20 years old, and I was so scared I couldn't spit. One member of our patrol had a defective flashlight on his belt that blinked on from time to time. We all had cautioned him about this, fearing that the flashing light would alert the Germans to our position should there be a break in the snowstorm. That's exactly what happened, and we were immediately bombarded with mortar shells. Two other soldiers and I ran toward the German lines, while the rest of the patrol sought cover under three burned-out American tanks. The Germans gunners knew exactly the coordinates of the tanks' location and fired a salvo of mortar rounds on them. I never saw my six friends again.
>
> The other two men and I managed to get away, but we were lost, although we knew we were close to the German lines. By five or six the next morning, the snow stopped and the skies cleared enough for the stars to become visible. That was a beautiful sight because I knew I could use the constellations, which I had to learn to obtain my astronomy merit badge, to find our way back to the relative safety of the American lines. And every step of the way, I gave thanks for my Scout leaders and merit badge counselors.[86]

The next major objective for the 104th was Cologne, Germany's fourth largest city. The Timberwolves advanced across the Cologne plain, capturing 4,539 prisoners in two days.[87] Company L of the 414th Infantry entered the outskirts of Cologne at 9:23 A.M. on March 4, 1945. The Canadian First Army pounded those Germans who were protecting the last escape bridge across the Rhine River for the retreating army.[88] The 104th Division crossed the river. Resistance weakened, and the American troops moved rapidly. During this drive across northern Europe, John ate some food at an abandoned German house. It was a poor decision, for the food was poisoned. It took him days to recover, and he later would joke that it was the poison that made "his hair fall out."[89]

The 104th, moving east to link with the Russians, captured Nordhausen. John was one of the first soldiers to discover the large V-2 rocket factory that had been operated by 25,000 slave laborers housed in a concentration camp.[90] Few of John's letters were saved from this part of his military career, but one that he wrote on April 12, 1945, was published in its entirety by his hometown newspaper. After taking over the concentration camp John wrote his parents:

> I thought that I had seen just about all the horrible and terrible acts of man; many I've become accustomed to and accepted as part of war, which in itself is far more terrible and heartrending than you,

On March 16, 1945, John was in Paris on leave and had this photograph taken.

Near war's end, John stopped to pose by a sign pointing the way to Berlin.

as a civilian, …can possibly realize. But today I saw a crime so heinous that I'm ashamed to think that I'm a member of the human race. …

I am in a fairly large town that has fallen into our hands. The name is of no importance, for there are a lot of towns like this one, and the same crimes are being committed in the others. I believe what I saw today was on a minor scale compared to some of the others, for I never heard of this concentration camp before. I saw and spent two or three hours looking at the results of this concentration camp and talked to a Jew, who had escaped and returned to look for bodies of friends and relatives. I saw the results of a systematic scheme of starvation—thousands of bodies, mostly men, prisoners of war, political prisoners—Jews, Russians, and Poles for the most part. They were lying on the floors of concrete buildings where they crawled—nothing but skin and bones, young and old, half-naked, some with horrible wounds. In one place bodies were stacked like cord wood, all having died of starvation. The grounds were covered with bodies, parts of bodies. We got here in time to save a few thousand so weak that they couldn't eat. All our medical facilities have been busy trying to save as many as possible. When we arrived they were dying at the rate of 80 a day.

Here is my understanding of the system. The Germans have forced these people from all conquered lands to work, setting certain requirements to obtain food. As

Photographs taken by John in April 1945 at the Nordhausen slave labor concentration camp illustrate why he wrote a passionate letter to his parents after surveying the camp.

sickness and total lack of any useful productive strength catches up in the cycle, the prisoner is then thrown in the death house to die of starvation.

I can't make you visualize just what a terrible sight that was—acres of tortured bodies revolting to see. It's difficult to know exactly how one feels, one moment of extreme hatred and you want to kill every German over here. Sometimes I feel sorry for them. They are not a super-race. Really they are far from one. They have degraded themselves in the last ten years by their subjection and attempted degradation of others. No doubt there are some Germans who are decent. The fact remains that the German nation and the German race, as a whole, are responsible for these crimes. So I say to you, and I hope that you will pay heed to what I say: Make it your responsibility to see that we have no German lovers, forgivers, soft-hearted individuals proclaiming that the Germans have been mistreated, or the like at the peace table.

Let's have a harsh peace. Divide up, sit on them from now on. The harsher the better; in fact, probably the best deal is to let the Russians exterminate the German race. I don't care if I ever see another German prisoner, and I feel sure that there will be a lot less taken, especially SS boys.

The Germans have lost all right to be a member of the civilized world.

Don't laugh or take lightly what I'm saying. It is true—far worse than you realize. Don't accept as propaganda past atrocity stories. Millions of innocent people have died over here or lived a tortured life, and the Germans are to blame. The roads are full of refugees of all nations, aimlessly walking over the roads trying to return to their homes.

Pass this on. Tell everybody you can. Preach it! You need to know just what is going on over here. The American people need to share this suffering.

This is not as well written as I wanted to write it. Read it carefully. Iron out my errors. Make it stronger and pass it on.

Remember, we can't be too hard on the German people. They deserve all we can dish out. Don't subscribe to any "feed Europe" plan. The Krauts lived off Europe for the past five years and lived well. They will need food this winter. Next winter will probably be worse. Let them starve. Don't feel sorry for the children either. Let them starve. If you begin to feel sorry for them, stop and think of the tens of thousands of people they starved on purpose.[91]

John's harsh words were typical of American GIs who gave up two, three, or four years of their lives, who left home as innocent young men but came of age during the horrors of war. John would have agreed with war correspondent John Chancellor, who said of the German death camps: "What we saw is impossible to forget and necessary to remember."

During his months in Europe, John managed to see his brother Billy only twice. Once when the 104th and Billy's outfit, the Sixty-ninth Infantry Division, were close, the two were able to make radio contact, grab Jeeps, and meet near Krostolz, Germany. The second time was at the end of the war.

As spring flowers began to bud, Hitler's army was crumbling. The Russians were closing in on Berlin, and John's division was moving closer to the Mulde River, where they would meet the Russians. They were so close to the Russians at this time that both fronts halted their fighting while they waited for the "official link" lest they shoot each other. The first soldiers of the 104th met the Russians at Pretzsch on April 25 and again the next day at Torgau, fifty-three miles from Berlin. V-E Day was announced on May 8, 1945.[92]

Eight days later John's platoon leader, Second Lieutenant William O. Jones, wrote Mrs. Harbert to thank her for sending him a package of food. He told her about the tensions he felt trying to look after his men and enforce military discipline. He wrote that with the war over he could say that "all my men came through without a scratch," which must have been "providence" because "nothing else could account for the miraculous escapes." He wrote that John

> is honestly a very likable boy—he has a good mind and unbounding energy—All the men in the platoon are fond of him as are most of the officers. Undoubtedly, his mind is so far above the average enlisted man that at times he becomes a problem by wanting to know why. An answer that

When the 104th Division met the Russians in the spring of 1945, John and Billy ran into each other for the second time during the war. Here they pose with a Russian captain.

The Harbert brothers met once during the drive across Germany when a radio operator told Billy the 104th was nearby and he was able to borrow a Jeep to go find John.

For several weeks after Germany surrendered, the 104th Division was assigned guard duty around Halle, Germany. When John returned to Germany in the 1960s, he drew on his memory and photographs to locate many of the places where he had stayed.

Outside of Le Havre, France, the 104th Division set up Camp Lucky Strike as it waited for shipment home. During this time John and several other men managed to slip off to visit Paris one more time.

The 104th Division was expected to play a large role in the American invasion of Japan. On June 11, just over a month after the German surrender, John and his company loaded onto French "40 and 8" freight cars for the trip to Le Havre, France, to be shipped home before being transferred to the Far East.

> orders state it brings another why. His arguments never lack reason but truthfully, I'm on the spot. You see I'm an officer of the United States Army and must carry out orders without question. Battles can and have been lost because orders were questioned or countered. John's energy is another problem of mine. He is curious and his energy carries his curiosity into forbidden and often forbidding places and I'm constantly trying to alibi him out of trouble. These qualities are an asset and have proved so many times in combat. But sometimes they are most trying. He has no fear either of bullets or opinion. He stands up for his rights, lots of times when he is in [the] wrong. But I know that when John can turn his brain, energy, and stubbornness to work (of his own choosing) he will be a grand success. Maybe I better say he's a darn nice guy and getting nicer.[93]

With the end of hostilities the 104th Division was ordered to occupy an area north of Dessan along the Elbe and Mulde Rivers west of Halle. The men of the 104th turned from being aggressive fighters to being policemen, enforcing law and order, patrolling and helping displaced persons, and processing prisoners of war. Within days after V-E Day, General Allen began a systematic examination of the division's night attacks, which had enabled the 104th to seize objectives quickly with a minimum loss of life. The analysis helped the staff adapt the techniques of the 104th to a Japanese enemy and the Pacific theater where the division was heading. General Allen put his men back into training at Halle. By this time John was in Company D.

On the morning of June 11, 1945, the 104th Division loaded onto trains bound for Camp Lucky Strike, an army tent city near Dieppe, twenty-five miles northeast of Le Havre, France. They were beginning the first leg of their long journey home. The troops rode in old French "40 and 8" freight cars and were given two meals a day on the trip, mostly beans and coffee, which the soldiers swore was a "concoction of sulfuric acid and vinegar." The train stopped for two-hour breaks during meals, and the men were able to wash up with helmets full of hot water from the locomotive.[94]

During the ten days or so before the ships arrived in Le Havre, many men of the 104th had an opportunity to visit Paris. John managed to join John Risen Jones and his brother, Robert, and Colonel Fred "Pick" Hunt of Decatur, who were stationed at Enghein-Les-Bains with the 1151st Engineer Combat Battalion. After a few drinks, Hunt and John decided to visit some nightclubs, and Hunt loaned John his colonel's blouse so they would have the same rank. (It would be inappropriate for a colonel and a private to go bar-hopping together.) Robert, fearing both might get into trouble over the blouse and John's "impersonating an officer," went along. The young men enjoyed themselves, and there were no problems; however, it was an evening John enjoyed recalling.[95]

The men of the 104th Division boarded two ships, the SS *Monterey*, which sailed on June 26, and the SS *Ericsson*, which sailed on July 2. These young American soldiers left behind in Europe a worthy official combat record. The 104th Division had been in combat for 195 consecutive days, inflicted 18,000 casualties, captured 51,724 prisoners, including four generals, and 2,000 towns and villages, including the cities of Cologne, Eschweiler, and Halle. The division had lost 1,447 men and had 4,776 wounded. When the ships carrying the 104th docked in the United States the soldiers were immediately taken to Camp Kilmer and processed for thirty-day leaves. John returned to Birmingham. The memories of his war experiences were painful, and he was not eager to talk about them. As he gained perspective and began to adjust to life at home, John announced to his parents that he would not fight in the Pacific, saying he would go AWOL (absent without leave) if he had to. His mother, distraught and trying desperately to get John out of the army before he was faced with such a decision, wrote his commander that she had a wheat farm in Washington State, and she needed her son there to harvest the late fall crop and plant winter wheat.[96]

The furloughed men of the 104th were to report to San Luis Obispo, California, as their leaves expired during the first weeks of August. By August 29 all the men, including John, had reported for duty. That day he wrote to Fay Belt in New York City, telling her that he expected to be "going overseas again at the end of next month." John believed it was "a damn dirty trick sending us over again, especially when there are so many who have never been out of the United States for the first time."[97] John was "up for a lieutenant's commission."[98] However, the course of the Pacific war changed rapidly in mid-August. After two atomic bombs were dropped, the Japanese sued for peace on August 10, and on August 14 the Allies accepted. On August 30, General Douglas MacArthur reported that he would not need additional soldiers in the Pacific for occupation duties. General Terry Allen immediately put the men of the 104th Division into classes to aid them with their conversion to civilian status, and the army began checking each individual soldier's points to determine priority in processing discharges. Mae Harbert's letter and the wheat farm's need for labor bumped John toward the top.

John M. Harbert III, promoted by now to private first class, U.S. Army, was honorably discharged from Company D, 414th Infantry, on September 29, 1945, at Camp San Luis Obispo.[99] The war had had a profound effect upon his life. John understood the fragile nature of his humanity, and he had a greater appreciation for life. He had observed firsthand the worst of leadership and the best. He knew that teamwork was essential to success and that accomplishing small well-defined goals was a step toward achieving significant long-range ends. On the fiftieth anniversary of the Battle of the Bulge he reminisced with his secretary Sandi Falkenhagen and talked about the war and "how terrible it was to see men blown to bits." He told her it was a miracle he had lived through the war, that he guessed "someone up there wanted me to stay alive."[100]

4

FINDING A PLACE IN LIFE

"a soldier's vocabulary and little else"

When John Harbert left Camp San Luis Obispo, California, he headed north to Palouse, Washington, and the farm once owned by his maternal grandmother, Eva Lebold Hamilton Schooling. He spent the fall working on the farm, plowing and planting winter wheat, and thinking about what he wanted to do with his life.[1] In the past eighteen months he and Wayne Peake had exchanged letters that gave updates on what was going on in their individual worlds but that also were deeply philosophical in tone. Their attitudes toward the war, that it was "a nasty and in many ways pointless job," contrasted with Mak Peake's idealistic view. Wayne's brother thought that he was "holding aloft the torch of humanity," fighting a "clean and righteous" war. In 1944 John and Wayne had discussed going into business together, and when John brought up the question of financing, Wayne wrote back that "smart handling of money will always mean more money, but getting the nest egg, or the credit for one, will really be the test. About the only sure fire way apparent this moment are your crap games and my War Bonds, neither of which will endanger us with the stigma of Rockefellers."[2] They even discussed salaries and agreed that "it is far better to own one truck and haul firewood than to continue through life with a fractional cut of somebody else's profit on your ability."[3]

At the war's end, Wayne was stuck in the navy, while John went to plow wheat. John thought about transferring to a university in Washington, probably his father's alma mater, Washington State University, to complete his engineering degree. Wayne warned that he would lose credits and suggested he finish his degree at Auburn and then go to graduate school, maybe at Cambridge or the University of Chicago. Maybe they could go to MIT for an advanced degree. Perhaps, Wayne suggested, John should leave engineering behind in favor of law, economics, or medicine. But in any case, Wayne suggested, John needed to set his sights "on an entity, a purpose, a hilltop."[4]

Soon after the first snows came, John hitchhiked back to Alabama. He spent the weeks before Christmas helping his father. He took some golf lessons, repaired old cars, and thought about going back to college.[5] John spent some time in Mobile living on Bobby Radcliff's houseboat on the Tensaw River. Bobby, who had known John's father when Harbert and Cargile Construction Company was doing work at Coden and Monroe Park, invited John to go duck hunting and was surprised to see that the army and the war had made John "so thin he must have weighed only 135 pounds."[6]

John's exchanges with Wayne continued into the winter. In essence they agreed that a real education was not just engineering or the physical sciences but also involved the humanities, especially history, an appreciation of language, and the use of the written word. In early December Wayne sent John an essay clipped from the August 1945 *Harper's* magazine. The anonymous "Letter to a Seventeen-Year-Old Son" did not, Wayne wrote, "cast an entirely new light" on the discussions, but it did "bring out very clearly what we have been trying to say." The *Harper's* essay stressed the importance of a liberal arts education, of history and literature as a way to understand people and nations, and of the use of language, and it encouraged the young man, by reading and study, to increase the resources within himself.[7]

In later letters John and Wayne discussed being objective in setting one's goals, looking at life rationally, and achieving happiness and satisfaction. They shared apprehensions about moving as adults into a time when there were so many uncertainties and unknowns, "coping with a world when it isn't bathed in a khaki hue." John confessed he was "mixed up," and Wayne responded, "Hell, yes, you're mixed up, every young man is and much more so when he has to win a war in the mean time." John finally told Wayne of his decision to return to Auburn to complete his civil engineering degree, and Wayne recommended that when John got back to the campus he talk over his plans with civil engineering professor Wilfred Honour, who had quite a reputation for inspiring students to do their very best. The conversation with Honour, Wayne told John, would be an experience, "sort of an inspiration in itself."[8] John's initial call upon Professor Honour grew into many visits over the course of the next months, and John gave Honour credit for helping him adjust to being back in school and encouraging him to complete his degree.[9]

Years later John admitted that he "did not make the best adjustment to civilian life," for he was several years older than his classmates when he returned to Auburn. He recalled that he had fought his way through Europe and "came back with a soldier's vocabulary and little else." He had forgotten his "algebra, arithmetic, and how to think and concentrate." Adjustment to school was difficult. He worked for the college, doing odd jobs and grading papers, for which he was paid $84 in 1946.[10] The one course he needed to graduate was "indeterminate structures," the "toughest course in the civil engineering curriculum," he believed. Every day John wanted to quit, but, he once recalled, "somehow I stuck it out and passed the final `blue book' examination." He made the grade and graduated, but evidently the department head in civil engineering told him he was not graduate school material. Perhaps this assessment, as well as his "less than brilliant grades," discouraged John from trying to continue his education. In reality he had always been fascinated by what he once called "the romance of construction," despite the Auburn engineering dean's annual lecture, which John recalled as being on "the evils of the construction industry" and why it was not quite a respectable way for a civil engineer to make money.[11] It was some time before John sent in the $10 diploma fee, and he did not attend his API graduation ceremony on August 24, 1946.[12]

During his senior year at Auburn, John

made no satisfactory contacts with corporate recruiters. He later believed that his poor academic record was the reason.[13] He probably realized early on, certainly after his experiences in the U.S. Army, that he wanted to run his own business and be his own boss, but he had the good sense to realize he was not yet ready. In November 1946, John went to work for Dunn Construction Company for $50 a week as a superintendent on "a bridge and four miles of farm-to-market road." The road and bridge were near Coloma, a crossroads community nine miles southeast of Centre in Cherokee County in northeast Alabama. Although he had another job option with a higher salary, John selected the Dunn proposal because it offered him "the greatest responsibility and opportunity to learn." John was hired by Ed Bookout, who was executing the project in a joint venture with Dunn. John was given a 1938 pickup truck to use on the job, which he called the Coloma-Centre project. He rented a room in Centre and went to work designing the superstructure's false work, which John recalled as the most "over designed, strongest supporting false work anybody ever designed, but I was afraid to take a chance." His bridge design drawings are dated December 12, 1946.[14]

John completed the Cherokee County bridge and road project in twenty-five weeks and was paid $1,249 by Dunn. He managed the project so well that he had made "a substantial profit" for Dunn, but John believed "the experience and self-confidence" gained "in this job were more valuable to me than any financial compensation ever could have been." Despite the offer of a significant salary increase to stay with Dunn when the contract was completed, John returned the '38 truck to the Dunn machinery yard in June 1947 and quit.[15] For nine weeks John worked with his father's partner, Charles Cargile, "looking at small bridge projects and estimating them for Mr. Cargile." He had an opportunity to join with Cargile and his son, Jack, in a business arrangement, but it was not what John wanted to do. He wanted his own company. By late summer he decided to go into business for himself.[16]

John began his construction company as a proprietorship in 1947 with, in his words, "no meaningful financial resources or backing."[17] His only capital was several thousand dollars in cash from his war bonds and from money he had won shooting craps during the war. Of all the many stories about John Harbert, the one tale most often remembered by strangers and friends alike is the one that he started his business with money he had won gambling as a GI in World War II. Once when John was lecturing about business opportunities to a group of college students and told the story, a candid young man spoke up: "Mr. Harbert, I've decided I'm not interested in engineering any longer. But I sure as hell want to know your system of shooting dice."[18] Years later John confessed that it was "not a large sum of money, but it was enough to buy a two-bag cement mixer, wheelbarrows, hand tools, and a concrete vibrator" and leave him enough left over "to meet the initial payrolls for a crew of twelve unskilled laborers."[19]

The first job John acquired for his company was a subcontract for $21,335 from M. R. Thomason of Montgomery, Alabama, to construct a bridge in Autauga County. The five-span reinforced concrete girder deck bridge was over Bridge Creek. John was not able to gain bonding on his own recognizance, but his father arranged it for him through Harbert and Cargile from the United States Fidelity and Guaranty Company of Baltimore.[20] John recalled that at the time he "was young, undaunted," and "did not realize the hazards of skeletal financing, limited experience, no labor force, no skilled supervision, [and] a scarcity of essential building materials."[21]

John went to Prattville and hired men from the cotton fields, men who were strong but had "absolutely no knowledge of bridge

John's new company's first job was a bridge over Bridge Creek in Autauga County. It was completed in 1948. John hired day laborers, and he was the only skilled worker on the crew.

construction." Fortunately, they were "willing to learn," and what they "lacked in experience, they made up in loyalty and hard work." John designed a set of forms and "taught them to place and tie reinforcing steel and to pour and finish concrete." At one point during construction, John had no money for his payroll. He called his crew together and confessed his dilemma. The leader told him not to worry. From the way he had acted all week, they had already figured out his financial trouble, and they were prepared to keep on working until he could pay them. On Friday, John decided, very uncharacteristically, to go into town at lunch. He checked his box at the Prattville post office and found a $490 government check, a refund on his GI insurance. John had $60 more than he needed to make payroll.[22]

Before John completed the Autauga County bridge, he again had a cash flow problem, but this time he had collateral—the retainage that the state still owed him on his contract for the bridge. He negotiated his first loan from the Bank of Prattville, where J. W. Strange "ran the bank and made the decisions on all loans." Years later John remembered Strange as from the "old school" of bankers who "wore a green shade while at his desk." Strange asked him "all kinds of questions," but in the end the banker agreed to grant him a loan. John M. Harbert III, contractor for Autauga County project 318-B, had his construction company off and running.[23] Looking back in 1989, John noted that the first Harbert-constructed bridge would "be there forever" because "we built it right."[24]

During the first twelve months of his business operations, John took out only enough money to pay his $12.50 weekly boardinghouse bill. The $1,004.61 income from his interest in the Washington wheat farm helped him get by, and he was able to invest "every available cent" in his company. He was extremely protective of his first equipment investments, a one-horsepower concrete vibrator, which he purchased secondhand for $301.16, and his two-ton, "red, cab-over-engine, Ford flatbed dump truck with stake sides so it could be used to haul materials." John would drive the truck to the job site each day and home again at night and confessed that "it was only with a great deal of trepidation that I turned it over to someone else to

Sometime after John began dating Wita, he proudly posed at Wita's house in the Jones's parking area by his new source of transportation.

operate while I managed the job."[25] His brother was one of those whom he let drive his truck. Billy had worked with John on the Prattville bridge during his summer vacation, and after he graduated from Auburn with a degree in civil engineering in June 1948, he immediately went to work for John. Although the family continued to call him Billy, professionally he now became Bill.

The years following World War II were boom years in the United States and in Birmingham. Soldiers came home and found jobs or, in more cases, took advantage of the GI Bill and entered college, frequently becoming the first in their families to do so. By 1946 there was a coterie of young bachelors, veterans of the war, on the Birmingham scene. Belton Cooper, a Huntsville native and a cousin of John Risen Jones, was one of them. He was a survivor of the Third Armored Division, which had operated with the 104th Division in the drives both before and after crossing the Rhine. Belton met John Harbert through John Risen, and they frequently had lunch together. Belton recalled that when he first met John, he was unimpressed but soon realized how serious and intense he could be and how determined he was to succeed. Belton's roommate was a newcomer to Birmingham, Edwin M. Dixon, a naval architecture and marine engineering classmate of Belton's at the University of Michigan. Ed was born in Grand Forks, North Dakota, but Belton convinced him to apply for a position with Ingalls Ship Building Company in Birmingham. Both Michigan graduates went to work for Ingalls as designers and estimators, and it was through Belton that Ed met John at a debut party.[26]

John and Ed became close friends, but John worked almost all the time and his social life was limited. Because Robert I. Ingalls, Sr., did not allow his employees to work more than forty hours a week, Ed had blocks of free time. John recalled that "Ed was young and energetic and wanted something to do with his spare time." John confessed he was "trying to run a bridge construction project from daylight till dark while handling all the necessary paperwork, which included figuring estimates on future work after I shut down the job for the day. I obviously needed help." John inquired if Ed were interested in "doing my payroll," and Ed agreed. Soon Ed was working for John, at first without pay, running cost estimates and compiling bids at night.[27]

One day John asked Ed to take time off from

work to accompany him on a trip to Sumter County to check the sites of three bridges being proposed by the Alabama Highway Department on a rural road between Derby and Whitfield. John and Ed spent the day, as John later related, "looking over the proposed work, studying the plans and specifications, and evaluating the local conditions." In fact they "drove up and down the dirt road" so many times that a local man, Frank Derby, stopped them to find out what they were doing. Derby was interested in the new bridges, and he showed them around the area. He told how he was involved with the idea of a rooster auction in 1919 to finance the first bridge over the Tombigbee River. The Dixie Overland Highway from Savannah, Georgia, to San Diego, California, remained incomplete because the state of Alabama had no money to construct a bridge to span the Tombigbee River. Derby had promoted auctioning off donated roosters to raise money for the bridge. He explained that the auction in August 1919 raised $40,000 to pay for the bridge, known since as the "Rooster Bridge." Financing bridges with rooster sales intrigued both young engineers. Years later John speculated that the visit with Frank Derby made bridge building "more appealing to Ed than the design of barges."[28]

John decided to submit bids on all three bridges even though his company was still bonding through Harbert-Cargile and he did not have the men or equipment to construct all three bridges at the same time. John drove to Montgomery on a Thursday night and in the Whitley Hotel "put the final touches" on his bid proposals. He recalled that the next day "when the Highway Department officials began reading out the results of the submissions, my heart was in my throat. I was scared to death. Pretty soon they got down the list to the Sumter County jobs, and I was surprised to hear that I was low bidder on all three projects." Now that John had won the jobs, other fears set in: Had he made a mistake in his estimation? Was his bid too low to complete the projects? Would he go broke building the bridges? Just as he was beginning to worry about these prospects, "an established Montgomery contractor," Z. O. Riddle, pulled him aside and asked John to subcontract the bridges to him. Riddle had the crews, and they were out of work. He really needed the jobs, and Riddle said, "I'll pay you $30,000 if you'll subcontract those projects to me." Knowing he had no crews to do the work, John accepted his offer, and "from one Friday to the next on a combination of youthful bravado and dice-table luck" he made $30,000.[29]

For months while Ed Dixon was helping with the estimation and bid work on his own time, he and John discussed Ed's going to work for Harbert to work up bids, keep the books, run the office, and help occasionally in the field. When John told Ed about the $30,000 profit on the three bridges, Ed was impressed. Belton Cooper advised Ed to try working with John for six months because if "it didn't work out" he could always "go out and get more money than old man Ingalls was paying" him.[30] Ed decided to "gamble" on Harbert "being able to match his fifty dollars a week at Ingalls." But when Ed gave his notice to Robert I. Ingalls, Sr., the conservative businessman confided that although he "understood the attraction of the opportunity," he warned Ed that "young Harbert had a very high probability of going broke."[31]

Ed left Ingalls in the spring of 1948 and was immediately put to work on a bridge in Coalburg that Harbert was building over Five Mile Creek in northern Jefferson County. John recalled that Ed was running "the 16-S-2 Bag Concrete mixer" while the last bridge guardrails were being poured. Ed remembers his first duties were "estimating new jobs, making payrolls, keeping books, purchasing and picking up materials, and running a concrete mixer on the Coalburg Bridge. ...John Harbert was superintendent—it was the only job we had going at the time."[32]

John had no patience with Alabama Highway Department inspectors who were not fair, and he "didn't suffer fools gladly."[33] He was especially offended by the state inspector who was "very difficult" and after the second week wanted a quart of whiskey placed on the front seat of his automobile each Saturday. John later recalled that "I know now that it would have been far easier and less costly to have put the quart of whiskey, or even a whole case of whiskey, in his car every week; but being young and inexperienced, I became angry and told him to go to hell; he would never get a quart of whiskey from me. From then on, it was a contest of wills, and I lost every battle."[34] Ed was able to deal with some of these problems, freeing John for other responsibilities. Ed also supervised estimating and was responsible for the Harbert safety promotions. John was always protective of his workers, and their safety was a primary concern. He recognized the dangers inherent in all construction sites and appreciated that accident-free jobs were more profitable.

The Harbert Construction Corporation had its beginnings in this small building in English Village. The one-room office would hold three desks comfortably, but at one time a fourth was squeezed in.

But personally John's most dangerous situations were when he was driving a car. The Coalburg bridge could have been the last bridge for John Harbert. Never a slow or careful driver, John left Coalburg late one afternoon, headed home driving his new green 1947 Ford coupe, which was less than a week old. He collided with another car head-on and was thrown to the side of the road. Those who first arrived at the scene thought he was dead, and John remembered listening to the voices, knowing he could not be dead because he hurt so much. The occupants of the second car were injured in the accident, and because it was during the days of segregation and they were black, and John was thought dead, the police who arrived called for ambulances that specialized in transporting black patients. Only after the vehicles reached the scene was it determined that John was alive. But both his knees were crushed. He had to lie on the ground by the road until an ambulance that transported white people could come from Birmingham to carry him to the hospital. John was in a cast for weeks, but he was lucky to be alive. For the rest of his life the steel pins in his knees set off the metal detectors at airports.[35]

During his company's first year, John operated his business from a cardboard box on the front seat of his truck, but by 1948 he was renting a small brick structure off Diaper Row in English Village at 2337 Twentieth Avenue South. The 1949 *Birmingham City Directory* also listed Harbert and Cargile at this address with John M. Harbert III as "manager." The next year the directory listed John as president of Harbert and Cargile, brother Bill as vice-president, and Ed Dixon as secretary-treasurer, despite the fact that Jefferson County corporation records indicate John's father and Charles J. Cargile

John (on the left) incorporated Harbert Construction Corporation on January 18, 1949. He retained 480 shares. Ed Dixon (center) and Bill Harbert (on the right) owned ten shares each. This photograph was taken in the 1950s.

had dissolved Harbert and Cargile two years earlier on December 30, 1947.[36]

The building John rented in English Village was so small that the company joke was that the "Bachelors Four"—John, Bill, Ed, and Ted Randolph (who joined the company in 1949)—held "staff meetings at debut parties" because there was not enough room in the building, which had only a half-bath and one twenty-by-twenty-foot room large enough to hold three desks.[37] Ted recalled that when John hired a second secretary they "had to move every desk and filing cabinet in the office" to make room for her. That was one reason they stayed in the field so much—because they "couldn't all get in the office at the same time."[38] From the very beginning, the four engineers knew how to do whatever needed to be done on any construction project, and they dressed in work boots and khaki pants so they could do it. John's father was proud of his son's hard work, and during these years he often said that "John is either going to be dead broke or the biggest contractor in the world."[39]

In the fall of 1949 Rex Barrington came by Harbert Construction Company to inquire about a secretarial job. She had worked for J. W. Goodwin Engineering and had met John when he came to pick up plans and specifications for water, gas, or sewage treatment plants, projects for which Goodwin was the consulting engineer. Someone had suggested she talk to John, and he interviewed her but told her he already had a secretary. Rex took another job that began after January 1, and until then she worked during the holidays selling toys at Yielding department store. On Christmas Eve, Rex looked up and saw John

Harbert coming toward her, leaping over a "long line of bicycles" rather than walking around them "as everyone else did." She later observed that "this was typical of John; he didn't take the usual route to get what he wanted." John related that his secretary had quit, and he needed Rex to come to work for him on New Year's Day. She agreed and stayed for thirteen years.[40]

The year before Rex came to work for Harbert, on January 18, 1949, John incorporated his company as the Harbert Construction Corporation. A closely held corporation, John was named president and retained 480 shares of the company; Bill L. Harbert was vice-president, and Ed Dixon was secretary-treasurer. Bill and Ed owned 10 shares each, valued at $1,000. John invested $32,000 in cash and transferred the inventory of his proprietorship, valued at $16,000, to the new corporation. This list included such items as a tractor, three trucks, and a 1949 Ford custom club coupe with radio, heater, and plastic seat covers, as well as three wooden desks, three steel wastebaskets, one Burroughs electric typewriter, and assorted equipment and office furniture. Five hundred shares of capital stock were secured by $50,000 in cash and property.[41]

One opportunity that John maximized during the early years of Harbert Construction Corporation was to bid work designed by J. W. Goodwin Engineering Company. Jimmy Goodwin was a rough-hewn, hard-working, Auburn-trained engineer who drove a difficult bargain. After World War II, Goodwin Engineering cooperated with small Alabama towns, communities that were growing and needed new sewerage disposal systems and water filtration plants. John and Goodwin would "develop an economic analysis which would justify the facilities," and they would arrange a meeting with the city's government officials. Goodwin would present a design for the proposed system; John would estimate the construction costs; and they would bring along someone from a bonding company to explain how the system could be funded through city bonds. On "several occasions" John and Goodwin even agreed to purchase the revenue bonds themselves, investments that proved to be quite good over the years.[42] If the city agreed to the plan, it would employ Goodwin to design the systems, which were then placed for public bid. Harbert had to come in as low bidder to secure the job, and it was sometimes difficult because the engineering firm often used out-of-date cost lists. As consulting engineer, Goodwin Engineering would inspect the work done by the contractor and certify that the bid specifications were followed.[43]

Harbert Construction Corporation was unusual in its day because it was the only Alabama construction firm headed by three (soon to be four) graduate engineers. Rex Barrington recalled that "in those days there were four men in the office" and "no 'Mr. Harbert.'" To the workers in the field it was "Mr. John" and "Mr. Bill." Theodore F. Randolph, known as Ted, came to work on September 19, 1949, eight months after Harbert Construction was incorporated. Ted was an MIT engineer, and he joined John, Bill, and Ed in supervising jobs and checking on projects. As the months went by, Ed assumed more of the office work, purchasing materials, doing the cost accounting, and working on bids, while Ted did all the drawings for Harbert and became an expert on mechanical problems. "Ours was," John noted, "a small group of hard-working men and women who struggled together to make ends meet."[44] As the years went by John and Bill came to handle the outside work. The two brothers understood each other; John "trusted Bill completely," and Bill was "fiercely loyal to John." They all worked from "sunup until late in the night." It was "a dynamic and creative group" made up of strong individuals who worked well together, but everyone understood that it was John's company and final decisions rested with him.[45] John's perspective was expressed when he later noted that at this time he "began to gather around" him "people with intelligence, initiative, and spirit."[46]

In the summer of 1949 Harbert received its first big contract, a $67,000 water distribution facility for Demopolis, Alabama. It was a job that provided "priceless experience," because Harbert crews had to dig in the Selma chalk geological formation, and Ed practically lived in Demopolis to oversee the project. Harbert had two other jobs going at the same time. While Ed was in Demopolis, John was supervising a water treatment plant in Sylacauga and Bill was in Fort Payne with Ted superintending construction of a filter plant. Harbert Construction Corporation completed its first water purification plant in Newnan, Georgia, in July 1950. In the years that followed, Harbert built similar projects in Fort Payne, Centre, and Fairfield, Alabama, and in Jackson, Mississippi. Sewage improvement projects were completed in Jasper, Alabama, and Tarpon Springs, Florida.[47]

During these early years Ted Randolph owned a Culver Cadet airplane, which he flew around the Southeast looking for jobs. John, who often flew with him, called the plane a "flying coffin" and later commented that "the good Lord was looking after us in that coffin." Once when Ted and John were flying home from Pensacola, they ran out of gas near Jackson, Alabama, but Ted found a golf course, "with no players," and landed the plane. He and John walked to town and purchased five gallons of high-test gasoline, returned to the plane, poured it in, and took off for Birmingham. As John tells the story, a thunderstorm hit when they were close to Jefferson County, and the two engineers were lost with the plane's lights out, rain coming in the cabin, and only a flashlight to illuminate the instrument panel. Ted flew low to see if they could tell where they were, and John spotted the Childersburg bridge, telling Ted, "We've got it made now." On another occasion they had trouble leaving Tarpon Springs from the beach. The airplane got stuck in the sand, and John got out and pushed. Ted took off and met John at the Clearwater airport. They refueled in Tallahassee and were only two hours late for an engagement party.[48]

John worked from daylight until late at night in the field, and there were times when days would go by and no one in the office would see him. Although the office operated on an eight- to-five Monday-through-Friday schedule with half a day Saturday, never were such limited hours observed. Rex finally had to schedule a secretary to come in later in the morning and stay late in the evening "just to take messages" from John and the men who were off on jobs during the day. She recalled that if you worked for Harbert then it was a given that "when the men were gone, you were liable to have to do most anything from driving to a job—or meeting the superintendent halfway—with a needed part to delivering a check they needed." She never forgot the time she received a frantic call at home about a broken machine. She called the manager of a local parts dealership, sweet-talked him into meeting her at his store, picked up the essential part, and drove off into the night to meet the superintendent halfway to Georgia. The part was installed, and the equipment was working by daylight when the crew arrived at the job site. She remembered that these were "hectic" times, and "we felt an excitement. We felt we were helping to build something and that the company was going somewhere."[49]

By 1950 Harbert Construction Corporation had outgrown the one-room office in English Village and had moved to a new building John had erected at 2208 South Eighth Avenue. The construction progressed despite some problems, including a bombing. It seems that there was a plumbers' strike and John could not get a plumber. So he had Ted come from Fort Payne with some workers, and they put in the plumbing. The building was "mysteriously bombed," the police said when they woke up John in the middle of the night. He called Ted and told him to get the men out of town. The city plumbing inspector came out intending to arrest the culprits, but John managed to talk him "down to a $5.00 fine." John was cited for doing plumbing without a city license, but because he was able to find out who was involved with the bombing the charge was eventually dropped.[50] When it was finally completed, the new building had several rooms, enough desks for everyone, a private office for John, and a fenced-in area in back to park equipment.

John kisses Wita during a picnic at the old Dallas County Purnell Plantation of the E. E. and Evelyn Glass McCoy family during the summer of 1951.

Although the Harbert payroll carried a dozen or so skilled workers, the regular work force was supplemented with day laborers. At that time, unskilled workers who wanted jobs could be picked up in Birmingham at the corner of Eighteenth Street and Morris Avenue, and often someone from Harbert would take a truck downtown to hire workers for the day. Harbert Construction Corporation was always nonunion, although in some job venues union workers were employed. John wanted to make sure that his workers were paid good wages, but he resisted anyone other than himself trying to control decisions about his jobs or his company.[51]

Although John's personal life took a back seat when he started working, in the months after he returned home from the war and then from college in 1946, his mother "launched" him "back into civilization by having party after party." In warm weather she and his father would host his friends and their dates outside and in winter months in the downstairs trophy room.[52] Mrs. Harbert loved to entertain, and with the help of Edna Wilborn, who had cooked for the family since they returned from Mississippi, she provided lavish spreads of food for hungry young people. Frequently in the fall John's friends would gather at the Harbert home to drink beer and listen to football games on the radio.[53] In the winter of 1946-47, when John was working for Dunn Construction Company, he attended a debut dance at the Birmingham Country Club and ran into Impy Shook's Birmingham-Southern College roommate, Wita Jones. John had attended Phillips High School with Wita, and she had doubled-dated with John and Impy as John's army buddy's blind date in 1943. If John had been attracted to Wita in these school years, no one recalls him saying so, but it seems improbable that the shy boy did not particularly notice the vivacious brown-eyed red-haired tomboy with the unusual nickname. On this occasion John immediately asked her for a date.

John and Wita dated only a short while

before he asked her to marry him the following summer. Although Wita thought he was "interesting," she also knew that John was very "different." She was often surprised at crazy things John did and said. At the time, she was dating several boys and was seriously involved with a young man she had been going with off and on since she was a freshman at Birmingham-Southern College. She thought she loved him, but she was not yet ready to be serious with anyone. After Wita declined John's proposal, they dated only intermittently while both dated other people. Later that summer John came by the Jones house and asked Wita if she had changed her mind about marrying him, and she said she had not. In 1985 Wita wrote that "it took some years after his first offer of marriage for me to go down the aisle. No one in her right mind would not have given a lot of thought to life with someone as completely different from the norm as John; and, in those days, he didn't have a thin dime."[54]

As the years went by and all of Wita's friends were getting married, her father became piqued at his twenty-six-year-old daughter's indecision about her life. Mr. Jones packed her off on a Florida vacation to think things over and selected Treasure Island, where one of her beaus was working. A week's dating of the young man convinced her she was not in love with him but with John. However, when Wita returned to Birmingham she had trouble deciding how to let John know she had changed her mind. He had told her to call him if she ever did, but by the courting rules of the day, this simply was not done. After much soul-searching, Wita finally called John, and in 1949 they began to date again. However, John was working hard establishing his business, and he was not really in a financial position to get married. His company was, according to Wita, "his whole world." He had a job laying sewer pipes in Tarpon Springs, Florida, and was only in and out of Birmingham.[55]

When Wita finally told John she would marry him, he took her to Atlanta to Maier and Berkle, and together they selected an emerald and diamond engagement ring. Wita had always loved emeralds because they were her birthstone. When John had the ring in hand early in 1951, he showed it to Rex Barrington and confided that he was going to give it to a girl. Rex said the ring was lovely and asked John who the girl was. John replied, "Her name is Wita Jones, and she has red hair and she's tough, and I love her."[56] Because of John's sewer pipe-laying jobs, Wita's friends teased her that the "rumor in Mountain Brook was that Wita was marrying the Roto-Rooter Man."[57]

Marguerite "Wita" Jones came from an established Birmingham family. She was the daughter of Raymond McAdoo Jones from Murfreesboro, Tennessee, who was the son of James Jones and Eva McAdoo Jones. He attended Princeton University, spent the summer of 1913 in Santiago, Chile, living in the American Embassy, and graduated magna cum laude from Princeton in 1914. He was in Mexico during the early years of World War I and came to Birmingham to purchase a sand and gravel company. In Birmingham he met, courted, and married Marguerite Nabers.

Marguerite was descended from two old Jefferson County families. Her mother was Alice Pinckney Worthington, daughter of Benjamin Pinckney Worthington (1814-84), whose father, Benjamin (1774-1853), came into Alabama from Hopkinsville, Kentucky, in 1817 and lived on his large Jefferson County farm on the Georgia Road until his death in 1853. Benjamin Worthington sold portions of the family land to the Elyton Land Company, which founded Birmingham in 1871. Marguerite's father was Zach L. Nabers, one of four sons of Judge Zach Nabers of Mobile and Sarah Rebecca Nabers of Jefferson County. Sarah was the daughter of Francis Drayton Nabers (1804-53), who settled at

Carrollsville, where the first Jefferson County court was held in 1819 shortly after the county was created by the Alabama legislature. The Nabers property was west of the Worthington plantation. Francis Drayton Nabers's son, William F. Nabers (who had married Worthington's daughter Betty), also sold land to the Elyton Land Company.[58] Both Worthington and Nabers were original stockholders in the Elyton Land Company, which founded Birmingham on 4,000 acres, part of it original Worthington and Nabers land.[59]

Marguerite and Raymond Jones were married in Birmingham in 1917 and moved into a house on Twenty-eighth Street South. A daughter was born in 1920. Named Alice for her grandmother, she became known as Acky. A second daughter was born in 1923 and was named for her mother, Marguerite, but she was always called Wita because that was what Acky first called her. When Wita was twelve months old, the family moved over Red Mountain to Shades Valley to a house on Pine Ridge Road in what was to become Mountain Brook. In the early 1920s it was considered far out in the country.

Raymond Jones with his two daughters, Wita and Acky, and his wife, Marguerite, on the fishing pier at High Tide on the Gulf Coast in August 1947.

Raymond Jones enjoyed hunting and was often gone in the fall and winter on hunting trips to south Alabama, especially in and around Pineapple in Wilcox County. He raised hunting dogs and trained them, and he taught Wita to appreciate the skills of a good bird dog. He made her comfortable around guns and gave her lessons in handling a shotgun and in shooting. He was an excellent tennis player and avid golfer, but they played golf together only occasionally. Eventually Wita became as good a golfer as her father was. Because of her father's influence and the wooded area surrounding her home, Wita grew up enjoying the outdoors and was something of a tomboy. She was always athletic and well-coordinated. Wita played with the family dogs and learned to love animals. She climbed trees, hiked in the woods near her home, learned to swim well, and took golf lessons. For three summers she went to Camp Meenagha in Wisconsin on a scholarship awarded because of her athletic ability. At camp she was captain of two teams and won numerous honors. After three years as a camper, Wita returned as a counselor for three more years. For two of those years she was head counselor with a staff of fifteen people and was in charge of the waterfront.[60]

Wita was six years old when the New York stock market crashed in 1929, and she grew up in the Great Depression. For many years her grandparents lived with her parents, and although they managed to keep a cook and a chauffeur through most of these lean years, her family struggled through some hard times. Wita entered first grade with the first class at the new Mountain Brook Grammar School, which was then part of the Jefferson County school system. Rather than attend the local county high school, Shades Cahaba, her parents paid a tuition of $10 a month to the Birmingham Board of Education, and she went to Phillips High School, which was considered academically stronger than Shades Cahaba. Wita graduated in 1940 and was senior class poet that year. From her years at Mountain Brook and at Phillips she knew John, Billy, and Betty Harbert.

During World War II, Wita entered Birmingham-Southern College. She lived at home for two years then moved on campus. She pledged Kappa Delta sorority and soon acquired the nicknames "Queenie" and "Hot Top" for her flame-red hair. She was active in the college intramural sports program, and in her four years at Birmingham-Southern she was a pitcher and member of the all-star softball team, played basketball and tennis, and was a champion at long-distance golf, which was a driving contest. Wita won the intramural swim tournament each year, and by compiling the most points in various competitions, she remembers the honor of being chosen the top intramural female athlete at Birmingham-Southern College all four years she was there. In 1943 she was in charge of Sadie Hawkins Day and was president of Kappa Delta sorority. Under her leadership the KDs "enjoyed one of the most successful years in their long history on the Hilltop."[61] Although she completed her requirements in March 1944 for a double degree in liberal arts and in science, she received her diploma at the June graduation at which Wendell Wilkie was the speaker.[62]

After graduation, Wita worked for the American Red Cross as head of the safety service division, which included water safety, first aid, and accident prevention. She supervised all the Red Cross teaching programs in Jefferson County and perfected her skills at the Brevard College Aquatic School in North Carolina. Wita made her debut in 1945 because no debut galas were held the previous year since so many eligible bachelors were in the military. She was presented at the Redstone Club's ball held at the Birmingham Country Club.

When Wita began dating John, she learned early on what a fast driver he was. With several jobs scattered across the state, John found himself racing around trying to check on each job. He received so many speeding tickets that the state of Alabama suspended his driver's license for six months, and he had to hire a driver to chauffeur him to and from work and around the state. When he had a date with Wita, he and the chauffeur would pick her up, and the chauffeur would drive to his home, leave them, and then Wita would drive. When John was ready to take her home, they would pick up his driver, and he would drive them both to Wita's home on Pine Ridge Road and return John home.[63] John never liked having a chauffeur; he preferred driving himself. And although in later years he perhaps was more careful, stories abound about his fast driving. There were employees and dear friends who avoided being passengers in John's car. Neville Palmer, who came from Jamaica in 1970 to work for the Harberts, when asked if Mr. Harbert were a poor driver replied, "No. He was a good driver. He was just a dangerous driver."[64] Louise Hall, who worked for the Harberts in the 1990s, once caught a ride with the Harberts to her bus stop in town. She recalled that "Mr. Harbert was driving so fast I wondered if I would leave the car alive."[65]

During the time Wita and John were dating, Wita was often taken back by John's stories and his antics, and she was never quite sure what he would do next. He told her stories of having roomed with a magician while working on a construction job during college, and he had a whole repertoire of magic tricks, especially card tricks. John bragged that he could eat a light bulb, but Wita never saw him do it. He loved to shock people by telling accounts of the time he and a fellow construction laborer rented an attic room in a whorehouse in Chattanooga. Wita reasoned that John "loved to be different just to be different."[66]

When John was ready to give Wita the emerald engagement ring, he drove her to the spot in Mountain Brook where Beechwood Road meets Overbrook Road, the exact site where four and a half years earlier she had turned down his initial proposal. She accepted the ring, and they made plans for a summer wedding. Her sister, Acky, was pregnant. Acky and her husband, Pete McGriff, had married shortly after the war and had delayed having a family because her mother kept telling her she "had to be Wita's matron of honor." But after some years, they decided that "Wita wasn't going to get married," so Acky and Pete started their family. Mrs. Jones said Acky was "too poochy to be in the wedding." Acky enjoyed the parties and showers and the excitement of the event, but at

During the wedding reception at her parents' home on Pine Ridge Road, Wita and John relax with their friends and wedding party. Left to right on the floor, Joan McCoy Edmonds, Olivia Miller, Wita's sister Acky Jones McGriff and her husband, Pete McGriff, Ann Shaw Sharman, Anne Equen Ballard, and Bamie Edwards Williams. In back Ed Dixon, John and Wita, Bill Harbert, and Alice Marbury McCullough.

During their honeymoon travels across the American West, John and Wita stopped to eat a leisurely picnic lunch.

the wedding she wore a black maternity dress and felt like the "wicked witch of the wedding."[67]

After the typical round of parties, teas, and showers and a particularly rowdy bachelor's party, John and Wita were married at five o'clock on June 30, 1951, at Saint Mary's Episcopal Church. The reception was held at the Jones home on Pine Ridge Road. John had planned an extensive western tour for their honeymoon. Although the eventual destination was Lake Louise and Banff, Canada, John was taking Wita to visit many of the places he had been as a child and as a soldier in World War II. He was, observed Wita, "always one to retrace his steps."[68]

Following the wedding reception, John and Wita left for the Birmingham airport to fly to Memphis where John had parked his car all packed for the trip. They had reservations at the Peabody Hotel. At the airport John's friends had hired a small band to play "Deep Purple." The next day the couple drove to Hot Springs, Arkansas, where they tried out the hot baths separately in the men's and ladies's sides. Then they drove on through Oklahoma and to Wichita, where they turned west into Colorado. John showed Wita Pike's Peak, the Cave of the Winds, and Camp Carson. They visited Manitou Springs and Colorado Springs and drove through the mountains and north to Denver where they stayed at the Broadmoor Hotel and called on Aunt Bessie. John and Wita motored northwest through Jackson, Wyoming, and the Grand Teton Mountains to Yellowstone National Park. John wanted Wita to camp out and sleep on the ground, but she "wouldn't, for there were bears." After Yellowstone they continued northwest to Washington State to see Pullman and spend the night with cousins at the family wheat farm at Palouse.[69]

When they finally reached their destination, the Chateau Lake Louise, in Alberta, Canada, a letter from Harbert Construction Corporation was waiting for John. Although the letter appeared over the typed signatures of Bill and Ed, the spoof was actually written by Rex, who said she wrote it "simply because there was nobody left here to sign my paycheck."

In the letter Rex gave John a quick update on Harbert jobs, which were all "progressing very nicely" in spite of the superintendent at the Scottsboro job quitting. They had another man who had agreed to work for "a case of whiskey a week and an unlimited expense account." The new man had "fired all the personnel up there and hired his old drinking cronies to complete the job. None of them have ever done any sewer work but they plan on laying it in like water lines, so I guess it will work out alright." On another Harbert job the crew had hit quicksand, but "they will not have any trouble." In south Alabama a town had rejected the Harbert-laid gas lines because "it seems the pipe has all rusted out in the last two or three weeks." The company

On their honeymoon, John took Wita to Colorado, where he had been stationed during World War II. He revisited many sites and drove Wita up Pike's Peak.

was having some union trouble, and the office had been dynamited. Rex ended her letter with a cheery "have a good time, enjoy your honeymoon, give Wita our best regards and don't worry about anything back here. Everything seems to be going along just fine."[70]

After leaving Lake Louise, John and Wita traveled south to Seattle, then down to San Francisco, California, where they called on Aunt Nita Warren, who was then living in Menlo Park, and there they briefly saw John's parents, who were visiting California. John and Wita then drove through southern California and into the mountains where John once trained with the 104th Division. They took a southern route home, going by way of Las Vegas, where they enjoyed the floor shows and gambled some. They visited the Painted Desert, then went east through Dallas. By the time John and Wita reached Birmingham in mid-August, they had been traveling for six weeks. John had left his construction company in good hands, but he had been gone from his business much longer than he had ever been gone before, and for that matter, only one other time would ever do again. At the end of his honeymoon, John had fulfilled his wartime dream of returning to Colorado "for a vacation after the war."[71] When he and Wita arrived in Birmingham, they were ready to establish their home together.

ALITALIA
-DIWF

5

BUILDING HARBERT, A FAMILY, FLORIDA GAS, AND PENBRYN

"a risky game"

After the newlyweds returned to Birmingham, they moved into the Lane Park Apartments in Mountain Brook. Wita began organizing her home and adjusting to being a housewife. John went back to building Harbert Construction Corporation, working seventy-hour weeks at a salary of $20,000 a year. Wita remembered the first time John left her for an overnight trip. He was headed for Camilla, Georgia, to bid on a sewage disposal plant. This trip was the first of hundreds of "good-bye, travel safely" adieus they shared as John traveled the state, then the South, and later the country and the world seeking or inspecting construction jobs for Harbert. He knew exactly what it would take to be successful in the construction business, what he once called "a risky game."[1] Hanging on the wall of John's office was the motto: "The harder I work, the luckier I get." He once observed that he had made "an initial commitment to certain standards for my company: sound engineering personnel, progressive management policies, and visionary financing," which in the early years "was about the only kind of financing" he could obtain.[2] Despite the heavy responsibilities of his company, John found time to be a farmer. Working on the land brought about a release of his business tension. He had always loved farms and land, and he had dreamed of having his own farm someday. In 1951, after he and Wita married, he purchased "420 acres of eroded cotton land" south of the Coosa River and west of Childersburg for $40 an acre. John named the property Green Hill Farm. He constructed a large two-story barn from pressure-treated creosote bridge timbers that he purchased from Grayson Lumber Company at a discount because the Alabama Highway Department "had rejected the shipment and refused to pay Grayson." In October 1951, John bought thirteen head of cattle from two farms in south Alabama. On weekends he would personally drive the bulldozer and "level out the eroded ditches on the property." He improved the quality of the topsoil and built fences, cattle pens, and cattle guards. In 1954 John employed a farm manager and constructed a two-bedroom house on the property for the manager and his family. Because there was no drinking water on the farm, he drilled a 470-foot well and laid a water system to the barn, three cattle troughs, and the manager's house. He "planted trees and food plots for quail and other wild game."[3]

John gradually purchased other cattle and a champion bull and became active in Talladega County farming circles. He organized and was president of the Sylacauga Stock Yards, an entity established to market Talladega and Coosa County cattle and hogs. (Bill Nichols, later elected to Congress, was secretary-treasurer.)[4] John also dug two lakes on his farm and stocked them with fish. Fifteen years after he purchased the farm, fly fishing in the lake was the "main attraction" for his family.[5]

Wita and John wanted children, and because they married in their late twenties they decided to begin their family immediately. By September Wita was pregnant; unfortunately, she had a miscarriage at Christmastime. After the first of the year, John took her on a vacation to Jamaica. One of their early reasons to travel came from John's participation in the Young Presidents' Organization. During the 1950s John became active in the YPO, an international group of men and women who have become presidents of $1 million companies before reaching the age of forty. He and Wita attended YPO meetings in Atlanta; south Florida; Sea Island, Georgia; and in the Caribbean Islands. On his YPO forms John noted that his outside interests were his stock farm on the Coosa River and collecting rare books and maps. His favorite diversion was fly fishing, and he enjoyed a "fast round of tennis."[6]

John stocked his Green Hill Farm lake so friends like Nelson Brungart and his father, Newt, could enjoy John's favorite sport. This photograph was taken in April 1959.

By late summer Wita was pregnant again, but the baby almost lost its father in an automobile accident. John, on one of his "wild rides checking out a job," hit a mailbox and went into a ditch. He came back, shaken but unhurt, the car covered with red mud. His secretary, Rex Barrington, began to fuss at John, asking him, if something happened to him, "what will I tell Wita?" John only smiled and said "tell her she's tough and I love her."[7]

Wita would need to draw on all the toughness she had in the weeks and months ahead. After a complicated pregnancy, a cesarean section was necessary because the pregnancy had extended four weeks beyond the baby's due date. John M. Harbert IV was born April 19, 1953. The baby, called Jay, was very ill, but it was some time before an accurate diagnosis was made. He required around-the-clock attention, and Wita alternated spending time with her mother and John's mother so that she could have help with the baby, who rarely slept. When Jay was three months old, the doctors determined that there was a bile blockage and recommended that he be taken to Children's Hospital in Boston for an operation. Wita and John took the baby and flew to Boston. Wita's mother went with them to help with Jay. Wita recalls this period of weeks as one of the most difficult and trying times of

John and Wita moved into their new house when Jay was eighteen months old.

She always believed this condition was caused by Jay's not receiving enough oxygen in the last weeks of her pregnancy. For Wita, the tensions of dealing with a special-needs child were great, and at the same time the demands of Harbert Corporation were increasing for John, which limited his ability to help her. Although John paid every doctor bill without question, he left the decisions about health and eye problems, corrective shoes, motor difficulties, and proper schooling to Wita. Step by step, with unfailing patience, she began to teach Jay what he needed to know. And in the meantime she suffered three more miscarriages.[10]

her life.[8] Jay was operated on, and the duct was opened, but Wita was in Boston for one month before she could bring Jay home. Her mother was able to stay with her the entire time, enabling John to return to Birmingham after two weeks. The day before she was to leave Boston, John sent Wita an airmail, special delivery letter to the Sheraton Plaza Hotel. He anticipated that she would have good flying weather for her return and wished her a safe trip. "We will have a party when you get here," he wrote in his flowing hand. He sent all his love and told her how much he had missed her.[9]

The doctors in Boston assured the Harberts that Jay would be fine, and Wita returned home exhausted but thankful that all had gone well with the operation. As the months went by, however, Wita became convinced that something was wrong. Jay was not following the normal timetables for a baby's mental and physical development. By eighteen months he had not walked and he was not talking. It was soon apparent to Wita that he would need special help in learning to master simple tasks.

In the fall of 1954 when Jay was eighteen months old, Wita and John moved out of their small apartment at Lane Park and into a new house John had built on thirteen acres adjoining his parents' property on Shades Mountain. They called the house "Penbryn," which was the name listed on county maps where a small cabin once stood on the property. It is Welsh and means "little house on the hill."[11] John had Nelson Smith design the house, a contemporary two-story ranch with cedar-shake roof. Wita had several basic disagreements with John and the architect. She preferred a more traditional house, but John had his mind set on a modern one. Some arguments she won—she got her wide random-width oak floors—and some she lost—she did not get her pane windows. The house had five bedrooms and four and a half baths, a large formal living room, a generous-sized dining room, a library, breakfast room, screened porch, large kitchen, servants' rooms, and carport.

In the next forty years the house underwent several additions and renovations.

In 1954 Birmingham architect Nelson Smith designed for John and Wita a contemporary two-story house that John built on thirteen acres on Shades Mountain.

Wita redesigned the front entrance, changing the roof line, and she directed a major redecorating by Robert Hiden, who was a relative of the Mudds, a connection of Wita's Aunt Nellie Mudd. Hiden spent most of his time traveling between London and Birmingham. He had a special expertise in blending antiques with textured fabrics and subtle but striking color combinations. He typically used English fringes on silk fabrics for his drapery. He designed rugs in size and color for individual rooms and had them handmade in Spain or Portugal. Through Hiden, Wita acquired two sets of double-arched carved wooden doors that had once been in a French chateau, and she added them to the dining room and den entrances.[12] John's financial successes in later years would have allowed him to build a more lavish house, but he and Wita remained at Penbryn, where their children grew up and which contained so many memories.

The 1950s were boom years for the country as the United States caught up with its consumer needs, housing demands, and infrastructure construction. With its Birmingham location, Harbert Corporation was in the geographical center of the Deep South, and John, ready to take advantage of every opportunity, was willing to take calculated risks, a trait that became characteristic of him. He acknowledged that he had a gambler's instinct, which he said he perfected during his years as a GI in World War II. In reality John's business risk-taking was far more his willingness to wager that by his hard work and careful planning, coupled with committed management, competent superintendents, and skillful workers, he could be the difference in making any project successful. Wallace Malone, who as chairman of Birmingham's SouthTrust Bank in the 1980s was not always supportive of John's credit needs, nonetheless appreciated his talents. In 1989 Malone commented to a *Birmingham Post-Herald* business news reporter that "John does not mind taking a risk. ... He has over-the-horizon vision. ... He's educated but in addition to book sense he has common sense."[13] As Elmer Harris, CEO of Alabama Power Company, was later to observe, John was always able to "make a decision quickly, no matter how big the risk."[14] Such quick action was possible because John had often anticipated the possibilities and already contemplated what his proper response should be. The growth of Harbert Construction Corporation in the 1950s, as John himself noted, "was sporadic," and "on several occasions" the company expanded "too rapidly." However, its foundation was laid during these years.[15]

By the midfifties, Harbert had expanded in terms of both the geographical locations of its contracts and the "complexity of projects undertaken."[16] Harbert crews were operating at construction sites in four states, and simple five-span bridges and uncomplicated pipelines had been replaced by intricate designs and difficult engineering challenges. Despite successes, John was plagued by a problem common to all construction companies, and it was one that in the late 1950s was crucial for Harbert. Even in the later decades, when John's corporate and personal assets were extensive, it was absolutely essential to Harbert's success: the corporation had to have adequate cash flow to sustain its growth. John was operating in the riskiest part of the heavy construction business. Many of Harbert's jobs were on contracts to governments—federal, state, and local—and these entities were always slow to reimburse. Governments were especially dilatory in paying retainage and overruns that resulted from changed plans or altered specifications for which they were responsible. John once remarked that his company "made the mistake, more than once, of taking on major risks without the assurance of commensurate rewards."[17]

John's experiences on a construction job in Tarpon Springs, Florida, eventually led to his first major gamble. Luckily, it also proved to be a financial success and became one of his most significant long-term investments. In the winter of 1951 Harbert had a $218,000 contract, the company's largest job to that time, to construct a sewer disposal and collection system for Tarpon Springs, a small town twenty miles north of Saint Petersburg, Florida. Because the location was so close to the Gulf of Mexico, it was, John recalled, "a risky job involving a great deal of wellpoint work" to remove the water from the soil. John and Ted Randolph moved to Tarpon Springs and "shared the management of the 24-hours-a-day, 7-days-a-week job." They also shared "a tiny, two-bedroom apartment over a bar owned by a Greek guy named Mike."[18] The winter was severe. Florida, despite numerous resources, had no significant source of coal, oil, or gas, and energy resources had to be transported into the state by rail, truck, ship, or barge.[19] Florida homes either were not heated or had inadequate heat; there was no heat in John and Ted's apartment. They learned the hard way that Florida can be very cold. John and Ted resorted to using the electric stove in the kitchen to cut the chill in their apartment. This experience convinced John that there was "a market for natural gas in Florida, because in spite of what all the tourist agencies advertised," it could be "mighty cold there in the wintertime."[20]

Speaking before business students at Auburn University in 1980, John explained that Harbert Construction Corporation had acquired the engineering and construction proficiency to undertake a range of projects, from developing "potable water supply and distribution systems to natural gas distribution systems, oil terminals, and land development." And in order to take advantage of these skills, he "looked for a need for these kinds of services."[21] Before World War II, typical home heating in the United States was supplied by circulating hot water or forced hot air heated by coal- or oil-fired furnaces. Coal had to be shoveled from coal piles to furnaces or into a stoker that gradually fed the coal to the furnace. In the federally underwritten housing boom of the postwar period, floor furnaces fueled by clean-burning natural gas began to take the place of coal. John recognized that natural gas would be in great demand, and small towns would need extensive gas lines laid. To Harbert's sewer line and water pipeline laying expertise, Harbert added natural gas lines and began bidding on gas projects. In 1951 Harbert laid its first gas pipe system in Demopolis, Alabama.

Remembering his experiences in Tarpon Springs, John was convinced that Florida needed another source of power, but he had a "hard time selling" his idea because, he recalled, "Floridians themselves did not feel they needed this source of energy. They had plenty of cheap oil at the time, and the investment community did not perceive any demand for natural gas." Florida was, so the advertisements proclaimed, "the Sunshine State" and a warm-weather destination for tourists. Few civic or political leaders believed that Florida would ever develop an industrial system "that would need energy." To bolster his plans, John "gambled $5,000" to fund a market survey of energy users and energy costs in Florida. The Louisiana engineering firm of Barnard and Burk did the investigation and absorbed the other half of the expense of the six-month study. The results proved that Florida was a good market for natural gas, but it took John and his investment group "six years to convince the Federal Power Commission" to grant a certificate of convenience and necessity to permit the construction of the interstate natural gas pipeline.[22] The investment group also had to prove that there were "sufficient gas reserves to support that market requirement for twenty years and to affirm financial feasibility." The feasibility studies had to include "detailed engineering data, acquisition of twenty-five hundred miles of right-of-way, pipeline engineering and compression station designs, complete financial plans, and myriad other demanding details," all of which "required money."[23] John met Jack Bowen at this time. He was representing Delhi Oil of Dallas, which had responsibility for developing the gas supply and building the gas lines from south Texas to Baton Rouge.[24]

More than two decades later, John remembered the risky investment in this enterprise:

> As is usual in a gamble of this nature, you get wet a little at a time. You start with a small investment, and each step requires a little more money to stay in the game. It's exactly like draw poker: You have paid into the pot, have a reasonably fair hand, and you ante up to get another card and continue to play. Also to share the risk, you invite others into the deal, and in the early stages of a risk development, you seek individuals who can contribute talent in some fashion, as well as risk money.[25]

To complete the deal, John needed "engineering, legal, political, and financial talent." Despite the rough road, he had to provide the leadership to keep his "entrepreneurs working together harmoniously," especially when things were not going well. Soon John reached the limits of his risk money. He remembered investing "some $600,000," all of it "borrowed money."[26] In order to obtain more capital, John and Charles Barnard, the senior partner of the engineering company that had done the original survey, flew to Texas to convince a "rich Houston investor" that the Florida project was worthy of his money. As John told the story, to both of them the tycoon seemed perfect—a real gentleman with a fine office in downtown Houston, experience in the gas pipeline industry, and what appeared to be a good engineering staff. John signed a binding contract with the financier, enjoyed euphoria for several weeks, and then discovered that his new "Texas friend had out-promoted" him. The man was bankrupt. John first began to doubt the Texan's affluence and his liquidity while they were playing billiards at the elderly man's Houston home. He surprised John by asking him if he would consider taking a second mortgage on his house.[27] Although John now knew that the Texan was a liability, he considered himself "locked in" with his mistake because his hearing before the Federal Power Commission was "at a critical point" and "any internal conflicts creating an appearance of disunity could have a negative effect on our position before the Commission."[28] John's investment group had "to fight like hell" to receive the permits to build the pipeline. Years later he recalled that "every step of the way" he was thwarted "by an unenlightened press intent on stirring up a controversy in order to sell papers."[29]

In December 1956, the Federal Power Commission (in a three-to-two vote) finally approved construction of the 2,600-mile pipeline, including main line and laterals, across five states from Texas to Florida; however, it took the investment group another two years to secure the financing. Marvin F. Pixton, whose daughter Dorothy had once worked for Harbert, was the chief financial officer for the Ingalls Companies in Birmingham. He helped John by making contacts with New York financial interests, writing to the vice-president of Douglas L. Elliman and Company that

> As I understand it, Mr. Harbert is interested in getting a sort of construction loan commitment on a job which will run in the neighborhood of $30 million to $35 million so that he could carry the accounts which would arise in the work during the interim between actual construction progress and receipt of progress payments. It has been my experience in a contract for ship construction running around $10 million or $12 million that even on a prompt-pay basis the contractor is required to carry "on the cuff" so to speak a substantial amount, sometimes running around a million dollars or more even on a job of that size pending the time between submission of the progress payment requests and the actual receipt of the funds.[30]

Pixton recommended John as a man he had known for "a number of years," a "real `go getter'" who "has built up a very enviable position in the construction field." Pixton noted that the Harbert company "enjoys a very good reputation, both financially and as an engineering firm."[31] On August 28, 1958, the project was finally fully financed.[32]

In January 1958, John hired William H. Rossman as controller of Harbert Construction Corporation. The financial reporting and the sheer magnitude of the Florida project required more expertise than the company required when Ed Dixon ran the payroll alone out of the one-room office in English Village or when J. D. Sledge was keeping the books and Rex Barrington was making payroll and signing checks in the company headquarters on South Eighth Avenue. John

Bill Rossman provided skillful financial management for Harbert Construction Corporation from 1958 until his retirement in 1985.

To complete the Florida pipeline, Harbert Construction Corporation ordered $1 million dollars' worth of Allis-Chalmers equipment. John talks with the driver while Bill Harbert (left) and Ed Dixon (right) remain on the ground.

recognized that for Harbert to have credibility with its banks and bonding companies, he needed to have a certified public accountant in-house. Rossman was a CPA and held a Stanford University MBA; and although he knew nothing about construction, he had almost two decades of experience in the Texas and California oil and gas production industries.[33]

The Florida venture went forward under the name of the Houston Texas Gas and Oil Company, with Midwestern Constructors laying the Louisiana and Mississippi portions and Harbert doing the more difficult south Florida part—300 miles of main-line artery from the Kissimmee junction on the parkway to Vero Beach and Miami. Harbert also constructed more than 700 miles of distribution lateral lines over Florida.[34] Harbert's part of the pipeline was completed in nine months, but not without problems. On one occasion there was a disagreement about a right-of-way when a resident faced down Harbert men with a shotgun, threatening to shoot if anyone crossed his land. And there was so much equipment being shipped to Florida that Harbert had to hire a traffic man to make sure it went where it was supposed to be. Harbert once ran into a cash crunch when a load of expensive equipment was en route to Florida and payment was due when it arrived. With some fancy rerouting instructions, Harbert men were able to delay arrival in Florida until they had the payment check covered at the bank. Although there was much concern over snakes in the swamps, and Harbert Corporation took the precaution of researching snakebites and issuing snake boots and leggings to its men, the noise from the bulldozers sent the snakes and alligators running in the opposite direction.[35]

In order to complete the Florida pipeline, Harbert financed the largest peacetime equipment purchase in Alabama. John selected Allis-Chalmers and ordered one million dollars' worth of ditching machines.[36] Harbert had some equipment especially designed for the job. The high water table and sandy soil made for an "engineering nightmare" where a man could "dig a ditch then lose it while turning" his head. One piece of machinery was designed by Harbert to dig the ditch and slope and pack the sides at the same time.[37]

Stringing, welding, inspecting, and burying the pipe through Florida had to be accomplished through forests and swamps and over creeks, streams, canals, and tedious crossing of rivers. Stringing pipe in open fields and pastures went more smoothly, but in the Sunshine State a good rainy afternoon could turn a dry grassland into a lake. The crews had to work fast when they could, for there was "always a bog around the bend in Florida."[38] During peak construction in May 1959, Harbert employed more than 5,000 people and had a million-dollar payroll; throughout 1958-59 Harbert was operating twenty-two crews directed from thirteen offices.[39] Jack Bowen, who was closely associated with the Florida gas project, noted that when the FPC approved the project "everything was ready to build the pipeline and the necessary compressor station facilities," and "the entire line with all the lateral lines and compressor stations was built in nine months. You could not do it in nine years today."[40]

John wanted to promote Harbert and the pipeline for the benefit of his company and also because of his interest in the Houston Texas Gas and Oil Company. John purchased a sixteen-millimeter motion picture camera and put George Gambrill in charge of producing a film on the gas line construction. Working with a scriptwriter from New York, a Montgomery photographer, and a Washington, D.C.-based film editing and film-mix company, Gambrill created *The Florida Venture*. The film was sent all over the world to prospective customers of Harbert and was shown in small towns across Florida. John also made numerous speeches about the idea, the financing, and the construction of the pipeline.[41]

The financial strain of such construction almost put Harbert Construction Corporation under. Things were so close that there were times when checks could not be released until after 2:00 P.M. when the banks closed. When money was tight, John, Bill, and Ed "would make some rounds trying to pick up money that was owed Harbert." John always had difficulties with bankers and once told his secretary, Rex Barrington, never to let a bank know how desperate you are.[42] On the fortieth anniversary of Harbert Corporation in 1989, John looked back and clarified one point: "Some people have written that I have been bankrupt three times. I have never been bankrupt and everyone has always been paid, but I have been broke three times."[43]

The first few years were slow for the Florida Gas Company, which handled the distribution of the natural gas. CEO Jack Bowen directed the company through a crucial time with the aid of John, "who played a key role" in helping Bowen "in redirecting and restructuring the company and gaining the confidence of investors, creditors, lenders, and employees."[44] Eventually Florida Gas "proved highly successful" and saved Florida residents millions of dollars in energy costs. Once when John reminisced about the Florida project, he observed that "the ten-year battle resulted in a profit for the venturers, more for some than others. The estate of our Texas tycoon, as luck would have it, profited the most. And I like to think that the old man, who had so deftly outsmarted us, somehow knew how it all turned out. I'm sure he would have smiled."[45] The Florida venture proved to be an experience invaluable far beyond its dollar profits to Harbert, and the corporation's investment in the Florida Gas Company was Harbert's first diversification move. John developed an understanding of energy supplies and needs and laid the foundation for Harbert's move into the coal energy market, which would prove so profitable for Harbert Corporation in the 1970s.

While John was deep in negotiations for the Florida natural gas pipeline and Harbert construction crews were stringing and welding pipe across Florida, other Harbert jobs were being estimated, bid, won, completed, and collected. There were more natural gas pipelines and water lines, water treatment plants, and sewage systems constructed in Harbert's original operational region of Alabama,

Mississippi, Georgia, and Florida. Harbert completed its first government contracts for bulk fuel facilities at the air force base in Columbus, Mississippi, and a runway extension at Brookley Air Force Base in Mobile.[46] For the first time, Harbert moved outside the continental United States with a sewer line job in San Jose, Puerto Rico. The company also moved into the Northwest, winning jobs in Washington and Oregon.

In 1956, during the critical planning stage of the development of the Florida gas line, John made a personal investment that proved to be fortuitous. He joined two partners, Frank Smith and Rolland King, in purchasing a 2,000-acre Minute Maid citrus grove outside Sarasota, Florida. The grove was not profitable, according to John, because it contained "four different kinds of citrus fruit trees, none of which ripened at the same time; consequently, they had to harvest each grove four times a year instead of one."[47] John would have to make the purchase with borrowed money; however, he was not able to find support in Birmingham. His local banker told him there was "nothing down there but a bunch of coconut trees and monkeys in the trees." He even refused to join John and fly down to look over the property. John had no intention of harvesting oranges, but the banker was unwilling to risk a loan backed by John's vision. Eventually, John was able to secure financing in New York. What he planned to do was to take the $2,000-an-acre land and change its use and its value by creating a community of homes with a convenient shopping center.[48] Harbert Construction Corporation built the shopping center, which opened on January 15, 1957, as the South Gate Shopping Plaza. The center had a Publix supermarket, a drugstore, a W. T. Grant store, a dozen other stores, and a parking lot for 1,250 cars.[49] John took pride in the irony that after the property was developed "one small corner lot (less than half an acre) for which we paid $500 was sold for a quarter of a million dollars" to a bank.[50]

The bow-legged green and yellow "H," designed for John by George Gambrill, became the symbol of Harbert Corporation in the late 1950s; by the '70s and '80s it was recognized across the nation and in many places in the world where Harbert had construction projects.

At about the time the Florida gas line was nearing completion, John, with his keen eye for public relations, asked George Gambrill to design a logo for Harbert Construction Corporation. George set to work, but John rejected many of his creations as being too much like the International Harvester "H." Finally, Rex Barrington made a suggestion. Wita and a number of the wives and secretaries were pregnant; why not, she asked, "make it pregnant? Everything else around here is!" Gambrill's design, the famous "bow-legged H," soon emblazoned tractors, trailers, trucks, scrapers, bulldozers, and water buckets, as well as stationery, calling cards, and advertisements. The Harbert "H" was destined to be known and recognized the world over.[51]

With this pregnancy, which had helped inspire the "bow-legged H," Wita's doctor ordered extended periods of rest, and she "did not leave the house for seven months." Wita read, played bridge, did needlepoint, and visited with friends who dropped by or

On a Saturday in May 1959, John, dressed in his boots, plays with his two sons.

called on the telephone.[52] A boy was born on December 2, 1958, and named Raymond Jones Harbert for Wita's father. In January, John took Wita to Jamaica to rest. As a child Raymond suffered from asthma. Wita moved him to a small room just off her bedroom so she could hear him at night when he began to wheeze. She had a nebulizer that she worked with a tire pump, misting the medicine so Raymond could breathe it into his lungs.

During the 1950s Harbert Construction Corporation won several jobs at the Birmingham Municipal Airport. One called for large amounts of fill dirt, which would be very expensive to acquire and haul in. In surveying the proposed job site and working on the estimate for his formal bid, John noticed several small houses that occupied a hillside adjacent to the airport. He figured that the people who lived there would like to move away from the danger of being too close to the runway and the noise of the planes. John contacted a real estate agent and had him visit the people and acquire options for Harbert on the houses and the property. He then structured his bid to include purchase of the property, tearing down the houses, and moving the fill dirt from the hill to the airport across the road, a much cheaper process than buying the dirt and hauling it by truck from distant places. Harbert won the job and a hill site was leveled.[53]

John remembered this experience in 1958 when he was awarded another contract to build a 10,000-foot runway at the airport and ran into difficulty with materials. Construction specifications required "dense graded aggregate base course" because the Birmingham runway was to be used by Hayes Aircraft to bring in "the big B-29 planes for modification." Harbert had received a quote on these aggregate materials from Vulcan Materials, but after the bid letting, Vulcan's sales representative confirmed that although the company could meet the time schedule, the price had increased sixty cents a ton more than the figures John had used in his estimate. John refused to be bushwhacked. He drove around the eastern part of the county, located an abandoned quarry, acquired title to the property, and began "producing and stock-piling stone that met specifications." In the end John made $300,000 more on the project than he had planned, and Harbert had diversified into the rock quarry business, experience that would later be put to use in another state.[54] A year later Harbert won another contract to construct more airport taxiways at the Birmingham airport.

In 1958 John had attorney Ed Friend set up a profit-sharing plan for Harbert. Because of the volatile nature of the construction business, John believed it would be impossible for a construction company to fund a retirement plan, but he was convinced that a profit-sharing plan would provide a nest egg for his employees and be an incentive to make everyone work together toward a goal of greater profits on individual jobs. The plan was voluntary, and the Harbert employees who participated over a number of years enjoyed a comfortable retirement.[55]

As the first decade of the Harbert Construction Corporation drew to a close, the company was aggressively driving ahead. The extensive equipment acquired for the Florida pipeline, which had doubled the machinery holdings of Harbert, was being moved to other job sites. Harbert built a portion of Interstate 59 in DeKalb County. At $3.4 million, it was Harbert's "first multimillion dollar road contract" and was finished in March 1960.[56]

Harbert had moved into the international field in 1955. With "surplus goods—equipment and know-how—which we could not always profitably sell at home," John explained that Harbert went after jobs "in countries where we might be competitive because of special construction knowledge and experience."[57] Harbert's "Foreign Job #1," a small sewer job in Arecibo, Puerto Rico, that was completed in 1957, came about after the initial contractor went broke.[58] It was John's first business opportunity to use his Spanish.[59] In the following years, Harbert did additional work in Puerto Rico. At the end of the decade the company bid on a crude oil pipeline job in India and on some improvements for the Panama Canal. Although neither job was won, these early international experiences were the foundation for later successes.[60]

In recalling the early years of the Harbert Corporation, Ed Dixon attributed the success of the company to the "mix of personalities and talents" that complemented one another, men and women who had "not daily but hour by hour communication." They were all aware of "what was going on" at every job site and could take questions from the field and supply an immediate answer. But a most important point, he said, was that "a construction company is like an army and needs a visible leader." John, according to Dixon, provided excellent leadership. In these years everyone called him by his first name, and whether it was the foreman or the man on the machine, they all related to John. Dixon observed that John had "a distinctive sense about getting along with people. He knew how to relate to them, how to charm them, how to converse with people of all levels" of life. He knew how to lead.[61]

Harbert completed its $85 million portion of the Florida pipeline by September 1959, in a construction time of nine months. At the end of the year, Harbert issued its first newsletter, a small mimeographed legal-size sheet folded in half. John explained that he thought the Christmas season was an appropriate time to begin a company newsletter. He was "thinking of the great changes that have taken place in our company in the past five years. I am particularly conscious of the fact that I no longer have the personal contacts in our organization that I did a few years ago." He hoped the newsletter would "make up for this in some small degree," and he wished everyone a happy Christmas and a fruitful and prosperous New Year. He had every reason to believe the decade that would begin the following week would be a good and profitable one for Harbert Construction Corporation.[62]

6

PEARL RIVER, RED MOUNTAIN, AND LOCK AND DAM #18

"extended far beyond our means"

The years at the turn of the decade, 1959-62, were difficult times for Harbert. The construction of the Florida gas pipeline had strained the company's financial resources. Harbert had expanded "on pure nerve" and with little capital. John was "vulnerable."[1] Reminiscing about these bleak days in 1987 at a retirement dinner honoring Ed Dixon, John said that "we floundered around from minor successes to almost catastrophic failures," and "in the dark days" of the late 1950s and early 1960s, "we were extended far beyond our means."[2] In 1981 John recalled that his young company's "particular managerial style was sometimes termed `restlessness'—and, by some elders in the financial forum, `compulsive gambling.'"[3] Rex Barrington knew that at times during these days "John was [in] over his head, but I knew he wasn't going to drown."[4] In addition to the main office in Birmingham, in 1960 Harbert had offices in Seattle, Orlando, and Puerto Rico, produced gross revenues of $18.5 million, and was licensed to work in twenty-two states. Although the Florida gas pipeline had left Harbert with a massive amount of equipment, a remarkable group of experienced superintendents, and a valuable corps of trained workers, the profits from the construction were not commensurate with the financial risks Harbert assumed.[5]

In a 1960 midsummer memo to his Harbert employees, John encouraged each one to "find more to contribute than just the sweat of his brow—just as I believe it is important that an employer contribute more than a weekly paycheck." John wrote that Harbert especially wanted "to provide the opportunity for every individual member of our organization to find room for personal growth and development in his profession—realizing full well that in doing so we are also advancing the cause of our company's continued progress." John went on to point out that "it is only through the efforts of individuals dedicated to their own personal progress, and with a strong feeling of personal identity with their company, that we can continue to grow and prosper."[6] Throughout the decade, John would encourage a management philosophy that promoted individual responsibility, offered opportunities for those who exhibited leadership, and rewarded competence, hard work, and loyalty.

Despite the pressures of his business, John did find time to vacation with his family. During the mid-1950s Harbert had been involved with the development of Santa Rosa Island off Fort Walton Beach, Florida. The corporation acquired five lots on the Gulf of Mexico, and John constructed a large five-bedroom house on one. But Wita had difficulty enjoying the beach because there were so many people coming and going that it was too much for her to manage. As a teenager she had visited in the North Carolina mountains during the summers, and in later years she sometimes went there with friends and played golf. She longed for a house in Highlands, where many Mountain Brook people spent July and August. John agreed. The tiny community high in the Smoky Mountains of North Carolina was a popular summer resort attracting artists, writers, politicians, and affluent business people.

Wita and Jay enjoy playing in the gulf at Fort Walton Beach, Florida, in August 1957.

In 1959 when her mother was going to Highlands to visit friends, Wita asked her to see if she could find a house for sale. Mrs. Jones found one nestled on the side of Little Yellow Mountain with a lovely view of the valley and the mountains beyond. She called Wita and told her about the house, which was known as the James Hammett place but was owned by the Lowenstein family. John was unable to go to Highlands to inspect the house because he was suffering from hepatitis, which he had contracted on a visit to South America to check on a job. But after talking to the real estate agent, John decided to buy the house for Wita, "sight unseen." It was fall before Wita and John could travel to Highlands, see their new mountain retreat, and finalize the deal. Wita called the house "Shangri-la" after the remote and beautiful imaginary land in James Hilton's 1933 novel *Lost Horizon*.[7]

The two-story 1920s house sits on a ridge, with a view looking northeast to the Smoky Mountains. The grounds are covered with oak and pine trees and rhododendron, mountain laurel, and ferns. The uneven and bumpy driveway is made of slate rock and cement, and on the edges and along the side of the house, it is covered with dark green moss. There is a carport, held up by posts made from whole trees, their long-gone branches sticking out as stubs. Although it is too narrow to comfortably accommodate today's cars, the carport serves as a covered patio for barbecuing. Low rock walls separate the driveway, walkways, and the front patio from the woods, and a constant gentle breeze blows; the air is cool and there is no need for air conditioning. A small two-bedroom-and-bath servants' cottage is on the property, just beyond the kitchen, and when Wita went to Highlands, she had help with the cooking, the house, and the children. She often

The retreat Wita called Shangri-la was built in the 1920s and overlooks Highlands from Little Yellow Mountain. The North Carolina mountains were mostly a summer retreat, but occasionally before 1981, when they acquired Pinebloom, the Harberts hosted house parties here during the winter as well as the summer.

John supervises Will Rudolph with the barbecuing at Highlands during the 1987 Labor Day weekend.

During the summer of 1970 Margie and Raymond joined Justice Hugo Black at the Highlands Country Club after Black had finished a tennis match with their mother.

employed local women to watch the children or enrolled them in youth programs at the country club or in the community.

Each spring Wita would drive to Highlands, often alone, to check the house and make plans for opening it for the summer. Sometimes she would take friends with her. She would meet with contractors to inspect the house to see if repairs were needed. A Highlands gardener would come by, and he and Wita would plan what flowers would be planted in which beds and where she wanted hanging baskets of blooming flowers. She would see that the gutters were examined and that no pipes had frozen during the winter. The local cleaning company would send staff to schedule a housecleaning. Perhaps Wita would meet with a decorator to select new fabrics for curtains or a new color for the sun room. When she and the children arrived in mid- to late June, the impatiens and geraniums were blooming.[8]

The house has a large living room with a great rock fireplace, a two-story cathedral ceiling, and paneled walls. There are four bedrooms and four baths, a large dining room, and a bright yellow kitchen. But the favorite room is a converted screened porch with windows on the side and a picture window at the end overlooking the mountains and the valley. Here Wita and John enjoyed their morning coffee amid the antique wicker furniture that evoked the 1920s. She would needlepoint, and they both would make calls to friends and plan their day. Most often the house was filled with company, couples from Birmingham or friends from all over the South.

Highlands was always Wita's world, never really John's, although John came to the

Madeline Lewis and her nephew, Neville Palmer, assist Wita in gathering ferns in the woods around Highlands, North Carolina, in the summer of 1977. For many years Madeline and Neville worked for the Harberts, but Madeline returned to her home in Jamaica about 1993. Neville continues to make sure the Harbert household runs smoothly.

During the summer of 1964 John and Wita entertained Jack Tobias and his wife, Binky, and Betsy and Frank Plummer at Highlands. Jack, Betsy, John, Wita, and Frank enjoy the view from the Harberts' front yard.

mountains when he could. The town was a summer paradise for vacationers sojourning for a few days, but for those who came every summer there were parties and visiting and quite a regular social season. Wita played golf several times a week, much more than she was able to schedule at home. She had a reputation as being the best golfer on the mountain, and during the summer she took a leadership role in the Highlands Country Club. John did not like golf. It was too slow for him, and he played only when Wita insisted. He once said that he had given up golf because "my wife has a nine or ten handicap. She started beating me regularly so I got mad and quit."[9] John often joked about his poor golf, telling about killing snakes when his ball was in the rhododendron, and saying that although Wita had shot three holes in one, he had never "had one hole in five." At Highlands he occasionally was irritated by the conversations of golfers who were always talking about what they shot on what hole. But he loved tennis, and he and Wita played a lot of tennis at Highlands. John would fly up on Friday and occasionally stay until Monday morning. He would bring briefcases filled with work to do, and while he was there he would make dozens of telephone calls and dictate letters. Wita always believed John was more relaxed at Highlands than anywhere else. In the summer before he died, John created a small work area in their large bedroom and installed a fax machine and a computer, anticipating that with his retirement he would be spending more time in the mountains.[10]

As the decade of the 1960s opened, John was in demand more than ever to serve on civic and fund-raising committees. The Florida gas pipeline had received favorable publicity, and John had shown the film of the project or talked about it at numerous Birmingham and Florida civic and educational meetings and to engineering groups. In these years John found more time for community activities, such as his participation on the fund-raising committee for the University of Alabama drive to expand the engineering facilities at the Birmingham extension center, the forerunner of the University of Alabama in Birmingham. With Thomas Martin as chairman, the committee was able to raise $650,000.[11]

John was quick to help people in need, and one such occasion occurred in September 1961 after Hurricane Carla struck Galveston, Texas. Birmingham's radio station WAPI broadcast an appeal for a land-water vehicle to assist in the recovery process. Harbert had an army "duck," and John immediately made arrangements to send it to Galveston. He located an army C-124 transport plane at the Birmingham airport. The plane had been overhauled by Hayes Aircraft and was ready to return to duty. John had the army fly the duck to Texas.[12] In 1969 when Hurricane Camille hit the Mississippi Gulf Coast, John selected a group of Harbert's skilled people and pulled heavy equipment off every job in the Southeast and sent it to Mississippi to help with the rescue and repair work. The men "endured typhoid and tetanus shots and 14-hour work days, seven days a week." They cleared roads, brought in fresh water, and at the request of the L & N Railroad cleared their lines to restore service from Bay Saint Louis west to the Louisiana line. Birmingham kept in contact with the Harbert men by radio, as airplanes directed the Harbert crews over passable roads to trouble spots. The Mississippi Gulf Coast was the area of John Harbert's last high school days, and he wanted to help his friends.[13]

John and Wita were a popular young couple in Birmingham with an active social life, although on too many occasions to suit Wita, John was either late getting home or off on a sudden business trip, and she either missed an event or joined friends to go without him. The Harberts attended private parties at the country clubs, hosted parties in their home, Penbryn, and participated in various charity fund-raising galas. Wita spent time on her home and her gardens. She worked in her greenhouse and had a formal garden and a rock garden. In springtime the grounds were filled with color from blooming azaleas, bulbs, cherry trees, and dogwoods. The Harberts opened their home for the Church of the Advent's spring home and garden tour in 1962.[14] Although Wita's difficult pregnancies had convinced John she should not try to have another baby, she wanted a girl. On June 8, 1961, Wita gave birth to their daughter, Marguerite, who became known as Margie. This red-haired child looked like her mother and always reminded John of Wita.

Jay and Raymond with their sister, Margie, whose arrival in 1961 completed the Harbert family.

The Harbert family was complete. John was often away from home, but when he was there he enjoyed playing games with the children. He would tussle with them, pretending they were sacks of potatoes to be thrown onto the potato truck—the sofa. He would hug them and rub his beard on their faces in the mornings and pretend he was twisting off their noses, making his thumb appear to be a nose between his fingers. He would hold them and give them mule bites. He had, Margie thinks, an "understanding of the delights children take in simple things." He brought surprises home for them—apples, candy bars, small toys. Margie remembers that the one everyday question of her childhood was, "Will Daddy be home for dinner?"[15] In 1975 when John addressed the Samford University Business Majors Association, he remarked that construction

> is a business that requires a lot of travel and uprooting, and it takes a special kind of wife and family to put up with it. I hate to say it, but in many cases a man's wife and children must take second place in receiving his attention. I vividly recall my young daughter at a very early age asking me, "Daddy, why can't you stay home like other daddies?" She's probably thirteen now, quite a young lady, and although she probably still asks the same question to herself, she has learned to live that kind of life in which an emergency is a part of the normal routine. She knows I can't be responsible for building a power plant if I stay in our backyard, and she knows that if I say I have to go, I will go, even if it means missing her special banquet or leaving her in bed with the mumps. The life of a construction man means a sacrifice by his entire family.[16]

If the decade began ominously for Harbert Construction Corporation, things were about to get worse. In April 1960, Harbert announced it was bidding on a "rolled earth-filled dam of approximately four million cubic yards of earth with a spillway and ten tainter gates" that would be located on the Pearl River some eight miles north of Jackson, Mississippi.[17] By June, Harbert had won the $6.6 million contract and planned for construction to begin July 1 with an eighteen-month completion time. The dam, which would flood 31,000 acres and create a large reservoir and provide flood control for the river, water for Jackson, and a forty-three-mile-long recreational lake, was a project that Harbert was constructing in joint venture with an established Minnesota construction company, Johnson, Drake and Piper. The joint venture had two parts: the Pearl River Dam and the Hartwell Dam on the Savannah River between Georgia and South Carolina. Johnson, Drake and Piper owned 40 percent of Pearl River and 60 percent of Hartwell and was in charge of the Georgia operation, while Harbert owned 60 percent of Pearl River, only 40 percent of Hartwell, and was in charge of the Pearl River project. Things went well in Georgia, but nothing went well in Mississippi.[18] There were problems from the very beginning, and Harbert controller Bill Rossman once observed that "we have found over the years that if something starts to go wrong at first, then everything goes wrong."[19] Although the project began with an elaborate dedication ceremony, at which John and Birmingham bankers Frank Plummer and A. J. Bowron, Jr., appeared along with Harbert's equipment suppliers, Hall Thompson and James Waitzman, as things developed within the company Harbert people were soon calling it "Pearl Harbor."[20]

Mississippians viewed the building of Pearl River Dam with much enthusiasm. The dam would, said the Jackson *State Times*, attract industries "seeking a plentiful supply of water," and it would "be a wonderful boost to the economy of this area and the entire state." John noted in December 1960 that he was very concerned with speed because good summer weather had been lost due to the late bidding date. The Jackson newspaper took notice of John's Mississippi birth, saying the project was under the direction of a "state native" and "graduate of Gulfport High School," but Mississippi contracting firms resented the intrusion of an Alabama corporation onto turf they considered their own. Harbert soon had differences with local administrators, organized as the Pearl River Reservoir Board. They kept changing the specifications.[21]

Harbert bid on using rip-rap on the riverbanks, but the reservoir board changed the material requirement to asphalt. The estimate for moving the dirt for the dam was far too low because, as John explained it, "the dirt had a lot of `Yazoo clay' in it," which meant that it was "high in moisture and difficult to compact." Harbert workers had to use cultivators and plows to handle the dirt "so that the wind and sun could dry it out." John said that "we had to move it from place to place and handle it many times in order to educate it and get the densities required. `Educate' is not an engineering term; it's what my father used to call it when dirt had to have so much attention."[22] John's father had spent his early professional years dealing with Yazoo clay in Mississippi. If Harbert's difficulties with a board that kept changing its mind and with Yazoo clay that would not compact were not enough, a devastating flood in February destroyed much of the work already accomplished and damaged Harbert's equipment. Although Harbert crews sandbagged the cofferdam and moved construction equipment to higher ground to prepare for the flood, the water was higher than anyone expected and, in fact, set a forty-year record. At the height of the flood the spillway construction was under forty-two feet of water. The only way to access the site was by Harbert's own water taxi service. Harbert was "operating boats on a lake that wasn't supposed to be in existence until the dam was completed."[23] Rains continued to come in the spring and summer, with 7.2 inches falling in June, causing twenty-seven lost-work days that month.[24]

Harbert also had problems with the work force, missing equipment, and petty vandalism. As things in Mississippi were falling apart, the construction of the Hartwell Dam was going well in Georgia, and John was able to negotiate a deal with Johnson, Drake and Piper for it to buy out Harbert's share of Hartwell at a profit to Harbert, but John refused to release the Minnesota firm from its liabilities at Pearl River.[25]

Word circulated in the industry that Harbert Construction Corporation was broke, and on paper it was. During a crucial period in the summer of 1961 when Wita was at Highlands with the children and servants, John called and told her the dismal news that he was about to go bankrupt. She replied that she would "come home immediately." But John responded, "No, you stay up in Highlands with the children and play golf. Smile and pretend that nothing is wrong, and we can stop the rumors. I'm going to put on my boots and go over to Pearl River and finish that job."[26] John went to Mississippi and fired many of the workers. For the rest of that summer each Monday he would fly to Mississippi wearing his khaki pants and boots. If Pearl River was going to drown his company and take him down, too, then John was going to know exactly what was happening every step of the way, and he would do the best he could to prevent a total disaster. He had spent the last two years developing a "corporate image" and painting the new Harbert "bow-legged H" on every piece of Harbert equipment. The "H" was "rapidly" becoming "familiar to people in the industry and even to outsiders," but, as Charlotte Gafford so aptly put it, "John Harbert's good name and spiffy logo were about to take a bath in the Mississippi mud."[27]

John recalled that with "all our cash and credit resources" drained, Bill Rossman was responsible for handling the finances and dealing with creditors from the Birmingham office while he was in Mississippi. John sent the other senior management personnel into the field with the charge to finish as many jobs as possible in the quickest time with the greatest profit. In the interim the Harbert strategy was to go to major creditors, explain the situation, and ask "for additional time to pay our debts." The corporation tried "to buy time," often stalling and refusing to make commitments to pay by explaining that the federal and state governments were "substantially behind in their payments of contract estimates." Harbert's creditors knew this claim was true. On major accounts, John or Rossman made personal visits to explain that the

The yellow-painted Harbert trucks and heavy equipment with the new Harbert "H" logo were soon recognized all over the South. Margie and Raymond Harbert occasionally visited construction sites with their father.

company was temporarily overextended and short on cash, but "we were confident that they would be paid—plus interest." Most of the creditors were satisfied to wait, but as John recalled, "it soon became apparent that we had some vendors who needed to be paid. We also knew that our most realistic threat could very easily come from a small creditor, someone who might have sold us fifty dollars' worth of yellow pencils ... who could, if he desired, force us into involuntary bankruptcy."[28]

Bill Rossman recalled that at one time during this crisis he went to the bank to borrow money to pay bills and took with him the Coopers and Lybrand accountant who worked with Harbert. The banker studied the corporate financial statement and replied, "This isn't a bankable statement," to which the accountant replied, "There's always bankruptcy." Rossman turned and told him "never to use that word to me again."[29] Although John frequently said in his numerous speeches that he "had been bankrupt three times," in later years he clarified this remark and explained that he had been close to bankruptcy three times, but he had never been bankrupt. These months represented about the closest he came.[30]

At a particularly low point, Ed Dixon came into John's office one day and gave him a copy of the weekly pastoral message of his minister, Dr. Guy McGowan. In part, Dr. McGowan had written:

> *Among the most trying experiences of our life are those conditions and circumstances about which we can do nothing more and when we must carry on our ordinary routine of work while we wait on an uncertain outcome.*
>
> *... Incidents of financial stress, when it seems that all is jeopardized by impending loss, bring the spirits of men to grievous straits.*
>
> *While we await an uncertain outcome, above all else we should strive to carry on industriously and diligently, as though things would turn out according to our hopes. If they do not, we shall be in a far better position to begin again than if we yielded to panic, took drastic action, or sought to run away.*
>
> *One of the most helpful things religious faith does for people is to give them courage, stamina, and quiet strength for the long periods of waiting which must come in some form to every life.*
>
> *"Trust in the Lord," says the Scripture. "Wait patiently for him and he will give thee thy heart's desire."*

No words could have helped John more. During these trying times, John would open his desk drawer and read the Reverend Mr. McGowan's message. Years later John wrote an introduction to a collection of the minister's pastoral essays in which John pointed the reader's attention to this essay and its special meaning for him.[31]

After being turned down by two banks, John was finally able to negotiate a $200,000 loan from Frank Plummer, president of Birmingham Trust National Bank (now SouthTrust). Without that money "that very afternoon," Harbert Construction Corporation would have been "out of business," John explained. Harbert Corporation's fiscal year ended on January 31, and it was due an $800,000 tax refund, which could be used to pay the loan. Plummer made the loan, and Harbert stayed in business. After January 31, Harbert filed its tax return and on February 12 received a check from the government.[32]

During this crisis Bill Rossman came up with imaginative and skillful financial presentations for Harbert's Baltimore-based bonding company, United States Fidelity and Guaranty Company. One of Harbert's assets during the financially difficult times was the confidence that Birmingham USF&G representative Ed Beal and bonding agents Leroy Monsky and William P. Engel had in John Harbert. When cash flow was tight—or nonexistent—Rossman carried the stress, for as John once said, Rossman "had to stay in the office and ... caught most of the telephone calls and personal visits from worried and demanding creditors, while the rest of our executive team was in the field running jobs and trying to increase cash flow any way we could."[33] In one of his financial reports, Rossman warned John that "we are in a situation where our creditors own more of the business than we do, and they might decide that they can run it better than we can." Things were grim. John knew it, but he sometimes put Rossman's financial report, in its sealed envelope marked CONFIDENTIAL, in the bottom of his desk drawer unopened. After all, John reasoned, he was doing all he could do and knowing how bad it was would not help.[34]

Years later when Rossman retired, he looked back on his career with Harbert Construction Corporation and told his wife that the time he most enjoyed working with John was when the company was in the greatest financial trouble because it was such a challenge and called forth every bit of the talent he had.[35] In several of John's speeches and media interviews, he said that during these critical years his company's financial statements were "not worth the paper they were printed on." When Andrew Kilpatrick quoted this statement in a *Birmingham Post-Herald* column in October 1990 (when he wrote about John's inclusion in the *Forbes* list of the nation's wealthiest men), Rossman, who had retired five years earlier, was offended. He clipped the article and sent it to John with the quote circled and only the notation: "Bull Shit."[36] In the late 1980s, Rossman said that John always knew the true financial condition of the company because he told him. John may not have read the figures, but Rossman knew John read his written comments.[37] Rossman once told his wife that John always asked for his opinion and that he always told John exactly what he thought. Often he advised John *not* to do something, explaining that the company could not afford it. But after listening to Rossman, John usually went ahead and did what he wanted to do. In the end, Rossman admitted, John was right in the first place because he had such vision.[38] And, Rossman could have added, such guts.

In the fall of 1962, Pearl River Dam was finally completed, and water began filling the reservoir in November.[39] The *Harbert Newsletter* reported that "the landscape at Pearl River has undergone a remarkable change. Where two years ago the swampland marred the view, [there] now stretches a completely cleared reservoir that sweeps away as far as the eye can see ... 32,000 acres of it. The trees and bog, the rattlesnakes and copperheads are gone. Soon there will be a vast blue lake rippling in the sun and dotted with white sails, motor launches, and fishing craft of every description. ... [Harbert engineers] can truthfully say they changed the geography of Mississippi forever."[40]

Although Harbert Construction Corporation won the suit it filed against the Pearl River Reservoir Board for cost overruns and improper specification of materials, the jury award of $320,000 was not near the $2 million that John believed was justified.[41] Harbert auctioned off surplus equipment in October to raise cash. In the meantime, John was glad to get out of Mississippi with lessons learned and his business and corporate life intact.[42]

John's losses in the Mississippi mud were compounded in February 1964 when his father died at University Hospital in Birmingham from heart failure complicated by diabetes.[43] The man who had been such an inspiration to his son had lived long enough to witness John's success as an engineer and a businessman.

The year 1964 marked Harbert's increased interest in the international business and construction arena. For the first time since the war, John went back to Germany in early December 1964 with forty-five American and Canadian businessmen, members of the Young Presidents' Organization, through which John had built an excellent national network of friends.[44] This YPO trip was sponsored by the West German government. John's visit to West Berlin and West Germany signaled his increased interest in foreign investments and in opportunities for Harbert construction projects overseas. He was very impressed with the standard of living of the West Germans but not with conditions in East Germany, which he said was ten to twenty years behind West Germany despite heavy Soviet investments in the East German economy.[45]

In the mid-1960s Harbert completed several jobs that helped bail the company out of its financial troubles, including work on Lay Dam on the Coosa River and improvements for the Alabama Power Company at Lock #17 on the Warrior River. Harbert worked on two jobs during this time that were unique and especially challenging and required all the talent and ingenuity of Harbert's engineers, superintendents, foremen, and equipment operators. Both brought widespread acclaim to Harbert and became models of successful construction ventures. The first was a stretch of Interstate 40 through the Smoky Mountains in eastern Tennessee and western North Carolina, and the second was a Birmingham expressway, a daring cut through Red Mountain with a route designed to go between two high-rise apartment buildings in deep excavations that were to come within feet of the two buildings' foundations.[46]

Harbert's construction on I-40 brought its crews into an isolated area. Before this cut through the mountains, no road joined Cosby, Tennessee, and Lake Junaluska, North Carolina. The people who lived there were proud men and women, many of whom had never in their lifetimes gone more than six miles from home. Flour-sack dresses and overalls were their Sunday best, and their only cash income came from distilling whiskey. Harbert's men were accustomed to communicating with each other and with the Birmingham office by radio, but because their two-way radios were the same style as those used by sheriff's deputies and revenue agents, Harbert men were advised to take the whip antennas off their cars and put them in the trunks when they were working in the mountains.

John loved the area and had a deep affection for the people who lived there. He checked the job as often as he could. He was fascinated by the mountain culture and took pride that Harbert had employed a large number of local men, who were tough and loyal and who for the first time were able to earn a decent wage close to home. John felt good about Harbert bringing dollars to the local families and was happy that the interstate would bring doctors and stores closer to the mountain people.[47]

The toughest part of I-40 was a stretch of 3.4 miles through the Pigeon River gorge that involved cuts as deep as 170 feet. This part of the highway is known as the "Pioneer Road" and was to Harbert foreman C. M. Branam, a forty-three-year veteran of highway construction, the "roughest work I've ever seen."[48] The job required the "excavation of approximately a million cubic yards of material per mile" and a total dirt removal "in excess of 3,300,000 yards." The frequent use of explosives needed to move slippery rocks made the project site particularly dangerous, and crews worked around the clock in good weather amid mountain scenery that "was unbelievably beautiful."[49]

One of John's superintendents, Bill Barnett, remembered the day that John showed up at the Pigeon River job: "I was inspecting a piece of equipment and I climbed off of it just as Mr. Harbert appeared on the scene. He was 'walking the job' even though it was bitter cold and snowing. I said, `Mr. Harbert, if I had your money I wouldn't be out here on a day like this.' And he said, `If I weren't out here on a day like this, you might not have a job.'"[50] Much of the construction at Pigeon River was accomplished a half mile above sea level "with early winters and late springs and snowfall up to ten inches." Despite these conditions—cold, sleet, and snow—the project went forth with such precision that Harbert executives rated the project "number one" because of the excellent utilization of equipment and manpower resources. This was the third and most difficult stretch of I-40 constructed by Harbert.[51]

Until Harbert Construction Corporation began the highly visible and well-publicized Red Mountain Expressway project, John Harbert and his company were hardly known in his hometown beyond the construction industry and his immediate circle of social friends and business acquaintances. Although John had acquired a number of contracts in the Birmingham area, projects like the Birmingham airport extensions and improvements, the construction of several bridges, and some work at Lock #17, most of his sewer, water, and gas line work and his bridge and dam projects had been accomplished far from home and with little fanfare. Even with the publicity surrounding the successful completion of the Florida gas line and its coverage in the Birmingham newspapers, Harbert had not received much attention from the average city resident. The *Alabama Roadbuilder* noted that Harbert's $3.2 million contract for the Red Mountain Expressway Phase II made it the "most expensive half-mile (it's actually .6 mile) in the Alabama Primary Highway System." One reason was the six-lane-wide tunnel between the two high-rise apartment buildings that required extensive structural steel and concrete reinforcements for the buildings' foundations.[52] In a 1967 interview Wita noted that "most people had very little idea of the scope of John's business operation until recently." Recognizing that John had a "natural proclivity for public relations," Wita had suggested that John mount an up-front campaign to inform citizens about the Red Mountain Expressway construction. This public relations program made Harbert Construction Corporation a familiar name and its "bow-legged H" a recognized symbol in Birmingham and in Jefferson County. The program would win national and international attention for John and his company.[53]

Going into the project John was aware that the Red Mountain job could be a public relations nightmare. Residents on the mountain would be concerned about blasts cracking their plaster and their foundations, while elderly residents living on Highland Avenue would suffer noise and dust and would worry if the foundations of the two apartment buildings near the expressway would be affected. Bridges would have to be constructed over Arlington Avenue, over the intersection of Tenth Avenue and Twenty-sixth Street South, and Eighth Avenue South, and commuters would be inconvenienced by detours and would be angry at street closings that changed by the day. Soon after the state announced that the contract went to Harbert, John began receiving letters of concern from residents. John later explained that "we reviewed all of our problem areas and tried to anticipate everything that might happen. We made a basic decision that an educated, and therefore knowledgeable, public would more readily accept inconveniences and changes in travel routes than a public that did not know or understand what was going on."[54] To counter these anticipated problems, John planned a "good neighbor" policy and a massive public relations campaign. He gave a party at the Highland Plaza and the Highland Towers, the multistory apartment buildings that Phase II of the expressway would divide in a tunnel 100 feet wide by 300 feet long and 24 feet deep with some excavation as deep as 40 feet. John invited all the residents. He made Ted

Randolph responsible for "not having two leaning towers of Pisa," and Ted designed the underpinnings for the buildings with help from some consultants.[55]

The details of the construction were presented to all the apartment residents and their neighbors at the party. With diagrams and posterboards John and his engineers and superintendents explained what they were going to do. They polled the residents about working hours and asked for input about the best blasting times. Before the project began John wrote a personal letter to presidents and CEOs of Birmingham business concerns that employed a large number of workers. He outlined the project and offered to provide updated flyers and posters warning about street closings for each upcoming week.[56]

As the project went forward, Harbert constructed bleachers so residents could watch the excavations, had workers put their names on their helmets in large letters, and held weekly briefing sessions for apartment residents. Harbert ran special advertisements in the Sunday *Birmingham News* announcing what streets would be closed and provided maps and suggested alternative routes. Flyers called "Harbert Plan-Ahead-Memos" were distributed in the area. Large bumper stickers that read "Harbert: Slow Go Today, Go-Go Tomorrow" were placed on all Harbert equipment.[57] In May Harbert moved in five Caterpillar 657 scrapers and three Caterpillar 641 scrapers, huge earth movers from other construction sites. Working around the clock, Harbert managed to move 130,000 cubic yards of earth in nine days instead of the twelve weeks scheduled.[58]

When construction was completed, the tenants at the "fashionable apartment houses" gave a party to honor John, and the story of the tenants and the road contractor went around the world. Harry B. Brock, Jr., passing through Montreal, Canada, picked up the *Montreal Star* and read about his Birmingham friend on the front page. The story also made the *Detroit Free Press* and the *Chicago Tribune*.[59] Harbert won national and international recognition for the way the project went forth with the cooperation of neighbors, something heretofore unknown in the construction industry.

In the fall of 1967 John and Wita planned a special trip to Europe so John could retrace his footsteps in World War II. Wita's close friend, Joan McCoy Edmonds, and her husband, Bill, were living in Brussels where he was head of Coppee-Rust, a joint venture between a Belgian firm and Bill's Rust Engineering Company. Wita flew over early to visit with Joan, and John was to follow in a week, but two days later he showed up in Belgium. The two couples drove east in the Edmonds' car through the area where John had fought with the 104th Division in World War II—Aachen, Stolberg, Eschweiler, Weissweiler, Gey, Birgel, Düren, and then to Cologne. They had lunch at Birgel, and John visited the house where he spent six weeks during the Battle of the Bulge. John had taken all his war photographs with him and was able to find "many of the old scenes along the streets" and match them up with his photographs. John wrote his mother that he even "went in and met the Father of the Catholic Church that we had to shoot the top out of because of snipers." John noted that although "it had been some twenty-three years—I still remembered much of the landscape." After spending the night in Cologne, the two couples drove south to visit the Remagen Bridge. They saw Bonn and returned to Brussels. A day later John had an old friend drive him to Antwerp, into the areas where he served in south Holland, and then north to Amsterdam. Wita recalls that John had a wonderful time stopping people and showing his photographs and knocking on doors of houses he remembered visiting and introducing himself to the occupants. Later John and Wita rented a car and drove into Germany and Switzerland.[60]

Five months before John went to Europe, Harbert had won a huge contract to build a dam in Oklahoma. Things had been looking up for Harbert since the success of the Red Mountain Phase II operation, and John was gratified that Harbert was recouping some of its earlier losses. With the spring 1967 contract of $9.6 million from the U.S. Army Corps of Engineers for construction of Lock and Dam #18 on the Verdigris River in Oklahoma, John was able to leave the country with little worry. The project involved a lock 600 feet long, 110 feet wide, and 45 feet high that would raise the Verdigris River 21 feet. The June 1967 *Harbert Newsletter* announced the job, noting that "in the construction of this work, we will pour 170,000 cubic yards of concrete, place 2,500,000 pounds of reinforced steel, excavate five million cubic yards of earth and rock, and install the necessary lock gates and operating machinery."[61] An elaborate ground-breaking ceremony was held on June 24. Construction would take three years, and John expected the returns to push Harbert into the 1970s with a cushion of profits. But this was not to be.

The summer was hot and dry, and then came the rains. By late fall when John returned from Europe, "the job was in trouble." John replaced the entire management team and fired many of the workers. In December, with two of Harbert's top men, he "flew to Tulsa, rented a car, and drove to the site where, in a morass of rain water and mud, equipment sat idle—broken down." The wind was blowing thirty-five miles an hour, the temperature was zero, and if it was not snowing, it was raining. With John's attention the site was ready for concrete by spring 1968, but there were still problems. The concrete forms could be constructed during the day, but with temperatures rising to 120 degrees by midday, the concrete had to be poured at night. Harbert added a snow machine, which produced 80,000 pounds of fine ice to the batching plant to cool the concrete to a proper pouring temperature. Floodlights illuminated the construction area. However, problems mounted, and the government was slow paying. Looking back on the job, Rossman observed that "when we had trouble it was usually our own fault," but the "conformations out there required that the forms had to be nearly works of art. They cost us a bundle of money. We probably lost more cash on that job than on the Pearl. We'd been coming back financially—and then this one got us."[62] By fall 1969 Lock and Dam #18 was nearing completion, and at long last for Harbert that job was "downhill all the way."[63]

The fiasco on the Pearl River Dam at the first of the decade and problems at the Verdigris River Lock and Dam #18 as the 1970s dawned convinced John of several things. First, the construction business was not a very reliable way to make money. As Ed Dixon observed: "The nature of the construction business requires more dedication to longer hours. There is less dollar reward to effort in construction than in other areas. People in construction understand this, but the general population does not understand."[64] To ease the burden of the construction risk, John started moving his company toward diversification. His first venture into diversification had been with the Florida Gas Company in the late 1950s; in 1966 he went into the limestone quarry business by purchasing the Three Rivers Rock Company in Livingston County, Kentucky. Harbert bought the company from the First National Bank of Springfield, Illinois, which held title through defaults. Three Rivers was strategically located on the Cumberland River near the confluence of the Ohio and Tennessee Rivers and controlled limestone reserves estimated at 100 million tons. Harbert sent a top management team to Three Rivers, modernized the operation, and brought in new equipment and barges. Soon Harbert had the business in the black with profits flowing.[65]

In 1967 Harbert tried to purchase a small coal mining operation south of Birmingham

John directs a management meeting seated with Harbert attorney and board of directors member Jack Bingham and (standing) Joe Nelson, James Stone, and Bill Bolton.

but John was unable to work out the financing for his corporation. He was not able to secure loans from several banks because they considered the price of $700 an acre too much for land that had formerly sold for $50 to $100 an acre. However, John was able to put together an investment group composed of Harbert officials, and this group did purchase the mining operation and 2,300 acres in Shelby County. John later accused the bankers of having "set mentalities" when "there is no such thing as set values. Values constantly change."[66] This investment would eventually move Harbert into land development and would become the nucleus for the Riverchase community of the 1970s, but Harbert Corporation would not be involved until 1974.

The near disasters of the decade convinced John of a second precept he had believed in all along but now articulated: construction profits depended upon competent management, close supervision of projects, and dedicated workers. John had a favorite saying: "There is no fertilizer like the farmer's footsteps."[67] John himself had gone to Mississippi and personally fired a number of people on the Pearl River job. He had flown to Oklahoma with his top engineers and equipment people and replaced the original Verdigris team to put this project back on track. He knew that Harbert Construction Corporation needed to do a better job of selecting employees and giving them the direction and leadership they needed.

As Harbert Construction Corporation grew beyond John's physical capacity to maintain hands-on control of his projects, he recognized that competent management became even more crucial. His own management style grew and developed over time. He used the *Harbert Newsletter* to send messages to boost the esprit de corps of his work force, offering opportunities to his employees who were interested in assuming leadership roles and anxious to increase their responsibilities.

John placed enormous trust in relatively young engineers, such as twenty-seven-year-old Gordon Denton on the I-40 project and twenty-nine-year-old Walter Morris on the Red Mountain Expressway job. Yet he also depended upon experienced project managers almost at the age of retirement, men like L. L. Stephenson, who had spent a lifetime in the construction industry and came to Harbert in 1965. "Double L" was an important "trouble-shooter" for Harbert, straightening out the Verdigris River job and becoming head of the Three Rivers Rock Company.[68] To bring youth and experience together, John held a Harbert Construction Corporation management meeting in March 1968 to follow up on the 1966 meeting and to establish new goals. These goals were to improve the profit margin, implement long-range planning, strengthen management personnel, develop training programs for every job, increase the annual volume of work, continue to diversify the corporation, and complete a plan for the sale of Harbert Corporation stock to members of the management team.[69]

To encourage young engineers and to give Harbert the opportunity to seek the best, John initiated a summer intern program through which college students worked with Harbert's best engineers and business leaders during the summers, usually before graduation. He instituted the first management conference for his executives in 1965 and sought occasions for them to attend seminars and educational programs sponsored by universities. Brother Bill attended the Advanced Management School at Harvard in 1965, and Ed Dixon went in 1967. John himself went back to college to attend a week-long seminar on long-range corporate planning at Stanford University in California in 1965 and the next year completed a Young Presidents' Organization course, "Innovation, People and Money" at Harvard University.[70] John believed that "to be competitive and successful in today's world, one must always be an active student. Success requires a constant educational process."[71] Associates recall that John was always reading a book, a technical periodical, or a professional journal, especially when he was traveling. He never read fiction—he preferred history and biography—and he had a complete set of the *National Geographic* magazine bound in leather. He frequently sent his secretary, Sandi Falkenhagen, to the library to locate books and articles on a particular subject. John was always looking for new information and seeking knowledge.

He also recognized the need for Harbert to stay on the cutting edge of the latest technology. He upgraded the fiscal operations of Harbert by installing one of the first IBM office computers with programs designed especially for construction operations to help with bidding and cost management. He wanted the latest and best-designed construction equipment to help his crews work fast, efficiently, and safely. But despite John's efforts to provide training and educational programs for his employees, in 1966 he was still lamenting that his "greatest disappointment has been our inability to develop personnel *fast enough* from within our own ranks to provide the necessary leadership for our expanding responsibilities."[72] As Harbert Corporation moved into the 1970s, John continued to stress the necessity of developing more leadership within the company, and he became even more convinced that he must promote from within Harbert's own ranks.

Finally, the experiences of the early 1960s caused John to look elsewhere for opportunities. He discovered that outside the United States there was less competition for construction projects because operating abroad was too complicated except for the most highly organized and well-funded operations. However, on many jobs the financial risks were less than first glance might suggest, because some, but certainly not all, of the work was done through U.S. aid programs. In 1964 Harbert Construction Corporation increased the number of its bids on overseas projects, and Harbert International began to grow steadily. But construction projects in foreign countries had their share of difficulties. There were unanticipated obstacles, potentially dangerous environments, and language problems. There were questions about foreign labor crews and their skills and productivity. Living and working conditions for American superintendents were hard and uncomfortable, and sometimes political situations and revolutions put their lives in danger. Currency exchanges fluctuated widely. A foreign job bid in local currency could turn into a disaster overnight if the legal tender suddenly inflated. Despite these problems, Harbert was successful in making profits in overseas construction, causing one writer to assess that in his international projects John Harbert "had found his best crap game of all."[73] But as lucrative as Harbert's international construction was to be, the single most profitable venture for John was actually to come from Kentucky, a story that began in 1964 when John was seeking ways to diversify his company.

In an editorial in the February/March 1969 *Harbert Newsletter*, John urged the Harbert corporate family to look toward the decade of the 1970s. He cautioned that the construction industry must meet the demands of the country "or the government will take over." He cited projected statistics for the 1970s and listed the needs of the country as rebuilding cities, solving the transportation problem, expanding the services of all public utilities, clearing slums, and constructing new roads, parking lots, and bridges. He advocated plans for the next decade as well as "realistic projections for the thirty years between 1970 and the year 2000." The population increase alone "offers vast opportunities to individuals and to industry," and he suggested that technology would improve the American standard of living. What all this meant was that it was "both necessary and worthwhile for America to train more and more skilled workers, managerial personnel, and creative executives so that they may participate with confidence in the challenging years to come."[74] John expected the Harbert corporate family to rise to the challenge. But as much as John might dream, and as bleak as things were for the company in 1971, he never could have imagined how successful the decade of the 1970s would prove to be for him and for Harbert Construction Corporation.

→7←

COAL MINES AND RIVERCHASE

"I don't gamble anymore"

The turning point for his company was reached, John believed, "in late August of 1971" when he gathered his brother Bill, Ed Dixon, and Bill Rossman for a weekend retreat in Miami at Bill Harbert's condominium at the Jockey Club. "We really were," John said, "on the brink of financial disaster.... We worked all weekend, rehashing our past mistakes and charting a course for our future."[1] Ed Dixon recalls that the four men discussed at length the main strengths of Harbert—knowing how to use men, machines, and money—and considered how the company might use more long-range planning and how it could continue to diversify and move away from construction as its only base.[2] In 1974 John wrote that "Harbert has embarked on a carefully structured plan of internal and external growth, seeking new opportunities in both construction-related and energy fields."[3] The next year when *Engineering News-Record* asked him about his famous World War II crap game, which provided the capital for his first business venture, a confident John replied: "I don't gamble anymore. The construction field is a big enough game."[4]

Although the list of construction jobs printed in the occasional issues of the *Harbert Newsletter* remains impressive and there was never a waver from construction on John's part, he was bent on diversification for his company. He assured people that "I'm not getting out of the business, I'm trying to change the type of business that we're in so we're not taking any big risks." He observed that "the construction industry is geared for a man who is willing to pit his energy and his brawn" against the odds and who "really doesn't have anything to lose." John added that "once you've got a lot to lose, you'd better think about it."[5] By diversification John could hedge his bets. He was convinced that world demand for energy would only increase and that providing various alternative sources of energy offered the best opportunity for long-range profits.

After the Florida gas pipeline was completed and John had served on the board of the Florida Gas Company for some years, he realized that natural gas could not indefinitely supply the energy needs of the United States. He began to study energy supplies, and he became involved with a joint venture to drill for oil and natural gas in the Gulf of Mexico, but the results were mixed.[6] Then, as John explained it, he "began to look at alternate energy sources and concluded that, although it was not profitable at the moment, coal was the most available, economical choice."[7] Wita recalled that "long before OPEC and the oil glut, John had decided that coal was coming back."[8] John brought to Harbert a Birmingham man with wide experiences in coal mining, Charlie DeBardeleben, to help him find the right investment. After searching for five years in Alabama, Tennessee, and Kentucky, John learned about some coal reserves in Bell County, Kentucky, through contacts with the Georgia Power Company. Harbert had done business with Georgia Power beginning in January 1950, when the company completed a small ditching and excavation project outside Atlanta.[9] The power company was in a bind because management had elected to ride down its coal supplies, and now the company was having difficulty obtaining coal because the independent companies were refusing to deal. Georgia Power, which knew that Harbert had earth-moving equipment and could retrieve coal by surface mining, encouraged John to look into a coal operation in Bell County, Kentucky, that might be for sale.[10] John obtained a copy of a report on the Kentucky company's reserves written by J. A. Hagy, a mining engineer in his late seventies or early eighties who had worked in Alabama and lived in Birmingham but now spent most of his time in Kentucky working with Dr. Houston St. Clair of Virginia and his mining interests in Kentucky.[11]

Bell County is in eastern Kentucky, in a section of Appalachia at the southeastern corner of the state where Virginia meets the Tennessee-Kentucky border. Pioneers moving west on the Cumberland Gap road passed through the area in the late eighteenth century, and coal was noticed there as early as 1750. The region remained isolated and the people poor. Men worked hardscrabble farms in the fertile river bottoms and occasionally dug coal in the hollows for their own use. During the Civil War the people were starving, and Abraham Lincoln sent food, thus becoming the first president to send relief to the Cumberlands.[12] Commercial coal mining began in 1911 after the railroads came, and the United Mine Workers arrived in 1917 to unionize the miners. However, workers remained mostly nonunion, despite twenty-two years of strikes that routinely turned violent, especially in Harlan County, Bell County's northern neighbor. Eastern Kentucky people were divided on union membership: some were strongly antiunion and fiercely independent, while others were so pro-union they were willing to die for it. About the only employment was in the mines, and the coal industry rode a yo-yo string of high and low prices, which only increased the poverty of the region and the despair of its people. In the 1960s the area was economically depressed.[13] One writer noted in 1962 that "in community after community one can visit a dozen houses in a row without finding a single man who is employed."[14]

On a "cold winter day in 1969," John flew into eastern Kentucky and landed at the Middlesboro Airport in a single-engine plane. He had come to meet Cecil Gibbs, a man to whom he had spoken only on the telephone. They had discussed "some 10,000 acres of available coal reserves near a place referred to locally as Colmar." The land was actually owned by the Asher Mining Company but was leased to two men, Cecil's father, Les Gibbs, and Paul Hart; they had subleased it to the BellCoal Company, which in turn had subleased it to Gibbs and his brothers, who were operating the mine as the Mountain Drive Mine Company.[15] Cecil Gibbs, driving a four-wheel-drive Jeep, picked John up at the airport and drove him uphill, bypassing Colmar for the moment by taking a back road

As the Harbert Construction Company evolved, John took the leadership role in the coal mining investments, civil construction, and the Riverchase development, while his brother, Bill, supervised Harbert's overseas projects.

into the coal reserves by way of Varilla, a mining area with ground leases owned by Dr. St. Clair. Gibbs then drove to the adjacent area of Colmar. The back road was covered with ice and snow, and along the way John and Gibbs passed deserted mining areas with equipment sitting silent, blanketed with snow. John found it difficult to evaluate operations that had been shut down for several weeks, and from the Jeep it was hard for him to distinguish the coal seams under the snow. But as he and Gibbs walked the area, John could see open seams of the black gold and realized that earth-moving equipment could open up the coal efficiently and economically. Before 1947, no strip tonnage of coal was produced in Bell County, but by 1957, 32.2 percent of the coal in the county came from strip-mine operations. Everywhere John saw desolate bald areas in the mountains, and nowhere was there any attempt to reclaim the land.[16]

John spent several days with the Kentucky coal mining expert and later said that each day that passed left him more impressed with Gibbs's knowledge and more confident of his judgment. But John's personal file on the coal mines indicates that he was back-checking in a variety of ways everything Gibbs told or wrote him, especially inasmuch as Gibbs and his family had much to gain from selling to Harbert. When John made the decision to move into coal mining, he had a wealth of information before him and had studied this particular area for some time.

Although John had been told by a few Middlesboro citizens "that all the economically recoverable coal had been mined and the property had no value as a coal reserve" and the reserves on the land had been questioned by others, such as the Southern Company, he decided to purchase the coal leases and to buy out the Gibbs family's equipment and assets on the BellCoal Company property.[17] As John visited the isolated coal mines, he recognized that no one was using state-of-the-art heavy earth-moving equipment in their strip-mining operations, and he understood immediately that the experience of Harbert crews in moving earth for dam and highway construction "could be used to remove the overburden to expose coal that could be mined and sold for a profit."[18] John avoided using the term *strip mining* because it had the same negative connotations for him that it had for the general public. He preferred *surface mining*, which was the term used by the industry.

Sometime later, John returned to Kentucky, and his hand-written notes, made in pencil on a yellow legal pad, are dated December 20, 1969, and include a list of equipment—draglines, tractors, trucks, drills, and so forth—that Harbert would acquire for $1.5 million. The financial aspects of the deal were recorded in pencil on the back of a Harbert pocket card on which Sandi Falkenhagen had typed John's United Airlines flight numbers and time of departure from Birmingham to Knoxville and return, along with the confirmation for a Hertz rental car John would drive to Middlesboro. The handwriting is not John's, but probably is Cecil Gibbs's, and the deal disclosed a payment of $50,000 earnest money, the assumption by Harbert of various bank debts of the Mountain Drive Mine Company, and cash on closing of $248,850.[19] Such are the simple ways big deals begin.[20]

Because of Harbert's contract with the Georgia Power Company for construction of a fossil-fuel plant called Plant Bowen located at Cartersville, Georgia, John knew the Georgia company would need major sources of coal to supply the new 3200-megawatt power plant. Harbert had also done work with Hardaway Construction Company on Plant Hammond, another of Georgia Power's plants, and John knew firsthand that the power utility was having difficulty acquiring coal and maintaining reliable delivery of coal from eastern Kentucky. He realized that long-term contracts to supply coal would be profitable and could also be used for collateral for loans to jump-start any coal mining enterprise.

Harbert had been closely involved with construction projects for Alabama Power Company, and John's friends John (Jack) Bingham and Eason Balch and their firm were closely associated with Alabama Power and its parent company, the Southern Company, which also controlled Georgia Power. He felt he had inside contacts, as well as a reputation for delivering on his commitments.[21] John had in his file a study made by L. L. Stephenson, known as "Double L" and one of Harbert's most trusted geological engineers, and by the Harbert man who had been working on the Georgia Power Company's construction project. Stephenson analyzed for John the Hagy report on the Colmar coal reserves in regard to the cost of transporting coal from the mines to rail lines and to the power plants. He put forth a two- to twelve-year plan for Harbert, along with a suggested budget.[22]

Many people, especially Harbert's bankers, told John he was "making a big mistake," but Georgia Power was backing Harbert all the way. One of John's Auburn friends ran into him in North Carolina at about this time and recalls John confiding that he was going to invest in coal leases. The friend told John he was "crazy."[23] Coal had been a significant factor in the economic success of Birmingham's industrial district, and a few of John and Wita's friends came from families with fortunes originally built upon coal; however, coal had been in decline for some years and many men were trying to get out of the coal business just at the time John was deciding to get in. As John put it, "coal mining was considered a dirty business without profit opportunities." Wita recalled that John knew coal had to "come back because of what was happening to oil in the Middle East."[24]

Birmingham coal men were shaking their heads at John because "the coal industry was in the doldrums" and no one was "making any money by mining coal."[25] John thought that the coal "situation would change in time—and it did, more quickly than we or anyone else anticipated." When John purchased his first reserve, coal was selling for $4.73 a ton. Three years later the price had risen to $9, and by 1975 it was $18 a ton.[26]

Governor George C. Wallace had appointed John chairman of his governor's Energy Advisory Council, and in January 1974, in a speech at Auburn University, John said that the United States had "been living next door to [the energy crisis] for five years." His analysis of the crisis was that a more affluent world was using more energy and that antipollution devices on cars and the Clean Air Act had created "disruptions in familiar patterns of fuel use in this country."[27] After the fact and offhandedly, John observed that his decision to enter the coal business "was a case of being at the right place at the right time and reinforcing our knowledge and convictions with positive actions."[28] True, but it was also another example of John finding a need and placing his company in a position to fulfill it.

John had difficulty putting together the finances for the purchase of the coal leases, but he was able to get some financial backing from Georgia Power, and Rossman came up with a plan to sell Harbert's expensive heavy-construction equipment and lease it back. But the magnitude of the coal transaction still caused some concern on the part of Harbert loan holders.[29] And there is no question that in 1969 his timing proved fortuitous in another way, because when cash was needed he was able to finance the first lease purchases from an $800,000 state check on an Alabama Highway Department contract to Harbert Construction Corporation to clear and grub a segment of I-59 and I-20 in Birmingham.[30]

In the first year of its Kentucky coal operations, Harbert employed 120 men in Bell County with an annual payroll of just under $800,000, and they produced coal worth just under $5 million.[31] Within ten years, Harbert had accumulated more then 240,000 acres of coal lands that contained "in excess of one billion tons of reserves." The company averaged a major acquisition about every fourteen months. With these leases Harbert came to control more and more mines, such as Star Fire, Lost Mountain, Straight Creek, Stoney Fork, Squabble Creek, Buckhorn, Roaring Fork, Brownie Creek, and Savoy Coal Company.[32] To fly management personnel to the mines, Harbert used helicopters, first renting them and then buying its own in October 1973. On one helicopter trip around the mine area when John was aboard, the pilot misjudged his position and almost flew into a 44,000-volt power line. This near miss was one more of many brushes with death in John's life.[33]

The Savoy mine produced the highest quality coal, and it was sold as premium coal. Although Harbert acquired leases on both underground and shaft mines, which were labor intensive, most of its Kentucky mining involved

Raymond joined his father and brother on a visit to the mines on July 3, 1974. The next day Harbert entertained all the miners and their families at the annual Fourth of July picnic.

John invested heavily in draglines and equipment that could harvest coal quickly and efficiently, and he revolutionized the way coal was mined in eastern Kentucky.

surface-mining operations. Harbert was able to increase the productivity of the mines by investing in heavy and expensive equipment. In the 1950s and 1960s, big stripping shovels were popular for removing overburden, but John early on invested in a large Marion dragline with a forty-five-cubic-yard bucket on a 275-foot boom at a cost of $500,000. No one had ever before used such large equipment in eastern Kentucky mining because of its cost and because, as John noted, the "prevailing opinion was that such a machine was too big for contour mining in this area." The dragline proved very successful, enabling Harbert to handle deeper overburden. Harbert was able to turn the small "string of pearls" two-acre mines into one large coordinated and well-managed operation.[34]

Speaking before business and civic leaders of Bell County gathered at Lincoln Memorial University in Harrowgate, Tennessee, in 1980, John noted that

> When we started our coal mining operations, we were well aware of the history of poor employment practices in the industry. To understand the coal work force, one must remember the decades of mutual distrust between labor and management, the historic poverty of the eastern coal fields, the dangerous and humanly exhausting nature of the work itself, and the miners' feeling of exploitation. The effects of endemic poverty are also powerful impediments to labor peace and stable production.[35]

The Harbert labor philosophy of paying top wages and benefits and providing training and leadership to workers was another reason Harbert was able to increase coal production. Harbert's long-term contracts made work steady, and wages increased from an annual average of $7,000 when Harbert arrived to $21,000 by 1980.[36]

The mines on John's leases had a nonunion history, which suited him well considering his personal aversion to labor unions and his experience that 90 percent of Harbert's nonunion jobs made money and 90 percent of its union jobs lost money. Harbert's miners were "subjected to a lot of pressure and intimidation" from union organizers, but the men were "for the most part extremely anti-union."[37] On more than one occasion, especially in the early years when Harbert was pouring money into equipment and gearing up production, there was trouble at the mines and pickets were thrown up by organizers for the United Mine Workers. At these times, John flew into Kentucky wearing a side arm, and Wita worried constantly about his safety. She had good reason to worry because Bell County borders

Jay Harbert has a love of construction and is happiest on a construction site around large machines and wearing his Harbert hard hat. He often visited sites with his father, such as this one near Augusta, Georgia, in April 1974.

"bloody" Harlan County, probably one of the most infamous areas for labor violence in the United States.[38]

On October 26, 1971, during a United Mine Workers national strike, UMW strikers came to Mountain Drive Mine to try to unionize its workers. John had been told they were coming with some "600 men from five states," so he flew to Middlesboro and tried to get an injunction from a local judge. When he failed, John joined a meeting of his men and told them that "each man should decide for himself what he wanted to do" about running the picket line. The men were adamant that they intended to work and asked who would lead the convoy through. Without thinking, John replied, "I expect to lead you through." John spent a busy evening talking with union leaders, law enforcement officers, and anyone else with authority in the state of Kentucky. Dozens of Harbert men stayed at the mine that night.

The UMW pickets were on the curvy mine road and could not see the mine entrance. In the early morning the union pickets were surprised to see a caravan of cars and trucks coming toward them with heavily armed men inside. John was riding in the lead car and said later that he had not "seen so many weapons since World War II."[39] "The convoy of six Mountain Drive coal trucks hauling armed men" surprised the UMW people. Longtime Harbert executive Don Cook recalls that the Harbert miners were "armed to the teeth." There were Kentucky Highway Patrol officers observing from the side. With "several hundred people involved," anything could have happened. One man who was there commented that "if a car had backfired, a battle would have taken place and someone would have been killed—probably John Harbert."[40] John later thanked the commander of the state highway patrol for his troopers' professional "performance in handling a very delicate situation" when "unemployed coal miners ... were attempting to create a disturbance near our property."[41] After several weeks the organizers left, but UMW organizers reappeared at the Harbert mines during the 1973-74 Brookside strike in Harlan County and in the winter of 1978, when the UMW went on strike and sent armed men back to a picket line at Harbert's mines. But they did not stay long, and John joked of the wild rumor spreading through Middlesboro about "some crazy man from Alabama by the name of Harbert" who had "come up to the area with 12 machine guns to aim at pickets" who cause trouble. Eventually the UMW miners left, and the situations were defused.[42]

Harbert had men, like Cecil Gibbs, Dick McFarland, and Dan Penny, who knew eastern Kentucky well and who advised John on labor issues. Although the Gibbs family members lived across the state line in Tennessee, they had worked in the eastern Kentucky coal fields most of their lives. McFarland had many years of experience in surface mining. Penny was a native who first went into the mines at the age of twelve, and he appreciated the culture of the region and understood why the people distrusted outside authority.[43]

But John played an important role. He, too, appreciated the mountain culture of the people, and he genuinely enjoyed his visits to the coal mines. He spent a lot of time at the mines and knew the miners on a first-name basis. John often took his oldest son, Jay, along with him, and Jay recalls with fond affection the Kentucky people and remembers these trips among his happiest memories with his father. Jay was fascinated by the huge machines and draglines, and he worked on equipment at the Harbert machine shop when it was sent to Birmingham for overhaul. Jay especially enjoyed going into the mines and accompanying his father at Christmastime when John personally was there at the end of every shift to hand out turkeys to all the men.[44] In December 1979, John addressed the Mountain Drive miners and their families at a Christmas party, expressing how meaningful his association with them had been through the 1970s and praising them for their safety record, which was number one in the nation. When they left the party, these men, whom

On the Fourth of July 1974, John attended the barbecue that Harbert held for the miners and their families. He made certain that there were special gifts for all the wives and that they were personalized, with an enclosed letter from him thanking them for their support during the year. He enjoyed being there to give out the gifts personally.

John had called "the most dedicated damn bunch of miners in the world," surely felt good about themselves.[45]

One of the biggest events in the coal fields was the annual Appreciation Day Celebration on July Fourth. Harbert rented the campus of Lincoln Memorial University in Harrogate, Tennessee, and provided dozens of prizes, including rods and reels, sportsman lanterns, coolers, and hunting vests. Harbert planes flew in barbecue from Ollie's Barbecue in Birmingham. There was plenty of ice cream and watermelon, volleyball, pole climbing contests, and helicopter rides for 800 people. Each wife had a special box filled with an assortment of gifts. Each box was personalized with the woman's name on it and included a letter from John thanking her "for your own contribution to the success we have had this year." He was usually there to hand the box to each wife. Harbert hired a photographer to come and take family pictures, and a few weeks later John would send complimentary eight-by-ten color photographs to all workers along with a note of appreciation for their work during the past year.[46]

John's ability to relate to workers is evident from his coal mine files, which are filled with personal letters from workers thanking him for favors or detailing problems they were facing. One wife wrote about her husband—the oldest man on the job—being passed over in his request to move from the night to the day shift. John investigated and reported in a warm letter to her that the day job that had opened was not as responsible a position and it paid a lower wage. He did not recommend that her husband take the pay cut; however, he assured her that he would see that her husband was given the first opportunity to move to the day shift when there was an opening suitable for him.[47] When another worker wrote to John complaining that he had been treated unfairly when he was fired, that he needed his job back because he was in debt and had a wife and baby, John responded with concern "that we are always interested in being in a position to help people," but that in his case he had "made this difficult to do." John advised him to try to find another job but noted that "it is unreasonable not to try and give a man a second chance," and he would discuss with the superintendent the possibility of rehiring him at a later date.[48]

On his visits to eastern Kentucky, John observed that many of his people had problems with their eyes, something he particularly noticed because he had suffered eye problems himself. He was also more aware of vision complications because he was serving on the Eye Foundation board at the invitation of Dr. Alston Callahan, who had educated John in the foundation's work and the exciting new developments in eye surgery. In Kentucky John was disturbed by the crossed eyes, abscesses, and other problems he saw in his workers and their families. He knew firsthand what miracles could be "wrought at the hands of skilled surgeons," and he began making arrangements with the Eye Foundation Hospital staff to bring the miners and their families to Birmingham for treatment. Harbert would cover the cost of transportation and expenses, and the doctors would donate their time. This arrangement became known in eastern Kentucky as the "Harbert Eye Clinic."[49]

One miner wrote a letter thanking John for his eye surgery: "My eye is straight and I find that this affects my whole being, confidence, thought. Possibly even my personality, at least I think so."[50] John was especially touched by letters from children, who, while thanking him for the eye surgery, were more apt to share the thrill of their first airplane ride. The superintendents of Straight Creek Mining Company wrote to thank him for helping eight of their employees and one dependent, assuring John that the 151 other employees were "very cognizant of the fact that they have an employer and a friend that they can depend on should they require help."[51]

John and Bobby Radcliff stand in one of the huge buckets of a dragline at one of the Harbert coal mines. John often took friends to visit the mines.

John received praise for his concern with the eye health of his workers, but in the words of his secretary, Sandi Falkenhagen:

> Mr. Harbert brushed it off in his usual inimitable fashion: "Well, hell, it's hard to carry on a conversation with these guys when I can't tell who they're looking at!" But his brash demeanor melted at the outstretched arms of a child who had never before seen his mother's face or the beauty of a sunset. The program continued for more than two years, while hundreds of men, women, and children were brought to Birmingham for treatment. For many, it was their first and only time in an airplane or nice hotel; for most, it was an opportunity to face each new day with hope.[52]

John wrote a friend that "if we can give one person self-confidence by improving her vision or appearance, make it possible for someone to learn and grow, then it is worth everything to me."[53] Through the eye clinics and other programs and the leadership provided by Harbert people, the loyalty of workers and their families was won by John, and union pickets never came back to the Harbert mining operations.

John had his coal mines well-organized and producing smoothly when coal prices went through the roof because of the Middle East oil embargo in the fall of 1973. Unfortunately, Harbert's long-term contracts set the price of most of his coal; however, by increasing production Harbert could sell more on the open market. In Kentucky, Harbert engineers, using the large draglines, pioneered a mining procedure they called mountain-top removal. This procedure enabled Harbert, as John explained, "to surface mine coal seams as deep as 450 feet, thereby greatly increasing the number of tons of recoverable coal."[54] By 1979 Harbert's purchases for its coal operations in eastern Kentucky boosted the local economy by more than $110 million, and Harbert had retrieved ten million tons of coal from Colmar alone. In 1980 Harbert ordered two more large Marion-Dresser 8050 draglines with sixty-five-cubic-yard buckets on 325-foot booms at a cost of approximately $10 million each. Harbert was employing more than 1,600 workers, and its coal production exceeded $215 million.[55]

John was convinced that land that had been surface mined could be reclaimed, made beautiful, and put back into productive use. Long before federal laws required it, John implemented a program in eastern Kentucky that turned former strip-mining areas into cattle ranches and groves of fruit trees.

From the very beginning, Harbert had in place a plan to return the land to nature and to turn the "abandoned pits into level land which could be used for orchards and pastures."[56] John considered himself "a conservationist and I am against any wanton destruction of land or other natural resources." But he knew the nation needed the "coal [and we] will have to do more strip mining" to get it.[57] John was proud that "long before the Federal Surface Mine Reclamation Act became law, we implemented a reclamation program." He commissioned one of the premier land planning and engineering firms in the South, Harland Bartholomew and Associates of Atlanta, to study the eastern Kentucky hills and the mining area. The same firm would later create the master plan for Harbert's Riverchase development and, at John's instigation and expense, provide a master plan for the Auburn University campus.

The design that Bartholomew created for Colmar and Varilla's 10,000 acres guided Harbert in its land reclamation work. After all the recoverable coal was removed from an area, the land's surface was leveled and planted. U.S. Department of the Interior statistics show that in 1971 "only 5 percent of the land stripped in Kentucky had been restored."[58] At the end of the decade, John estimated that Harbert's reclamation programs had created 20 percent of all the level land in Bell County. The orchards, cattle ranch, and demonstration farm that Harbert created were frequently visited by state officials studying reclamation.[59] For three years Harbert worked with a forestry graduate student to create ground moisture conditions to promote tree growth.[60] In 1990, John looked back at his coal mining experiences and observed that "for the first time in decades, wildlife returned to the area that had been only barren hills and valleys before we came. As an Eagle Scout who has long practiced the maxim of leaving a place better than I found it, our years in the coal industry were, to me, a most productive and gratifying period in our history."[61] When John decided to sell his coal leases at the end of the decade, it was for a substantial profit.

In December 1971, John and Wita took the three children to Europe for Christmas because Wita wanted to make sure that "the children saw the world." She insisted on staying at the Brown Hotel in London because it was so typically English, and she arranged to have a Christmas tree decorated and put up in their suite. But the Brown did not work well for the children. Jay was eighteen, Raymond thirteen, and Margie ten, and it was unacceptable that there were no hamburgers available.[62]

After Christmas the Harberts flew to Madrid, where they stayed at the Lux Palacio, a small hotel where the children enjoyed riding the elevator up and down and driving parents and hotel management to distraction. A guide was hired to escort the Harberts to historical and cultural sites around the Spanish capital. Once they were caught in the snow after visiting the Roman aqueducts, and it was touch-and-go getting back to the hotel. At the Valley of Fallen, which commemorates the dead of the Spanish Civil War, there was a terrible traffic jam. John got out of the car and directed traffic—in Spanish—which, Wita noted, "he was quite good at but under these conditions in the street no one could understand a word he said." The guide's wife thought he was "crazy."

When the family left Madrid, John was driving a rented car, and it took both Wita and John to find their way to Toledo to see El Greco's home. From Toledo the Harberts motored down the Mediterranean coast to Granada to see the Alhambra Palace and stopped along the way to picnic under olive trees. Then they went south to Málaga, then to the Rock of Gibraltar. Wita's arm ached from holding on to the strap as John drove across the Spanish countryside at his usual fast pace.

From Gibraltar, the family departed for Seville, where they stayed at an old hotel, the Alfonzo XIII. From her reading and study, Wita was aware that there were some paintings by Spanish masters in a Seville hospital, and she planned to take the children to see them. With John and Jay resting at the hotel, she, Raymond, and Margie set off walking to find the hospital. Wita began to stop people on the street, asking in her rather weak verbal Spanish—she is better at reading the language—where the hospital was. When no one understood her, Wita began to cough and act sick. Finally, in the middle of the town, she "fainted enough for someone to get her there." As typical teenagers, Raymond and Margie were mortified by their mother's tactics to find the hospital, but they will never forget Seville nor the paintings of El Greco, Goya, and Velásquez.[63]

From Seville they drove up the Atlantic coast to Portugal and Lisbon where they checked into the Ritz Hotel and managed to see the historical sites around the Portuguese capital before flying home. John had enjoyed the trip because he had been speaking Spanish since he arrived. "John thought," Wita laughed, "that his Spanish was wonderful, and he didn't mind making a fool of himself. At least he could make people understand him."[64]

After John's secretary, Rex Barrington, quit in 1962 to move to California with her family, John went through a number of secretaries. They stayed only for short periods and left exhausted, unable to keep pace with John, turn out the perfect work he demanded, or assume the responsibilities he expected. Then in February 1973, a young graduate of the University of Montevallo interviewed for the vacant position. Sandra Watson, called Sandi, was an English major who was pretty, pleasant, bright, and highly competent. She interviewed with the personnel manager, and he had her spend time with an industrial psychologist to determine whether "she could get along with Mr. Harbert." She later was sent down to John's office. His door was open and he was on the telephone, but he motioned her to come in and sit down. He was having a heated conversation with a Harbert office manager in Jamaica, and as Sandi recalled, he "was livid." His desk was piled high with papers, and he was frantically searching for a special document. Sandi saw the paper he wanted, pulled it from the pile, and handed it across the desk to him. He smiled, put his hand over the telephone receiver to muffle his voice, and said, "I don't know who you are but you're hired." Needless to say, her interview went well.

The next morning, which was Valentine's Day, she received a call, was offered the position, and was told to come in after lunch. She declined because she had an appointment at one o'clock. She said she could start the next morning. The personnel manager replied that if she did not come she could not have the job, but Sandi refused to change her plans, thus making clear the tone that she was also independent. Until John's death twenty-two years later, Sandi was John's secretary and administrative assistant. One reason John was able to accomplish so much was that she directed his office so efficiently, especially while he was in the coal fields, flying to check on a construction site, or globe trotting with Wita.[65]

In the fall of 1974 John decided to make a move to purchase a large block of stock in Alabama By-Products Corporation and its subsidiary, Alabama Chemical Products Company. This purchase was something he had been contemplating for some time.[66] Known in industrial circles as ABC, it was an old Birmingham firm that was organized by Horace Hammond and Morris and Albert Bush in 1920. Four years later Erskine Ramsay merged his Pratt Consolidated Coal Company and its six-million-dollar holdings with Alabama By-Products Corporation and its affiliate company, Alabama Chemical Products Company. The 1924 company held millions of tons of coal reserves, the equipment to convert coal to coke, gas, and other by-products, and vast timberlands. In 1974 Mrs. Horace Hammond, widow of a company founder, her daughter, Catherine Collins, and her granddaughter owned about one-third of the ABC stock.[67] John knew Mrs. Hammond because they both were on the Board of Directors of the Birmingham Museum of Art. For some time Mrs. Hammond had been donating small amounts of ABC stock to the museum, and John had quietly been purchasing the stock, providing the museum with cash needed for operations and acquisitions. John was interested in Alabama By-Products because of its coal reserves, and as a stockholder, he was watching ABC management closely. He became convinced that its operations could be made more efficient and more profitable.[68] John realized that he needed to speak with Mrs. Hammond and her daughter.

Mrs. Hammond spent much of her time in London, where she had a suite at the Savoy

The Harberts celebrated New Year's Eve with a house party at Pinebloom. In 1987 Wita (second from left) and her sister, Acky McGriff, with Evalina Spencer and Bubbles Brungart cheer the New Year.

Hotel and where her daughter frequently visited her. In the fall of 1974 John knew Catherine was in London with her mother and that she was accompanied by her friend Margaret DeBardeleben Brungart, known as "Bubbles," who also happened to be one of Wita's closest friends. On September 10, John had a certified personal check for $1,200,000 drawn on his account with Birmingham Trust National Bank and flew to London to try to meet with Mrs. Hammond and Catherine to convince the ladies to sell their stock. He believed that the Alabama By-Products stock would present problems for Mrs. Hammond's estate, and a cash sale would give her more flexibility in managing her finances and in her estate's administration. He reasoned that with a stronger board of directors, ABC management could be convinced to improve the company's performance and the company could be made more profitable for the stockholders. He was also in the coal business, and Alabama By-Products would be a strong addition to Harbert's coal holdings.

When John arrived in London, he discovered that the ladies had gone to Scotland, but he was not able to find out exactly where they were. He called Wita in Birmingham and asked her to call Bubbles's husband, Newt, and inquire where Bubbles was staying in Scotland but not to tell Newt why she wanted to know. Wita laughed. She told John: "Nothing doing. I am not about to call Newt and tell him my husband is in Scotland and wants to know where his wife is staying without telling him why you want to know!"[69] John agreed Wita could tell Newt that he needed to speak with Mrs. Hammond and Catherine Collins about a business matter.

When John found out where they were, he flew to Glasgow and checked into the Central Hotel, where he just happened to run into Mrs. Hammond in the lobby. He invited the ladies to dinner; however, they insisted upon taking him. Mrs. Hammond was evidently concerned over whether John could afford to wine and dine her in the style to which she was accustomed, which included very expensive Lafitte Rothschild wine with dinner. The next evening, John again invited them to dinner, and this time they accepted, but only after Mrs. Hammond was reassured by John that he "could afford it."

The following day Mrs. Hammond finally asked John just what he was doing in Scotland. When John told her he had come to talk to her about purchasing her Alabama By-Products stock, she was rather angry. However, the next day she changed her mind, and the group departed Glasgow together. They were headed for Dromnadrachit with John sitting next to her driver in the front seat of Mrs. Hammond's purple Rolls Royce and with the three ladies in the back seat. John had come to England with twelve typed letters all stating different terms for the potential purchase. Negotiations between John and Catherine Collins went on all day, September 13, at the Hotel Glenurquhart. After John upped his offer half a million dollars, Catherine agreed. Mrs. Hammond's attorney and a tax expert had flown in from Birmingham and were there to advise her and oversee the sale.[70] Although the purchase price was never announced by either party, Irving Beiman, the business editor of the *Birmingham News*, wrote that "reports in financial circles" put the figure at "around $12 million," not far from the actual amount, which included about an $18-per-share premium above the current market for ABC stock.[71]

With the public announcement of the sale, John praised Mrs. Hammond and Mrs. Collins for their "outstanding contributions" to the cultural life of Birmingham. Employees and stockholders of Alabama By-Products were concerned about John's stock acquisition, but he stressed his confidence in the "efficient operation" of the company. In the long run, management stayed in place.[72] John, along with Ed Dixon, became active on the board of directors. Profits increased, dividends went up, and ABC stock increased in value. When John purchased Hammond's ABC stock, it was selling over the counter for $28.50, and by the corporation's annual report common stock was valued at $38.20. In the final transfers some of the stock was owned by John personally, but most of it was owned by Harbert Construction Corporation.

John and Catherine Collins corresponded for some time after the sale—she addressed him as "Dear Bullmoose"—and in one of his letters from September 1975 John reminded her that although ABC stock had increased in value he had put her affairs "into a more flexible situation" and he was "still carrying the debt load and the interest cost is appreciable."[73] Three years later ABC stock was "listed over the counter for $74 a share bid," but no stock was offered for sale. In March 1977 Alabama By-Products announced that its earnings were the highest in the history of the company.[74]

In 1977 John became increasingly concerned about environmental issues and the impact that the new federal statutes regulating air emissions might have on ABC coke operations. For these and other reasons, in September 1977 John sold his and Harbert's ABC stock to the Drummond Company of Jasper for a handsome profit, some of which he used to develop another project he had going at the time, the Chase property in north Shelby County.[75]

For several years after the investment group of Harbert executives purchased the 2,300-acre Chase property in 1967, they operated the coal mines but then had trouble with the United Mine Workers trying to unionize the mines. The management group took the issue before the National Labor Relations Board but lost, and then John decided to close the mines. John had long planned that at the right time he would shut them down and reclaim and develop the property, but the strike and the labor relations board verdict merely put the plan in motion sooner. The group of investors sold the property to Harbert Construction Corporation, and the corporation purchased another 700 acres, anticipating that the eventual construction of an interstate highway around the south side of Birmingham would make the development of the land more feasible.

Harbert hired Charles Franzman of Harland Bartholomew and Associates to develop a master design for the land that would include a variety of uses, a planned community, and a golf course and country club. Harbert entered into a joint venture with the Equitable Life Assurance Society to finance and develop the land. The Cahaba River flowed through the property, which was a heavily wooded area of rolling hills covered with trees and moss-covered rock outcroppings. When asked why he decided to develop Riverchase, John replied simply, "it needed to be done." Then he added that he was excited about the opportunity to design and build a community from the beginning. "We'll have all the things the community needs, but still have the patches of green, the fresh air, and the birds."[76]

Joe Lee was selected to design a championship golf course, and South Central Bell, Western Electric, and Harbert Construction Corporation announced that they would be building new offices in the commercial portion of the specially designed community. The name selected for the environmentally and architecturally planned area was Riverchase. John promised that it would be a place where "trees, grass, and flowers are just as important as buildings and parking spaces."[77] Builders were required to work around trees. Before the roads went in and the woods were disturbed, Harbert landscape architect Roger Yanko organized the local Blanche Dean Chapter of the Alabama Wildflower Society to walk the area, identify wildflowers that would be destroyed, and transplant them to the Botanical Gardens in Birmingham. Some of the species the group found had never been identified, and at least one had never before been reported in Jefferson and Shelby Counties.[78]

John selected a prime site on Hope Mountain for a new Harbert corporate office. Before he commissioned the architect, Neuhaus-Taylor of Houston, John met with employees to gather ideas about work spaces they thought would make them more productive as well as present a pleasant work place. As John put it: "We spend a great deal of our lives in a work environment. Making that environment pleasant takes commitment, but it tells employees and business associates that you value their time and services."[79] Ground was broken on October 17, 1975, and throughout the construction process, John was impressed with "the obvious enthusiasm of practically everyone involved."[80]

The building has open spaces, which John felt reflected the openness of Harbert. There are four garden areas complete with waterfalls. Artwork is placed through the gardens and the building. Large skylights flood the interior with light. When Judy Johnson was asked about working in the building, she responded that although working by a waterfall was nice and she loved it, "people make up a building, and this is really a great group of people." The open design to her "reflects the open doors to Harbert." She could never recall "a time that any of the offices closed a door to anyone, and that's very important." She noted that any employee could "walk into John Harbert's office and sit down as easily as you can sit down and talk to me."[81]

In 1975, John helped clear an area on top of Hope Mountain for the construction of the Harbert corporate office in Riverchase. Harbert vice-president Billy Land rides shotgun.

The exterior of the Harbert building is made from iron that has "oxidized to the red of the soil," and its "long glass windows reflect the trees and sky of a hundred acres." Charles Franzman, the landscape architect who worked on the outside designs, noted that "everyone involved in the project, including the construction crew, wanted only the best for the site as well as the structure. They were so careful that the day the building opened, branches of wild dogwood trees were brushing against the windows."[82]

Wita worked with Robert Hiden, who had redecorated Penbryn, to decorate John's new office, and nearly all the paneling and furniture were shipped from England and Italy. John was not particularly fond of Hiden, and the feeling was mutual, but as Wita explained, "one liked to be paid and the other liked what the other one did." John and Wita traveled to Europe to approve special antiques and art pieces Hiden recommended. It was during one of these trips to London that Wita and John met the sculptor Enzo Plazzotta and a close friendship developed. John and Plazzotta enjoyed playing chess, drinking port wine, and discussing art and great men, while Wita did needlepoint and she and Plazzotta's wife, Gillian, or Gilly as she is called, visited. John selected four Plazzotta bronzes for the Harbert building—*Icarus* in the arbor garden, *Venus* on the patio, and both *The Three Graces* and *The Ustinov Composition* in John's office.[83]

Hiden was able to find a seventeenth-century

The west gardens in the Harbert corporate headquarters in Riverchase feature a magnificent carved world globe created especially for Harbert by Jorge Lopez of Ecuador. The six-foot-diameter globe, which rotates every three minutes, was created from a cedar tree.

The Harbert corporate office is located on Hope Mountain in northern Shelby County. The large trees on its 100-acre site were preserved, and the modern building blends in with its heavily wooded surroundings.

John was especially proud of his office in the Harbert Corporation building. It was decorated by Birmingham-born Robert Hiden, a London-based decorator who worked closely with Wita as he collected antiques in Europe for John's office.

Matthew Boulton desk for John's office, as well as an eighteenth-century Korean vase, which he had made into a lamp, and sofa cushion fabrics from Antwerp. Wita needlepointed two exquisite birds that were made into sofa pillows. Hiden kept reassuring John that he was "in good hands." In October, Hiden wrote John that he wanted to be involved in getting everything perfect in his office. He would help decide "what goes in the planter, as well as arrange and/or rearrange furniture, pictures, sculpture, etc., etc., as planned." John responded by telex on November 26 that for five days he had been operating from his new office, and Hiden had better "be ready for work Monday morning, November 29."[84] The formal dedication was scheduled for December 3. John moved out of his office while Wita coordinated the decorations with Hiden.

Harbert Construction Corporation celebrated with four wine and cheese parties that stretched over two weekends. Harbert people from every job site came with their families to one all-day party. In his brief dedication remarks John paid tribute to the personnel in the field "who pour the concrete, tie the steel, lay the pipelines, mine the coal and dig the limestone; the equipment operators and the men who keep the equipment running; those men separated from their families and homes while working on our foreign projects. It is to every one of them … and to each one of you … that I dedicate this building."[85]

The corporate headquarters was frequently used for receptions and parties, especially fund-raising social activities. Employees took pride in the new building and felt at home in it. Walter Rowe, who was one of the company's longtime employees, had worked in the field for years and was devoted to the Harberts. He came in the front door of the new office "to see Mr. Harbert," but the receptionist "fussed at him about all the mud on his boots." When Rowe left the building after seeing John, the corporate president walked him to the door and told the receptionist never again to worry about mud being tracked in because it was "all that mud that kept Harbert in business."[86]

Throughout the late 1970s and into the 1980s John watched the growth of Riverchase; however, in 1977 its development was threatened by two small fish that swam in the Cahaba River. In November of that year, the Federal Register included a proposal that the Cahaba shiner and the goldline darter be listed as endangered species. The Department of Fish and Wildlife Service of the Department of the Interior recognized that the research upon which the fish were placed on the proposed endangered listing was several years old. Environmentalists were concerned over the continued development of the Cahaba valley and were active in pushing for the two fish to be added to the endangered species list.

John rallied the Birmingham Area Chamber of Commerce to argue the economic impact that a construction freeze would have for the Shelby-Jefferson County area.[87] He assigned Harbert attorney Bill Satterfield, a recent Cumberland School of Law graduate, the task of becoming an expert on federal environmental law in order to protect Harbert interests.[88] John was supported by Chriss Doss, Jefferson County commissioner, who strongly opposed rigid environmental restrictions being imposed on the Cahaba River because such directives would have the effect of virtually stopping development in the fastest growing area of Alabama—the south Jefferson County–north Shelby County corridor. With the organization of an Environmental Economics Committee of the Birmingham Area Chamber of Commerce, research was funded to reexamine the status of the fish and to see if they indeed lived elsewhere. The group also began a frontal attack on the provisions of the Endangered Species Act with the help of Alabama's congressional delegation. This effort resulted in 1978 amendments that required procedural steps and public hearings before action was taken.[89]

Since his Boy Scout days John was dedicated to protecting wilderness areas and considered himself an environmentalist who loved and appreciated nature; however, he recognized that his own view of a particular situation was sometimes at odds with the opinions of other people. In both the strip mining in Kentucky and the development along the Cahaba, John ran into conflicts with conservationists. While he resolutely demanded that his corporation act in a responsible manner and do the right thing, he also deeply resented any government entity issuing fiats and entangling him in regulations and red tape.

In a February 1975 speech, John shared that as a child Margie was always asking him "Daddy, why can't you stay home like other daddies?" John recognized that "the life of a construction man means a sacrifice by his entire family," but he tried to find special times to be with his children and Wita. In the summer of 1981, the family took a long rafting trip down the Salmon River in Idaho.

On September 15, 1981, Amoco Minerals Company purchased Harbert Construction Corporation's coal leases and related businesses. Gathered for the official photograph of the occasion were, back row, James Spencer (Balch, Bingham, Baker, Hawthorne, Williams & Ward); Dick McFarland (Mountain Coals, Inc.); Bill L. Harbert and William Rossman (Harbert Corporation); Donald L. Cook (Mountain Coals, Inc.); James Hughey, Jr., Mack Beal, and S. Revelle Gwyn (Balch, Bingham, Baker, Hawthorne, Williams & Ward); and William Powers (Harbert Corporation). Seated left to right, C. B. Stone, Jr., and K. J. Barr (Amoco Minerals Company); John M. Harbert III and Edwin M. Dixon (Harbert Corporation).

John continued to develop his coal mines with long-range plans and ambitious new projects. In the spring of 1979 he addressed the Congressional Coal Group in Washington, D.C., urging it not to overlook coal as a means to make the United States independent of foreign oil. He advocated a long-term stable price for coal to make worthwhile the recovery of every available source, and he assured the group that land that was surface mined could be reclaimed. He pointed out that the United States already had the ability to transfer coal-powered electricity through grid systems to areas using oil and gas for electricity, and he suggested that the nation invest in the South African technology that converts coal to oil and gas.[90] John moved ahead with plans for a coal-loading operation on the Tennessee River at Pride, Alabama, where coal or rock could be transferred from river barges to the railroad. Recognizing the foreign demand for American coal, he was planning and designing a modern coal port for Savannah where coal shipped by railroad from the Kentucky fields could be offloaded and transferred to ships for overseas transport.[91]

A number of companies and entrepreneurs watched with serious interest Harbert's success in mining coal, and occasionally representatives of a company would feel John out about the possibility of his selling. In 1981

John was talking seriously with a French oil company that wanted to acquire an interest in the coal mines and with Standard Oil of Indiana, known as Amoco, the American company that pursued a deal with the most enthusiasm. The two proposals on the table were very different. The French arrangement was to be a partnership with Harbert, while the deal with Amoco was a straight sale, and Harbert would be out of the coal business. John entertained representatives of the French company in Birmingham and at Pinebloom, the Harberts' south Georgia plantation. Wita recalls that once when they were flying from Pinebloom to Birmingham, the Frenchman, who chain-smoked, asked her if it would be permissible to smoke on the plane. She delayed answering because John did not allow smoking, but she knew he would not wish to offend the French businessman, so she held her breath for his answer. John spoke up and said: "No. The flight is less than an hour and we will be on the ground soon." To John the main questions on the deal were whether the Harbert people could get along well with the French (he was also concerned about the recent French election that had resulted in a socialist prime minister) and whether he wanted to stay in coal or get out of it all together.[92]

John insisted on total secrecy because he feared what the rumors of a sale would do to his employees. A possible divestiture of its coal properties would change the company mix because by the late 1970s coal sales were accounting for 65 percent of Harbert's business and generating 90 percent of its profits.[93] One year after the OPEC embargo of 1973 caused the price of coal to rise, Harbert's total volume of business increased 85 percent to $75 million, and coal mining accounted for $45 million of this total.[94] Yet as Byron Chew, Birmingham-Southern College business professor and former Harbert coal executive, observed, "John always had a good sense of when to get into something and when to get out."[95] With the history of coal being one series after another of highs and lows, John must have figured a slump was coming.

At any rate, John began secret talks with Standard Oil's chairman of the board, John E. Swearingen, and others from Standard's subsidiary, Amoco Minerals Company, organized in 1969 as part of Standard's diversification program. Standard Oil had been broadening its holdings for some time and had moved into strategic mineral investments because of Swearingen's concern that the United States was too dependent upon foreign sources for strategic minerals and because he believed it was a sound investment policy.[96]

Swearingen, a South Carolina native, was a chemical engineer who went to work for Standard Oil when he completed his master's degree at Carnegie Tech (now Carnegie-Mellon University) in 1939. He was married to Bonnie Bolding, a 1955 Howard College graduate from Birmingham, a vivacious blonde former cheerleader and beauty queen who was, as Wita recalls, with her two siblings known locally as "Birmingham's Gabor sisters."[97] Swearingen, smart, efficient, and articulate, started his move up the corporate ladder from Standard's research laboratory in Whiting, Indiana.[98] He and John Harbert had much in common, and during 1980 they frequently enjoyed each other's company. Swearingen was one of several Amoco Minerals people present at Harbert's Starfire mine on June 21, 1981, when the giant Marion-Dresser 8050 dragline first went into operation. Amoco representatives were also present when Harbert broke ground for the state-of-the-art coal port at Savannah, which Harbert was constructing in a joint venture with Elk River Resources. This transloading facility on the Savannah River was expected to handle twelve to fifteen million tons of coal a year, was projected to cost $110 million, and was planned to be in operation by 1983.[99]

In August, the discussions between Harbert and Amoco entered the final stage, and the Louisville *Courier-Journal* quoted Ed Dixon on August 22 that the consideration was five million shares of Amoco common stock with the sale to be completed in thirty days. Two days later *Coal Outlook* reported that John Harbert had confirmed the sale as a stock swap deal worth $400 to $500 million. On September 15, 1981, Amoco Minerals Company bought Harbert's Kentucky coal leases, all of its mining equipment and huge draglines, and its Three Rivers Rock Company, Louisiana quarry operations, Harcon Barge Company (which ran barging operations on the Ohio and Mississippi Rivers), and its interest in the new Savannah coal port (which was under construction). The deal was finalized by a stock transfer that left Harbert Corporation, and thus John Harbert, as the largest single stockholder in Amoco. At the time the deal was finalized in the fall of 1981, Harbert's Amoco stock was worth close to $270 million. The sale was a major American business transaction of 1981.[100] There was brief discussion among the Harbert stockholders that, considering the fact that they were all into or approaching their sixties, maybe the Harbert Corporation should be dissolved and the assets divided. But John would have none of this, and Harbert pushed on into the new decade.

Many people remember John always talking on the telephone. He was very good about staying in touch with people, and he called the office, friends, and family when he was traveling. With so many far-flung business operations, the telephone was his favorite way to find out what was going on.

The divestiture of the coal mines caused what the Harbert newsletter *On Site* termed "a sea change, a shift in corporate direction that was to affect each of its people." The restructuring of Harbert Construction Corporation into Harbert Corporation as the parent company for various diverse companies, including Harbert International as the construction arm, was necessitated in 1981 because the coal leases were in the corporation's name. The new name better recognized the more complex and diverse holdings of the corporation in the 1980s. In a 1989 fortieth anniversary look at the history of the company, *On Site* emphasized that the divestiture of the coal mines "left the company holding two major assets: a large infusion of capital and many talented and seasoned people, some of whom were looking about with trepidation as a new company emerged from the chrysalis of the old one." John reassured his managers and key personnel that new opportunities were ahead for those who had faith and were willing to work hard.[101]

The purchase and sale of the Kentucky coal leases neatly brackets the 1970s for Harbert Corporation. The divestiture of its coal operations gave Harbert the resources it needed to move into the 1980s as one of Alabama's and the nation's premier corporations. But liquid assets can also be a liability, enticing a company into risky adventures.

8

CIVIC DUTY, PUBLIC SERVICE, AND PHILANTHROPY

"better get involved"

John once confessed that, during the years he was building his company, whenever someone asked him to assume a political responsibility, he would reply that he was "too busy. ... I don't have time to get involved in politics."[1] Except for occasional campaign contributions, he left politics alone and avoided public service. He was an active member of the Young Presidents' Organization, which gave him a powerful network of friends and the opportunity to attend a variety of educational programs and seminars, but YPO was not a civic duty.[2] He had been involved with the Birmingham engineers who raised funds to strengthen the engineering program at the University of Alabama extension center, the forerunner of UAB. He made appropriate donations to various civic causes, and in 1966 he was elected to the Birmingham Area Chamber of Commerce. In 1969 John was a zone chairman for the Lurleen Wallace Courage Crusade, a fund-raising drive to generate $5 million for UAB's Lurleen B. Wallace Cancer Hospital. He worried at the time whether those efforts would affect his simultaneous fund raising for the YWCA.[3]

In 1966 John joined the Birmingham Rotary Club, and in 1982-83 he served as its president. During his presidential year John made a special effort not to miss a meeting and arranged his travel schedule to be back in Birmingham for Rotary. That year was special to the members, too, and attendance was high because, according to Betty Morrison, Rotary executive director, "no one ever knew what Mr. Harbert was going to say or do, so no one wanted to miss Rotary that year."[4] John hit the bell so hard to begin the meetings that he ruined the gavel and it had to be replaced. One time, while his back was turned, someone stuffed the bell with a napkin so it would not ring when John banged it.

John made no bones about the fact that he did not like lawyers, so he began every Rotary meeting with a lawyer story. Attorney Harold Apolinsky remembers one of those jokes: "What's black and brown and looks good on a lawyer? Answer: a doberman."[5] In

When John ended his term as president of Birmingham Rotary on June 29, 1983, the club presented a skit entitled "The Dictator and his Gong," poking fun at John's hard bangs on the club bell and his heavy-handed way of keeping things running on time. With John in dunce hat and secured by stocks, Ed Dixon demands the execution of the dictator. The room was packed for this program.

Foster "Buck" Etheredge, former Rotary president, presents flowers to Wita following the program.

fact, John's aversion to lawyers caused his good friend and attorney, Ed Friend, who drafted the profit-sharing program for Harbert employees, to dress as a doctor when he came to ask John for a donation for his favorite charity. He wore a green scrub suit, booties, and hat, with mask and stethoscope hanging around his neck. Needless to say, when "Doctor Friend" was announced at John's office door, he got a hearty laugh and a generous contribution. Through Rotary John supported a wide variety of civic projects and developed a network of friends and business contacts.[6]

Although several early associates suggest that John made an abrupt change in his attitude toward civic responsibility, others believe it was only a matter of time before his business matured and he was able to step forward into a leadership role in civic affairs. Beginning in the early 1960s, John made a commitment and assumed a more visible role in the civic, cultural, and political life of his city and state. However, it was the 1970s before

Wita worked to build a strong volunteer board for Spain Rehabilitation Hospital. In March 1974 she and Betsy Rackley assist a patient who is leaving the hospital. This photograph appeared in the Birmingham News *on March 31, 1974.*

he really found the time to be a dedicated civic leader, and it was 1973 before he assumed any political responsibility. Only five months before he died, John looked back on his life and his experiences and advised young contractors and engineers that they had "better get involved" in ways to assure that "we maintain our democratic form of government."[7] He believed that the way to do this was "to develop strong and capable leaders ... visionary in their thinking, global in their approach to all matters, unwavering in ability and integrity."[8]

In the early years John was influenced in developing his civic sense by the example of his friend and bonding agent, William P. Engel, who was devoted to Birmingham and was one of the finest civic leaders and philanthropists of his era.[9] Engel often involved John in his own causes, getting various contributions from John or from Harbert Construction Corporation. John once thanked a friend for the fine tribute he had given to Engel at a Rotary Club meeting, writing that "next to my father, Mr. Engel probably did more for me than any individual I have ever known."[10]

John was also encouraged by Wita and her mother, Marguerite Nabers Jones, and the examples they set. Wita was very involved in the Junior League before she married John, working with the Nearly New Shop and on the Follies. After her marriage, she helped at the Advent Day School and All-Saints School, where Jay was a student, and for a time she was a volunteer at Children's Hospital. She worked at the Center for Developmental Learning Disorders and diligently at Spain Rehabilitation Hospital, building a volunteer board and hosting benefit parties.[11] In 1978 she was on the committee that planned a Monte Carlo party to benefit the Birmingham Ballet League. She was a member of Linly Heflin and served on the Comprehensive Cancer Board. For two years Wita was head of the local American Heart Association fund-raising drive and was involved with the Birmingham Art Association before John was, and they served together as co-chairs of the first museum party. Wita's mother was an early leader in the Nineteenth Century Club, one of the city's oldest women's literary clubs. Club programs and activities increased Mrs. Jones's awareness of the needs of her city and her responsibility to make a contribution to the well-being of her community. Wita later became a member of the Nineteenth Century Club, along with her sister, Acky, and her daughter, Margie.[12]

Mrs. Jones was an enthusiastic supporter of the Young Women's Christian Association, and, except for two years, she served on its board of directors from 1945 until 1962. John was fond of his mother-in-law, and "Benny," as John and Wita called her, could convince him to do almost anything. So it is not surprising that the first civic responsibility John accepted was an invitation from the YWCA board of trustees made in January 1963 only weeks following Mrs. Jones's retirement from the board of directors.[13] In these years only women served on the board of directors, but the YWCA also had a board of trustees composed of men who helped direct the finances of the organization.[14]

Soon after John joined the board of trustees, he began to assume responsibility for advice and maintenance of the Y building, and almost weekly he sent Harbert men downtown to check on various problems, such as malfunctioning hot-water heaters, equipment failures, and leaking windows. John was soon committed to the acquisition of property for a branch Y on the north side of town, sending Miss Ethel Gibson, the director of the Y, a personal check for $500 to hold an option on some property the Y wanted to purchase from an estate.[15] John realized that the YWCA building, which was formerly the Birmingham Men's Athletic Club and then the Dixie Carlton Hotel, at the corner of Third Avenue and Twenty-third Street North, needed complete renovation. The YWCA had purchased the ten-story building in 1948 but had not renovated it since moving in.[16] Estimates from Harbert engineers and outside architectural consultants put the cost of renovation at $1.5 million. The YWCA was barely solvent; such a capital investment would require loans and a fund-raising campaign and would be extremely risky for the association. As Donald Boomershine recalls those days when he and John served together as YWCA trustees, such an investment was opposed by "several powerful members of the board," but John recognized that "it was now or never for the YW." Boomershine observed that "as was always the case when [John] believed in a project—he vocally and monetarily committed himself to it."[17] John agreed to serve as chairman of the drive.

The initial campaign began the summer of 1968 and raised some $800,000, about half the goal, so it was necessary to secure loans for $600,000 to complete the renovations. A portion of the money was borrowed from Birmingham Trust National Bank and part of it from First National Bank of Birmingham. To repay these short-term loans, another campaign began in 1972, and throughout the year John took a major role in calling on prospects on behalf of the Y. However, this campaign, too, fell short of paying off the loans. Boomershine recalls that as the loans became due, John would plead with the banks to roll over the loans and not foreclose, "which they had every right to do." By buying time, continuing to raise funds, and using new federal programs, the YWCA was eventually able to stabilize its finances. When the YWCA honored John in 1973 for "his vital leadership in the YWCA development program during 1972," few individuals really knew or appreciated the crucial role he had played in saving the Birmingham YWCA.[18] When John spoke to the annual meeting of the YWCA in 1969, he addressed the critical need for society to be concerned with "the spiritual, the emotional, the social and intellectual needs of American women—particularly young women." Aware that by the dawn of the twentieth-first century "80 percent of our population" will be living in cities, he recognized the importance of strengthening YWCA so it might meet its future challenges.[19]

Wita had always had an appreciation for art and a curiosity about art history, due partly to her mother's interests and the influence of her Birmingham-Southern College liberal arts education. She supported the Birmingham Art Association and encouraged John's involvement with the group. John and Wita co-chaired the Beaux Arts Ball in 1967 with Tee Dee Johnson. In September 1966 John was elected second vice-president of the art association, and at this time the president and two vice-presidents of the art association automatically became members of the Birmingham Museum of Art Board of Directors. John remained a member of that board, except for a two-year period, until his death. He was chairman of the Museum Building Committee in 1977, working closely with the design and construction of a new wing. At the time John was very concerned about having enough room in the budget to adjust for the inflation that was prevalent in the American economy and making construction so difficult.[20] Margaret Livingston, who worked closely with John on the museum board for almost three decades, appreciated the energy and enthusiasm that he brought to the board and admired his commitment. His expertise in construction was valuable as the original museum grew during the years he was a board member from the original building through wings and additions all the way to Twenty-first Street.[21]

In 1974 John addressed the Rotary Club on the Birmingham Museum of Art, and four years later he decided that because many members of the Birmingham Rotary Club had not been to see the museum he would have the club hold its meeting at the museum on October 4.[22] Box lunches were ordered and special short tours followed John's talk, which traced the history of the museum and highlighted its most valuable collections. In 1978 Wita and John donated two very fine paintings to the museum: *Grand Canyon, Yellowstone River, Wyoming*, 1886, by William L. Sonntag, Sr., and *Pines in the Mountains*, 1895, by Hermann Herzog.[23] In August 1984 John and Wita gave the museum a ten-foot-high bronze sculpture of Leonardo da Vinci's *The Vitruvian Man* by Enzo Plazzotta. Originally it was placed on a plinth on the western side of the building overlooking the garden walk where it was visible from the street. But when the northern addition was built, the sculpture was stored and later placed in front of the Civic Center's Medical Forum.[24]

While John's role in saving the Birmingham YWCA and his support of the Birmingham Museum of Art were known in limited circles, his first and most visible civic contribution to his city was, typically for John, made on his own terms and with a project he conceived and directed himself. As the story unfolds, John was driving to work in late spring 1973 and noticed "with disgust all the trash and debris" on the roads—beer and soda cans, cups, pop bottles, pieces of paper and plastic. Because Harbert had built many of these highways, John took pride in them and resented having them littered. He decided to do something about it. He hired thirteen high school boys, seventeen years old or older, and a coach to supervise them for the summer. He dressed them in yellow and green Harbert work clothes and hard hats, supplied them with tools and plastic bags, gave them training in traffic safety, and set them to picking up trash along the interstates and highways leading into Birmingham.[25]

John had several goals. He wanted to clean up the roadways, provide summer jobs for young men, and keep records to show the state highway department and Alabama citizens what the cost was to clean the roads on a

In 1973 John initiated an antilitter campaign by hiring high school boys, and coaches to supervise them, in cleaning up the public highways around the city. The project continued for many years and brought favorable responses from the community. The program made citizens and students more aware of the need to keep the city's roadways clean of litter.

per-mile basis. He also wanted to make citizens aware of littering and convince them to heed antilitter slogans. John hoped "that other businesses and groups might see what we're doing and voluntarily sponsor young men to so the same thing in other areas."[26] Unfortunately, this never happened.

But Harbert's antilitter campaign did not go unnoticed. It was the topic of conversations at offices and in homes as people began to observe the cleanup crews and wonder what was going on. There was widespread praise for Harbert that summer. One newcomer to Birmingham who drove Highway 280 to work each morning looked up Harbert Construction Corporation in the telephone book one day after she arrived at her office and called to say thank you for removing the garbage from the roadside. Radio station WBRC broadcast an editorial at the end of July commending John for "his unselfish, community-minded, worthwhile project." The *Birmingham News* published an editorial praising Harbert because "talking about needs to improve the community's and the state's environment is helpful. Doing something about environmental problems is a great deal better."[27] In every way, it was another public relations coup for John Harbert.

Over the next few summers the program was expanded. More coaches and more boys were hired and more praise was heaped on Harbert. Union Carbide Corporation supplied plastic trash bags, and more Harbert trucks accompanied the teams. Signs went up along the roadway: SLOW DOWN. HARBERT CLEAN-UP CREW AHEAD.Birmingham mayor George G. Seibels, Jr., wrote John to thank him for his "spirited attitude" in providing jobs for young people and cleaning up the "mess" on some of the interstates. There were more editorials of praise and some criticism of the state for not doing a better job of enforcing antilitter laws and cleaning up the highways with state crews or convicts.[28]

In 1977 Harbert set up antilitter booths at local shopping malls and hired girls to distribute litter bags. Harbert coordinators of the program began working with community beautification boards, and the corporation ran full-page advertisements on antilitter education. The next year John wrote each young person who had been part of a team and asked for suggestions. Considering John's strong belief in leadership training, it is not surprising that the best reply was judged to come from a young man who thought that changing the foreman occasionally would let teams have a variety of leadership examples.[29] In 1979 when a Gardendale man wrote the *Birmingham News* criticizing the program as free advertising for Harbert on the state right-of-way, supporters countered that the program picked up 400,000 pounds of trash the previous year, that Harbert had spent more than $100,000 on crews, that jobs were provided for fifty teens, and the program saved taxpayer money.[30]

The outside company that first invited John to sit on its board of directors was the American Cast Iron Pipe Company. In January 1969, on behalf of the board, Ken Daniel asked John to become a director. John accepted several days later, after reading materials on ACIPCO founder, John J. Eagan. A requirement for board membership was to understand Eagan's remarkable plan for employees and management of ACIPCO.[31] ACIPCO was recognizing John's business acumen as well as his long experience with laying cast iron pipe. As one of ACIPCO's largest customers, John took an active role on its board. In 1974, he was elected to the First National Bank board, something he thought ironic because the bank had been so lacking in support when Harbert had needed loans in the past. John said that banks were willing to lend to those who really did not need loans and that those who *did* need loans could not get the money.[32]

John had managed for years to avoid politics and political appointments by pleading that his business needed him and he was out of town a great deal of the time. He turned down Governor George C. Wallace's request to accept an appointment to the Alabama Air Quality Commission and the Water Improvement Commission. John "begged off with the excuse that either would pose a conflict of interest" because Harbert constructed water, sewer, and power plants and might be affected by rulings from these agencies. In 1973 when Governor Wallace was at UAB Hospital being treated for wounds he suffered in the 1972 Maryland assassination attempt, he summoned John to his bedside to discuss a vacancy on the Alabama Alcoholic Beverage Control Board. John had discussed the prospect of an appointment with Wita, who was opposed to his accepting the job, and he had asked for advice from several of

Wita was a member of the Mountain Brook chapter of the American Needlepoint Guild and took part in its project to work special needlepoint chair seats designed to reflect the history of the state of Alabama. These were placed on the dining room chairs in the Alabama Governor's Mansion. In the fall of 1977 there was a presentation of the chair seats and a reception recognizing the ladies responsible for the work. Wita, who worked one of the chair seats, joined Governor George C. Wallace and Barbara Blackwell, on her right, and Marilyn Milstead and her mother, Flo Thompson, on her left.

his close friends and business associates, all of whom advised him to stay away from the ABC Board and from the Wallace administration.[33]

When John saw the governor he made his usual excuses to Wallace, saying how busy he was and explaining how his wife disapproved of his involvement in politics. But as John readied himself to leave, Wallace raised up on one elbow and said, "John, that's the trouble with all you *nice* people from Mountain Brook. You are extremely vocal in your criticism of the way the government is run, but when somebody tries to get you to take part, you give all the arguments why you can't. How can I get honest people to run an agency of the government if honest people aren't willing to take on the responsibility?" John could do nothing but accept. The appointment was effective February 1, 1973, with John filling a vacated position. When interviewed about his appointment, John stated that he was optimistic about the future of Alabama and said that his "aim and desire is to do anything I can to help the state."[34] At this time there was no way he could have envisioned just how much effort and time his work with the ABC Board would entail.

Some months after John accepted the ABC appointment, he invited the governor to meet quietly with sixty-five Birmingham business leaders. With Tom Bradford, Arthur Callahan, and Wallace Malone, John set up the three-hour dinner meeting at the Relay House. John invited Democrats, Republicans, and independents, noting that there needed to be better communications between business and state government. John pointed out that a lack of involvement and a failure to communicate with the governor's office for the past twenty-five years had worked against the city of Birmingham. "You can't just sit on the sidelines. You've got to help coach. If you don't take part, you have no right to criticize the results." He said that regardless of political party affiliation, "you've got to be part of an administration to get results."[35]

In the spring of 1973 John busied himself with ABC meetings and tried to understand the history of alcohol regulation in Alabama. In the nineteenth century many Alabamians felt they had a God-given right to distill and drink whiskey. But temperance campaigns were strong after the Civil War, and by the early twentieth century prohibition sentiments held sway. The state strongly supported the passage of the Eighteenth Amendment, which established prohibition. Then in 1933 after Congress initiated the repeal of prohibition, Alabama approved repeal by a large margin. Wine and beer were available in the state after July 1933, but liquor sales were not allowed until 1937, when the legislature passed the Alabama Alcoholic Beverage Control Act, which created a board with responsibility for regulating the sale of alcoholic products in the state. The purpose of the board was "to promote temperance and suppress the evils of intemperance."[36] The board had the responsibility of issuing liquor and beer licenses and of revoking them if a community petitioned. The long meetings and conflicting testimony, opinions, and values must have tried John's patience.[37]

It is ironic that John was given and that he assumed such a responsibility, because philosophically he was opposed to government regulation of any kind, and he believed that the state should get out of the business of selling alcoholic beverages altogether and turn sales over to private enterprise. However, John realized that it was not practical to try to abolish the ABC Board at this time in Alabama. In his early years on the board he did as he had done so many times on other subjects: he began to educate himself about alcoholic beverages, their consumption, and the laws of various states and nations regulating distribution and sale. He tried to get a handle on the issues, where the problems were, and what solutions were possible within the framework of government and the political climate in Alabama.

State regulation was not working well when John joined the ABC Board, and there were many concerns. In past years, liquor agents walked the halls of the capital and generously supplied governors and legislators with the libation of their choice and funneled campaign funds in the direction of those who promoted their causes. The selection of brands offered to the public for sale in ABC stores was important for manufacturers, and stories about payoffs and bribes were commonly circulated on Goat Hill. Governor Wallace opposed liquor agents and even warned John that brown-paper grocery sacks filled with old $100 bills would turn up in front of him.[38] John never found any sacks of cash, but he did discover that the ABC Board's sale of alcohol was "the highest income producing agency of the state government."[39] Despite the fact that the ABC Board produced so much revenue, it was hampered by an antiquated law, which had been amended many times but needed to be completely revised and modernized. The budget of the ABC Board was established at $1.6 million a year when its transactions were $10 million; in 1975 the ABC stores were a $125 million operation, but the budget remained the same. This meant the agency stayed in a cash flow bind and could not pay its bills in a timely fashion.[40]

State regulation was not working well for other reasons. Alabama is the only state in the nation that allows local governments to tax alcohol over state taxation. Because local taxes on alcohol varied from county to county and city to city, retail distributors with state liquor licenses purchased quantities of beer and alcoholic beverages in areas where the tax was low and bootlegged it into high-tax areas. This practice was especially a problem for Birmingham and Jefferson County where the tax was high. Citizens were also purchasing liquor at lower prices outside the state and bringing it into Alabama illegally. Alabama's high-tax cities and counties were losing millions of dollars of tax revenue each year. John wanted laws that worked for the state, and he believed that "laws should be such that people are not encouraged to break them."[41]

With John's urging the ABC Board began studying Alabama laws, comparing the state's regulations and taxes with those of other states that controlled the sale of alcohol. In 1975 the board presented the legislature with an ideal bill, only to be opposed by the governor on three provisions: making beer tax the same statewide, returning an equal share of the tax to local governments, and prohibiting local governments from taxing beer; allowing the sale of table wine in grocery stores in any wet county; and allowing cities in dry counties to hold wet-dry referendums. John testified on behalf of the ABC Board before the House Ways and Means Committee, but the committee accepted Mobile Representative Sonny Callahan's substitute bill, which omitted those features of the ABC bill that Governor Wallace opposed.[42]

After the legislature failed to pass any act to reform the ABC laws, the board surprised the state by abolishing the requirement that miniature bottles of alcoholic beverages be used in establishments selling individual drinks, thus reducing the quantity of alcohol per drink and decreasing the cost of each drink, but the action was challenged in court and the ABC Board lost. However, five years later liquor companies were cutting back on bottling in small bottles and the state was forced to move to open-bottle pouring.[43] In January 1975, John shared his experiences on the ABC agency with the Conference Board, a businessmen's organization with which he had been involved for some years. At a meeting in Florida he told members that in past years at these gatherings there was a "repeated theme of the necessity of the businessman being involved with government one way or another," and after his experiences with the Alabama ABC Board, he was back to ask for "Lesson No. 2: How do I get uninvolved?"[44]

In 1975 the ABC Board voted to resubmit its reform package to the next legislature. Although John was disheartened by his failure to get the legislature to support reform the first time, he continued the fight. It was to go on much longer than he ever dreamed possible.[45] The next summer John tried again and failed. Montgomery political analyst Bob Ingram in his statewide column "The Alabama Scene," reported that "The most frustrated man in Alabama may well be John Harbert, the super-successful businessman-industrialist from Birmingham. As a member of the ABC Board, Harbert had worked for four years to have enacted some new laws which would put the state's liquor operation on a business-like basis. He got clobbered again last week in a House Committee. His entire package was killed."[46]

Each year the ABC Board would present its reform legislation, and each year the legislature would refuse to enact it. In 1980 John was chairman of the ABC Board, and he testified before the Senate Finance and Taxation Committee, listing the same problems and the same arguments for reform that he had given in 1975. But there was a difference. Wallace was no longer governor; Fob James was. James was a young man John had known through the Rebel Chapter of YPO and in Republican Party circles since the mid-1960s. Even though James elected to run on the Democratic ticket, John had helped finance his gubernatorial campaign. Governor James was committed to reforming Alabama's liquor laws, and John was more confident that he would be able to push reform through the legislature now because the governor approved.[47]

In July 1979 Governor James had asked John to serve as chairman of the ABC Board, and John accepted. Under John's leadership striking improvements were made. Besides lifting the requirement of miniatures for drinks, the board began to purchase directly from distilleries, allowing "industries fair and even access to the Alabama market and [expanding] the selection of products available in the State." John saw "that the ABC Board's operations were honest, efficient, and businesslike." He saw that the licensing process was smoothed and that a hearing commission was established to supervise this process, freeing the board to spend its time on other issues. John supported computer data entry at point of sale so that Montgomery would have inventory control and be able to monitor trade at every store. He saw that state stores adopted self-service sales and stressed efficient and courteous service. As John left the board, both Governors James and Wallace applauded his contributions to Alabama.[48]

In the spring of 1973 John accepted another government responsibility. Governor Wallace asked him to chair the governor's Energy Advisory Council, a group created because of the Arab oil embargo. For the next year John represented Alabama at special regional and national meetings on energy. He prepped the governor on energy matters, critiqued for Wallace energy reports of other southern governors, and made recommendations for the state's position. John advocated working toward acquiring an ample supply of energy at a reasonable cost and believed "that environmental restrictions represented one of the big problems facing this objective."[49] Testifying before the Federal Energy Administration in September 1974, John urged policies that would allow the United States to achieve energy independence and develop plans "to recover all of the hydrocarbons available." He urged Congress to establish a pilot program to reclaim coal in areas of Appalachia that had been stripped over from 1930 to 1950, a program that would include land reclamation. With coal selling in that era from $2 to $3 a ton, land reclamation was not feasible, but with the price of coal currently at $25 to $30 a ton, he anticipated that the project would be self-supporting.[50] John was deeply concerned about the energy crisis, telling the governor that the "fuel shortage has been caused by a more affluent world using more energy" and that it was not due to "a conspiracy between the major oil companies."[51]

In 1975 Dr. Alston Callahan called on John, who anticipated that he was going to be asked for a donation; instead, John was invited to join the Eye Foundation Hospital board of trustees. He was surprised and immediately began to ask questions about the foundation's work. He agreed to join the board. In 1980 he became chairman and led the hospital toward modernization, a professional administration, long-range planning, and a competitive and profitable operation. In 1983 he and Wita hosted a dinner to kick off a campaign to raise money to improve and increase the hospital's facilities.[52] The day before the dinner, Wita had told John that she had made a pledge of $7,500 to fund a Linly Heflin scholarship to Birmingham-Southern College and that she planned to pay for it over a period of years. On the evening of the Eye Foundation dinner, as they were riding downtown, John told Wita he intended to announce a $500,000 challenge pledge for the campaign. Wita laughed and replied, "Well, I think I'll just write a check for *all* of my scholarship tomorrow!"[53]

John rarely discussed with Wita his philanthropic gifts until he had made up his mind what he wanted to do. She was surprised by John's $5 million pledge to the Auburn Generations Campaign to fund a new engineering facility on the Auburn University campus, a building that bears his name. Wita was also surprised by John's $3.5 million gift that helped build the four-story classroom and office building that is named for her on the campus of her alma mater, Birmingham-Southern College. A gift that John considered "one of my most worthwhile investments" began in 1979 and involved an initial gift of $10,000 to the English department of the University of Montevallo "to promote better writing."[54] A composition lab and a tutorial program evolved from this gift. The Harbert Writing Center became a model program for other colleges. On the tenth anniversary of the center, English department chairman Dr. Norman R. McMillan attested to the success of the center in allowing students to reach their full potential as writers.[55] Wita often marveled at John's philanthropy. She explains that "John had a deep commitment to share," and she believes that his experiences in World War II, where he witnessed such physical devastation and human suffering, had touched his soul and made him appreciate his own good fortune, which caused him to help people so willingly.[56]

John's work with the Eye Foundation Hospital involved more than financial gifts. They proved "secondary to his contributions of time and leadership." For five years he was chairman of the board, and he "was often seen strolling the halls, talking to employees, encouraging the patients."[57] When construction was under way he checked the job frequently and thoroughly. Once when the parking deck was being built, he rode to the fifth and top floor and, as Dr. Callahan recalls the story, asked the construction foreman, Denny Blalock, how much it would cost to add an extra floor. The foreman replied $500,000 now, but a million dollars later. John ordered him to "go ahead and put on another floor." The foreman questioned whether Mr. Harbert had better have a committee meeting to obtain approval, and John smiled: "Committee has met. Go ahead!" When Dr. Callahan thanked him for such generosity in increasing his pledge, John replied: "Hell no! I know we need that floor. Alston, you get out and raise it." And Dr. Callahan did.[58]

Once when John was checking the job with Dr. Callahan late on a Friday afternoon, the elevator stopped between floors after the construction crews cut the power as they prepared to quit work. The two men thought they would be spending the weekend in the elevator, but after some time they were missed and the electricity was turned back on. As John assessed the situation: "We had plenty of air,

John and Wita frequently entertained at their home, especially for charity events. At a party in June 1977 honoring Charlie Boswell, John shows off his Battle of Waterloo chess set that features Napoleon and the duke of Wellington.

I knew it wouldn't hurt either of us to miss a meal or two, and Alston and I could never run out of conversation. We decided which corner we each would sleep in and agreed that there were worse ways to spend a weekend, but we surely were glad to hear the electricity kick back on and feel that elevator moving."[59]

John became involved with fund raising to support diabetes research beginning in 1968. His father had suffered from the disease and had died four years earlier from its complications. John wanted to see that a diabetes research and education hospital was built as part of the UAB medical complex. He worked closely with Dr. Buris R. Boshell in fund raising for diabetes and served on the board of directors of the Diabetes Trust Fund.[60]

John was also interested in education, and he believed strongly that the state's "leaders have an obligation to see that adequate funding is made available with minimal burden to tax-paying citizens to provide our children with a superior education."[61] In June 1977, he became a member of the Birmingham-Southern College board of trustees and in November of that year agreed to chair a committee to draft the mission statement for the University of Montevallo.

In 1979 Governor James appointed John to the Alabama Commission on Higher Education, and he served on the commission until 1985, although he was much less diligent about attending the twelve-member commission meetings than he had been about attending the three-member ABC Board meetings. At ACHE John supported the elimination of duplicate programs and the creation of cooperative programs that saved money. He was generally concerned with the cost of higher education and with making it more efficient for the students and the taxpayers.[62] After years of trying to influence the direction of higher education in the state, he described his efforts as "like pushing a rope," but he believed that the work of ACHE was important because the state was not getting its money's worth from the tax dollars poured into the large number of state colleges and universities.[63] Jim Vickrey, who was president of the University of Montevallo at the time, recalled that John "almost left [ACHE] in disgust on several occasions, but stayed on after talking with me and others."[64]

In 1978, as part of the Auburn Generations Capital Campaign, university development officer Buck Bradberry called on John to request a leadership gift for the College of Engineering, which had produced John, Bill, and so many other Harbert engineers. John committed $5 million dollars to construct a new civil engineering building, which was built by Harbert and named the John M. Harbert III building in a dedication ceremony on April 4, 1986.[65] On January 25, 1980, John had been elected to the Auburn University Foundation board, and he played a significant role on the

The John M. Harbert III civil engineering building on the campus of Auburn University is a state-of-the art facility used to train engineers for the twenty-first century. At its dedication on April 4, 1986, the Harbert family gathered to cut a specially decorated cake.

board, the development arm of the university, until his death in March 1995.

In 1986 John was serving on the board of trustees of Birmingham-Southern College when the trustees considered a renovation of seventy-year-old Erskine Ramsay Hall. It was evident that the old building was not adequate and that renovation would not serve the college's needs. Neal Berte recalls that "John quickly saw for himself the need for a new and much larger facility." After some discussions, John offered a leadership gift of $3.5 million to build the $6 million classroom facility. The gift in honor of Wita encouraged others to donate. Ground was broken on February 20, 1987, and the four-story brick building was named the Marguerite Jones Harbert Building and dedicated September 27, 1988.[66]

The University of Montevallo was the first university to recognize John Harbert by awarding him an honorary doctor of laws degree on October 12, 1978. Because John had not attended his graduation from Auburn in 1946, Montevallo was pleased to be the first university to dress him in academic regalia.[67] In 1981 Auburn University awarded him an honorary doctor of science degree, and five years later Birmingham-Southern College presented him with his second honorary

On February 20, 1987, Birmingham-Southern College broke ground for a building, to be named for Wita, which was primarily funded by John's leadership gift of $3.5 millon. Within the family, the children teased their mother, calling the stately structure "Wita's Wigwam." Handling the shovels are architect Harry Coleman, Birmingham-Southern College president Neal Berte, Wita, an unidentified student, John, Frank M. Dominick, chairman, Birmingham-Southern College Executive Committee, and Dr. H. Irvin Penfield, Birmingham-Southern College vice-president of academic affairs and dean.

When the Marguerite Jones Harbert Building on the campus of Birmingham-Southern College was dedicated on September 27, 1988, Wita's portrait was presented to the college as a gift of Harbert friends Houston and Frances Blount. John, Birmingham-Southern College president Neal Berte, and trustee president Carl Bailey join Wita in admiring her portrait, painted by William Draper.

University of Montevallo president Jim Vickrey congratulates John on October 12, 1978, after the University of Montevallo dressed him in his first academic gown and awarded John his first honorary doctoral degree.

doctor of laws degree. During his comments at this graduation ceremony, John praised a liberal arts degree and confessed that his own education had not included "the humanities, the fine arts, and communications skills ... areas which I have had to explore and study on my own." He noted that in "today's world, there is scarcely time for such self-tutelage; therefore a broad liberal arts experience as an undergraduate is almost essential for young people who hope to succeed in business or a profession."[68]

In 1978 John became a member of the board of directors of the Alabama School of Fine Arts and began working closely with its executive director, Jim Nelson. When John first heard of the school, he once confessed he thought it was "a place for weirdos" where the students were "a bunch of long-haired hippies who wanted to draw or dance or sing for a living." But he soon learned that the students were talented young people with self-discipline who worked hard, and John came to understand that the nature of the arts teaches "young people to think for themselves, to evaluate everything they do or everything that touches them."[69]

Nelson came to John asking help with financing a fence to protect the property and the students from the inner-city decay around the school. John hired a professional site designer to survey the school's property and recommend to John what was needed. After reading the report, Nelson remembered John's telling him, "Hell, Jim, you don't need a fence; you need a school." And John began to provide the leadership to accomplish that goal, contributing $1 million to the new school.[70]

John often flew to the National Boy Scout Jamboree. Here he joins Wayne Peake in sharing his memorabilia of the first National Boy Scout Jamboree with two Birmingham scouts.

John was always supportive of the Boy Scout program. He saw that Harbert Construction Corporation moved Troop 311's mountain to the Jefferson County Civic Center for the 1979 Scout-O-Rama so the scouts could give a demonstration of rock climbing, for which the troop received a blue ribbon. He served on the executive committee of the Birmingham Boy Scouts and in 1989 invited some of his scouting friends to fly with him to spend the day at the National Boy Scout Jamboree at Fort A. P. Hill in Virginia. In 1975 he was awarded the rank of Distinguished Eagle Scout by the Birmingham Area Council.[71]

John took a leadership role in developing a downtown civic club center that could serve a variety of purposes. The Birmingham Rotary and Kiwanis Clubs, significant in the civic life of the city since their founding in the early twentieth century, met for some fifty years at the Tutwiler Hotel. After the hotel was demolished in 1974, the clubs moved from place to place, never finding a suitable home. Aware that there were many diverse needs for a facility in the inner city, numerous joint committees tried to find a solution; then a committee of two—John Harbert and Hall Thompson—went to work. As John recalled, Thompson "kicked me" and said, "Let's don't listen to all the doubting Thomases."[72] In 1982 the two clubs founded the R & K Foundation, purchased a building on Fourth Avenue, and began a fund-raising drive to design and build a new multipurpose civic center. John contributed $150,000, and there were large and small contributions from members of both clubs, from Birmingham businesses, and from the city itself. Although committees from both Rotary and Kiwanis worked hard to raise the balance of the funds and every member of the clubs donated to the project, Elmer Harris, CEO of Alabama Power Company, observed that it "would not exist if John had not been so aggressive in supporting the idea and moving toward this goal."[73]

The sales transaction for the property was completed in the name of a new entity, the Civic Club Foundation, and the parking structure on the lot was razed in 1985. John, as chairman of the Rotary Club house committee, issued the contract through Harbert International, which undertook "the obligations as Prime Contractor for construction of the building at cost plus 2 percent overhead factor."[74] The modern three-story building was designed by Birmingham architect Charles A. Moss, Jr., who commented that "we wanted a building that showed the strength of the clubs and the strength of the community," thus the granite interior walls and support columns, a design that "carries the facade motif through out the building, and suggests solidarity." The "chrome-and-glass spiral staircase and spacious atrium give the building's interior an openness."[75] The facility was named the Harbert Center to recognize John's leadership in the project. Mrs. Dwight M. Beeson, who missed the dedication on May 28, 1986, wrote John after seeing the building that she was proud of having some part in the project and delighted that this meeting place is "one more bit of `magic' for Birmingham."[76] On the fifth anniversary of the center, John looked back and said that "it's unique maybe in the world of civic clubs. It's a well-kept secret and I'm proud to have been a small part of it."[77]

Despite his generous contributions, sometimes there were problems working with John, especially for university presidents and foundation heads who were restricted by state laws and institutional policies. They could not operate as quickly as John expected. John thought that once he had made a decision, everything should move forward to completion. He was often frustrated by the inertia that he perceived in state government and academia. University presidents found themselves explaining to John why certain things remained undone, not a comfortable position for either party.

In 1993 during his acceptance remarks when

John was proud of Wita's needlepoint art, which in 1972 was part of an International Needlepoint Festival exhibition at the Birmingham Museum of Art. Wita designed and worked John's vest, which included his favorite sports and activities. The pillow Raymond holds was purchased in Europe.

he was inducted into the Alabama Business Hall of Fame, John reiterated his personal dedication to "creating a better quality of life for all Alabamians." He regretted that he "never became deeply involved in politics or in providing leadership in government," and he recognized that his "hands off approach was not only narrow-minded, but often costly," resulting in poor leadership and ill-advised legislation. He urged business leaders to "become actively involved in the business of government."[78]

But there were many ways, especially in the last twenty years of his life, in which John was able to influence policy by the force of his personality and by the contributions of his money. Eason Balch was impressed with John's uncanny ability "to identify people who had power and who could impact what was going on" and to respect people with authority and position and know "how to influence them."[79] Elmer Harris watched John's civic involvement for years and noted that although "he pushed people hard, and expected civic leaders to contribute," he "was always willing to be out front, where leaders should be." Harris noted that John's "involvement in national, state, and local politics is an outstanding lesson and example of leadership that too few American business CEO's and executives ever learn and become actively involved in the world's best political system."[80] John explained to *Birmingham News* staff writer Dave White that he contributed to political campaigns because "we've got to encourage good people to run for office....I know there are favoritisms, but the higher caliber man you get in, the smaller chance there is of shenanigans going on."[81]

Many of John's contributions to his community are lost, for they were quiet and small kindnesses that remain unheralded and shared only with those he touched. When he accepted the Greater Birmingham Area Community Service Award on April 30, 1987, John stated that "as citizens we should be concerned with the total community; as human beings, with the whole human race," for "we harbor the basic need to seek a higher spiritual goal." He believed that "service is an outward manifestation of something deep within all of us. We know—each of us—personally and with certainty that *giving is its own reward*."[82]

9

HARBERT INTERNATIONAL

"we have to make our own luck"

John tried to visit the coal mines once or twice a month during the 1970s, but other people from one division of Harbert were flying from Birmingham to Kentucky every Monday or Tuesday to supervise the coal mines and coming home on Thursday or Friday. Meanwhile different Harbert vice-presidents and crews were continuing to build the original arm of Harbert Construction Corporation. Construction was moving forward in two directions, one domestic and the other foreign, and John was keeping his finger on both operations. Construction overseas was administered by Harbert International and after July 1975 sometimes by a new entity, Harbert International Establishment, which was incorporated in Liechtenstein with headquarters in London. It was created specifically to handle the complex projects in the Middle East and to give Harbert the ability to manage these distant job sites more closely. Bill Harbert concentrated on directing the international jobs and pipelines, while a new addition to the Harbert team, William F. Land, who arrived at Harbert in January 1971, focused on civil construction—bridges, dams, and interstate projects in the United States.

From the completion of Harbert's first international contract, a small sewer job started in Puerto Rico in 1955 and finished in 1957, Harbert bid and won contracts for projects in the Caribbean Islands, Latin America, and South America. There were pipeline projects in Trinidad, Colombia, and Ecuador, and by the mid-1970s Harbert had permanent offices in Bogota, Colombia; Panama City, Panama; San Jose, Costa Rica; Lima, Peru; Quito, Ecuador; and Luanda, Angola.

John had recognized a decade before that Harbert's capability offered underdeveloped countries an assurance of quality-engineered projects. For Harbert the international market afforded the possibility of greater profits because the greater the risks, the larger the profit margin. In a speech to the Saint Mary's Men's Club in 1965, John candidly admitted that. Then he explained that because the risk is so much greater "we limit the number of jobs we attempt out of the United States to one or two at a time"; "we feel, however, that

In November 1957, John led a team of Harbert Construction Corporation engineers on a trip to South America to investigate job prospects. With John were Jack Ward and Billy Edmonds; the trio is being greeted by the two men without hats.

the opportunities outweigh the hazards involved." Although, John pointed out, American "businessmen think of a gross margin of 10 percent as being more than adequate, most South Americans want to receive 30 to 50 percent mark-up on their investment," understandable in these countries where "the normal bank interest rate will be anywhere from 15 to 25 percent of a loan."[1]

In discussing the problems of construction jobs in South America, John noted the language difficulties and the cultural differences, especially attitudes toward petty graft and payoffs. Construction in many countries was further complicated by an inability to communicate with remote areas and the virtual impossibility of transporting supplies and equipment where roads were inadequate or did not exist. He also observed that it was much easier to see the heads of state in these countries than in the United States, "particularly if you are working on major construction projects that are of vital interest to the country." John noted that inflation and devaluation of currency were other problems a contractor faced in foreign jobs, but Harbert tried to protect itself by contracting in American dollars. High duties on imported equipment and spare parts also compounded the difficulties of the company's work. But the bottom line remained that if the profits were not far greater than the risk and worth the trouble of dealing with the challenges, then Harbert would not be running any "foreign operations."[2] When John was interviewed in 1975, he observed that a "person needs enough common sense to recognize an advantage when he sees it and then act on it. Knowledge without action is nothing." John saw in international jobs the opportunities to provide expertise, scarce equipment, and "materials that might not be readily available."[3] Then he pushed ahead, living by his dictum that "we have to make our own luck."[4]

Foreign jobs presented personnel difficulties as well. Harbert Construction Corporation provided superintendents and highly skilled workers, but laborers from the local area were recruited and trained in skills such as microwelding and pipe fitting. This training and work experience was valuable in creating a corps of workers who understood what Harbert expected. In isolated areas Harbert had to provide on-site housing for superintendents and camps for workers, complete with kitchens and medical support. John was

In September 1971, John and Wita visited Costa Rica to check on the work being done on the concrete bridge over the Rio Colorado.

adamant about safety on the job—his motto was that "safety makes money"—and many of his columns in company newsletters were about safety. Although federal regulations were stricter in the United States, he insisted on the same safety standards on Harbert's foreign jobs.

As the number of its international jobs increased, Harbert developed a special expertise in bidding jobs in foreign countries, in estimating local currency inflation and deflation possibilities, and in educating its American superintendents and foremen about local customs and labor practices. These Americans would live near the job site for the two or three years required to complete the project. Harbert kept in close contact with the U.S.

The installation of the precast concrete inverted arch bridge, designed by T. Y. Lin, over a gorge in the Rio Colorado in Costa Rica, was a dangerous project. But when it was finished, it became one of John's favorite accomplishments.

Department of State to monitor political and economic conditions in countries where employees were working, and John made sure that Alabama's congressional delegation, especially the state's two U.S. senators, were kept informed of Harbert's activities abroad and the impact these projects had upon Alabama. John developed a network of federal government contacts that provided information about conditions abroad.

One of John's favorite overseas construction projects—after it was finished—was a bridge designed by T. Y. Lin of San Francisco that Harbert built in Costa Rica over a 328-foot gorge of the Rio Colorado. Completed in 1972 as part of the Pan-American Highway and located twenty-two miles northwest of San Jose, the bridge was the first of its type in the world. Its designer claimed that the precast concrete inverted arch bridge had "the greatest advantages of suspension, arch, and cantilever bridges."[5] To John "it was one of the scariest damn jobs we have ever undertaken."[6] The bridge, built by using a cableway system to deliver men and materials, was constructed on top of suspension cables, "put together as though it were an oversized erector set."[7] Although Lin explained that he designed the bridge to make construction easier and cheaper in a country where concrete was cheap and imported steel costly, the architect did not anticipate the problems Harbert faced: an isolated job site in a jungle, rain, mud slides, insects, reptiles, and "heat so intense that concrete had to be poured at night."[8] Harbert completed the bridge ahead of schedule, part of a three-bridge contract in Costa Rica. Twenty-five years later, having survived earthquakes and heavy travel, the bridge stands as "one of the world's truly exotic bridge construction projects," a testament to Harbert's engineering and construction skills.[9]

Harbert constructed its first project in Ecuador, a pipeline from Guayaquil to Quito, in 1969. Many other pipeline projects followed, especially in Oriente province after oil was discovered there in 1971. Much of this area is wild, remote jungle inhabited by Auca Indians who are not cordial to intruders; however, Harbert's South American vice-president, Sol Lepp, found numerous ways to appease the Aucas, whose chief was fascinated by Lepp's ball-point pens. In 1981 John flew to Ecuador to visit a Harbert project. After a cocktail reception in Quito, where he had the opportunity to meet local business leaders and dignitaries and enjoy a Southern-style backyard barbecue hosted by the Harbert office staff, John traveled to the job site.

Harbert was constructing an offshore line to connect the refinery in Esmeraldas with tankers. The exportation of the oil was important, and the government had instituted tight security measures. John flew into the primitive Esmeraldas airport, boarded a dugout canoe to cross the swift Rio Esmeraldas, but was stopped short of the job site by a military policeman who asked for identification. John had left his U.S. passport in his hotel room in Quito, and although in his best Spanish he kept telling the man that he was the "presidente" of Harbert, the company doing the construction, the guard refused to believe him and would not recognize John's Alabama driver's license or his credit cards as proper identification. He insisted that to be in Ecuador John must have a passport and a work card. So John was hauled off to jail, where he stayed for several hours while frantic telephone calls flew between Quito and Washington, D.C., and government officials of every level in the two countries became involved. Eventually, John was released, "but not until he had a good chance to meet some interesting characters incarcerated for offenses not so benign as entering a construction project without a work visa."[10]

In 1974 Harbert had jobs under way in the Portuguese colonies of Angola and Cabinda, very politically unstable areas of southwest Africa that are rich in minerals and have an abundant supply of oil. Harbert had

Laying pipe in isolated areas with terrain from jungles to mountains was difficult. This Harbert-constructed water transportation system designed for the city of Quito, Ecuador, is one example.

contracts with Gulf Oil, Texaco, and Petrangol, a Belgian company, to lay oil pipelines. Chaos erupted after the Portuguese abruptly abandoned the country on November 11, 1974. John blamed the trouble on "Portugal's failure or inability to maintain a strong and viable government at home, which, in turn, made it impossible to control its colonial troops effectively."[11] Harbert supervisors reported that the Portuguese troops were "no more than an undisciplined and unruly mob" and were little use in maintaining order. Fighting among three factions began even before the Portuguese pulled out, and conflict escalated after the Europeans left.

Harbert's crews stayed and worked as long as they could. Then when their lives were in danger, Harbert asked the American Embassy to help get the Americans out; but the embassy refused. Harbert then turned to the British Embassy, which arranged for planes to fly in. Harbert personnel were evacuated by the Royal Air Force with some help from the French Consulate. Years later Bill Harbert observed that when you are in trouble in a foreign country, "you always go to the British Embassy first."[12] Harbert left behind equipment worth $1.5 million. Harbert crews did not return to Angola until 1981, when they were able to claim most of their equipment and property (except for a truck confiscated by the insurgents to haul ammunition). Work then resumed on the pipeline.[13]

The first major job Harbert won in the Middle East was a 1975 joint-venture contract with a North Carolina firm, Paul N. Howard Company, for construction of a water system and desalination plant for Abu Dhabi, the largest of the seven sheikhdoms of the United Arab Emirates, a small country with a booming economy based upon oil and gas.[14] After years of work and consultation with the engineers who designed the system, Harbert submitted its bid, using American-made pipe, but it was $8 million higher than the lowest bid from a Lebanese firm quoting Japanese and French pipe. A closer inspection of

During a visit to Abu Dhabi in 1975, Wita and John journeyed into the desert to learn more about the culture of the people. They stopped to visit with camel drivers.

the Lebanese bid showed that it failed to meet specifications. After nine months of working with the engineers and after rather long and interesting negotiations between Bill Harbert and Abu Dhabi officials, Harbert lowered its bid and eventually won the contract. The Harbert Construction Corporation was required "to put up an $8 million *cash* letter of credit," which made John sleepless some nights because, as he once noted, under the agreement the Abu Dhabi government could have cashed it in "if they didn't like the color of our hair or the way we blinked our eyes." The commitment to such a large letter of credit, John noted, "met with no favor from our banks or our bonding company."[15]

As part of the $52 million water system, American Cast Iron Pipe Company received a $25 million contract from Harbert for 33,000 tons of pipe and fittings, the largest order for pipe ever placed with ACIPCO. The pipe was moved from the Birmingham plant to Mobile by flatbed railroad cars and by trucks, and the pipe was shipped from the port in November 1975 aboard a Greek carrier. Other supplies and equipment worth $10 million were purchased in the Birmingham area and sent to the Middle East country because every earth-moving machine, shovel, and wheelbarrow had to be shipped from the United States. It was a two-year project, which meant that families of engineers and superintendents went with them. The joint venture hired a tutor to go along and teach the ten American children who moved to Abu Dhabi for the duration of the project.[16]

John and the Birmingham office were in constant touch with the Harbert people in Abu Dhabi through a telex system, far better than the old radio system he had used in 1967. John visited the job site in March and returned from Abu Dhabi with the news that Sheikh Suroor was pleased and wanted Harbert-Howard to bid on additional work. When the job was completed, John observed that Harbert had "received treatment from Abu Dhabi officials that was completely fair to us in all instances."[17]

Harbert's second job in Abu Dhabi was a $45 million joint-venture municipal water distribution and electricity project for the city of Al Ain. Both projects made a profit and encouraged Harbert to bid a job in Saudi Arabia. This project was to provide water transmission lines in Jidda for $54.3 million; however, problems with weather and rocks slowed construction and management did not adjust well, causing the job to lose money.[18]

A good example of John's ability to take charge and of his caring nature occurred after his brother fell ill in the Middle East in December 1977. Bill was in Abu Dhabi visiting Harbert jobs when he suddenly became sick and was in severe pain. The Harbert people called Birmingham and reported that

Bill was on a plane going home. John went with the company plane to New York to pick up Bill, but when the plane arrived from Europe, Bill was not on it. John finally was able to learn that Bill had been taken off the plane in Brussels in great pain, was in the hospital there, and was being prepared for surgery. John called Bill's wife, Joy, and told her to pack her bags and fly to New York to meet him. Wita found John's passport and delivered it to Joy, and in New York John made reservations for a flight to Brussels. Bad weather forced the plane to land in Frankfurt, and John and Joy took a bus to Brussels.

When they finally arrived at the hospital, Bill was in intensive care, recovering from surgery, but as soon as he saw his family, he gave an "OK" sign. John stayed four days with Joy, moved her to the Holiday Inn at the airport where everyone spoke English, and taught her what a cab to the hospital should cost and how to use her Belgian money. Two weeks later, Joy was able to bring Bill home to Birmingham.[19]

Little did John Harbert realize after the presidential election of 1976 that his company would benefit from President Jimmy Carter's foreign policy initiatives in a project that would be the company's most exciting and difficult challenge. Harbert had supported Republican Gerald Ford in the campaign. However, Carter's crowning diplomatic accomplishment, arranging a peace treaty between Israel and Egypt, led to Harbert's largest job, in both dollars and scope, and the most difficult and challenging construction project of the corporation's history. President Carter invited Egyptian President Anwar Sadat and Israeli Prime Minister Menachem Begin to Camp David in September 1978 for peace talks, hoping that "in a secluded place, away from the press" the two leaders "could come to understand the compatibility of many of their goals and the advantages to both nations in resolving their differences."[20] Toward the end of the discussions one of the sticky issues became what would happen to three Israeli air bases in the Sinai. Following its victory over Egypt in the Six-Day War of 1967, Israel had constructed air bases in the occupied territory and had built up "a vast infrastructure." Now Begin was concerned over Israel's defenses should the Sinai be returned to Egypt.[21]

In a breakthrough that occurred only the day before the Camp David accords were signed on September 17, 1978, the United States agreed to provide financial aid to Israel for the construction of two new air bases in the Israeli Negev Desert to replace the three bases Israel would give up by withdrawing from the Egyptian Sinai. Although the details had to be worked out, President Carter proposed that the United States through the Army Corps of Engineers construct new air bases and help move the Sinai airfields.[22] After the formal Treaty of Peace between Egypt and Israel was signed in Washington, D.C., on March 26, 1979, the Corps of Engineers got busy contacting potential American companies that had experience working in the Middle East. The project was so massive that Harbert was one of the few U.S. companies that was prequalified and would dare to bid on the $454 million project, and it did so in joint venture with a Massachusetts-based firm, Perini Corporation, with Paul N. Howard Company of North Carolina, and with Louis Berger of New Jersey, the design engineer.

Harbert's proposal was prepared with such a quick turnaround that the entire corporate office staff was involved. The company acquired its first word processor to produce the paperwork. The day the Corps of Engineers was to announce the winning bids in New York, tensions were high at Harbert. The word came down at two o'clock in the afternoon that Harbert had won, and all work ceased. Cheers rang out. The whoops and hollers of Billy Land could be heard from one end of the building to the other, and when he finally calmed and looked at his feet, he exclaimed, "My God, I've been all over town and I've got on one black shoe and one brown one." John was out of the office and received the news by telephone.[23]

Not only was the Israeli job large, it was also to be on a "fast-track" schedule with construction completed in record time—thirty months. There was no way the Israeli labor pool could supply the construction needs and any attempt to do so would devastate the local labor market, so Israel insisted that all labor had to come from outside the country. Because of high inflation, all building materials, supplies, and machinery also had to be imported. The corps engineer in charge, Major General James A. Johnson, invoked a little-used wartime priority to enable the corps to requisition equipment and supplies in the United States ahead of anyone else. Tractors, earth-moving machines, graders, trucks, compactors, and other equipment worth more than $2 million were shipped from the port of Mobile in the first shipment, and by the end of 1979 goods worth about $100 million, purchased in-state and across the Southeast, had been shipped from the Alabama port.[24]

Because the projects were of such a sensitive military nature, all personnel were required to pass security clearances and abide by certain rules—such as no photography. To complicate the construction project even more, Harbert had to work not only with its partners and the U.S. Army Corps of Engineers but also with the Israeli government and its engineers. Specifications, plans, and designs were changed weekly, sometimes daily, and they included runways, parking aprons, aircraft shelters, housing, utilities, roads, and other operational and support facilities.[25]

The base that Harbert was to build was located in the southern part of the Negev Desert at Ovda (Uvdah in Hebrew) where hills rose to the southeast and the mountains of Jordan peaked in the distance. The 8,000 acres selected by the Israeli government were in a valley on the soft soil of a wadi (a dry riverbed). Heavy buildings would have to be constructed on sunken pile foundations, and drainage and ditches would move rainwater—if it ever came—away from the base.[26] All supplies and materials were delivered through the nearest port, Eliat on the Gulf of Aqaba. Harbert sent its top superintendent, Thurlo W. Hooper, and his family to Ovda. Hooper had an easy-going, pleasant spirit, but he knew how to lead and direct men and to push a job along.

John recognized that because of the different entities involved—Harbert-Howard

Harbert mastered the task of shipping everything it needed to complete an international project—trucks, earth-moving equipment, supplies, machinery, and sometimes even food.

in joint venture, the U.S. Army Corps of Engineers, the Israeli government, and the Israeli military—he also needed to put the very best engineer he had on the project site, so he sent Vice-President of Engineering and Chief Engineer Ted Randolph and his wife, Jane, to Israel for two years. Not only was Ted a brilliant and creative engineer with years of experience, but he had the quiet personality needed to get along with difficult people and inspire them to work together well. Jane was excited about the opportunity to live in Israel and to learn Hebrew. The Randolphs and Hoopers and all the other Harbert people represented the corporation and Alabama well.

The project had everything that made John enthusiastic—the prestige of an American government project, origin in a famous international agreement, and a level of secrecy that required security clearances. The project was enormous in scope, had the challenge of a short construction timetable, was located in a historic land, and had a large dollar contract with profit in it. For this job everything had to go right. The only negative particular was that in the early years John was forbidden to talk about it, which was difficult for him.

A construction community rapidly appeared on the barren Israeli desert, but for several months it lacked electricity, water, and sewers. Contractors used 1,000 American and British supervisors and skilled workers and recruited 4,000 laborers from Thailand, who proved to be excellent.[27] Eventually the construction village had forty prefabricated houses with air conditioning for families, barracks for the workers, and two cafeterias—one for the Thais and another for the Americans and British, so each culture could have foods it ate at home. Almost daily Harbert flew in fresh foods from Thailand. Eventually there was a commissary, tennis courts, a movie theater, and a school. There was even a weekly newspaper, the *Desert Sun*. Harbert personnel were in virtually constant telephone contact with the Birmingham office.[28]

The prefabricated village was almost complete when John and Wita came to visit in October 1979. They enjoyed eating with the Thais, driving through the desert, visiting historic places, and seeing artifacts that the archaeologists were removing just ahead of the bulldozers. When he returned home, John wrote Harbert superintendent Hooper that he felt "the work camp will be used for the next ten or fifteen years after our people have come home." He asked Hooper to plant some trees and flowering shrubs around the houses and get Ted Randolph to design some way to use the gray water to keep them growing. He assured Hooper that if he received "a

In May 1981, when John and Wita visited Israel during the construction of the air base at Ovda, they rode with Jane and Ted Randolph into the Negev Desert and visited an ancient stone marker placed by the Turks to indicate the boundary between Israel and Egypt. Their guide, Alfonso, is to the right.

John Harbert enjoyed dressing up, wearing costumes and the clothing of other nations. When he visited foreign countries, he often purchased native dress. Soon after he returned from Arabia in the 1970s, he went visiting as "the Sheikh."

lot of flak from various directions," he would "handle that for you." He told Hooper, "I would hope that the Israeli Air Force personnel or other occupants of the building will have a pleasant reminder of Harbert for years to come." With construction moving ahead, John confided that "I envy you for the opportunity that awaits."[29]

Although John would have preferred to don his khakis and boots and stay in Israel, it was April before he was back again, this time bringing Jay with him. John took a special interest in the small school that had been established in the construction community for the children of American and British supervisory personnel. Before the air-base project was completed, he created and funded a writing contest for the students at the school. He and Wita enjoyed an all-day trip into the desert under the guidance of the school's teacher, Alfonso Nussbaumer, and John wrote him from the United States to ask him to arrange such a field trip for all the students at the school. John would pay all the expenses.[30]

One reason that the air-base project needed fast-track construction was because of the fragile nature of the Israeli-Egyptian peace agreement, which could come unglued at any time. The general tensions in the Middle East, especially as a result of the Ayatollah Khomeini's overthrow of the shah of Iran, had intensified activities of Moslem fundamentalists. In late 1979 the Iranian revolutionaries seized the American Embassy in Tehran, and anti-American mobs attacked American diplomatic missions from Turkey to Bangladesh. In Saudi Arabia radicals seized the Sacred Mosque in Mecca. The Saudi government reacted by cutting all international telephone and telex communications until it could get a handle on whether the gunmen were representing a foreign organization. Harbert's representatives on the Saudi job "had a little argument" with the government for two days before they could get their lines reconnected.

At the time Harbert had construction projects in five Mideast countries and was working in Israel as well as in Arab countries. Because of the Negev project, the corporation was added to the Arab blacklist of companies doing business with Israel; however, the Harbert name was misspelled on the list and so it continued to operate in all areas of the Middle East. This fact made the 1979 crisis even more dangerous for Harbert personnel. When asked about the situation, John told a local newspaper reporter that "there is a great deal of terrorist activity and we don't say much about where we are working, what we are doing, and who is going where and when." He noted that Harbert prefers "to be quiet and go about our jobs in an efficient manner. ... We have no problems with our host countries; they have paid us and have been reasonable to work with."[31] But these problems highlighted how perilous political instability could be to contract work in a foreign country. John was well aware that working with both Israel and Arab nations simultaneously was more than risky.

Meanwhile, life at the air base at Ovda was tense because of the Middle East political climate and the ten-hour six-days-a-week schedule to complete the bases. For the Camp David peace agreement to be successful, the Israelis needed to pull out of their Sinai bases by May 1982, and the Ovda airfield had to be operational by April.[32] In the summer of 1981 tensions escalated between Israel and its neighbors. John was again concerned for the safety of his people, and he asked Bill to make inquiries at the State Department about U.S. plans should Syria or Iraq attack the air bases that were under construction in retaliation for "Israel's bombing last week." John was probably referring to the Israeli air raid and destruction of the Osirak nuclear reactor near Baghdad on June 7, 1981. Israel had reason to believe—and later was proved correct—that the Iraqis were using plutonium fuel rods to produce nuclear weapons. John wanted to know beforehand what the U.S. position would be so Harbert might make contingency plans for its people at Ovda.[33]

There was no hostile incident, and the air base was dedicated in an impressive ceremony in November 1981. Prime Minister Begin spoke, and American and Israeli military brass came in full dress uniforms. Even though construction continued on the support buildings, the base was activated. At about this time, Ellie Copeland, who was working for Harbert in the construction office at Ovda, wrote John that "from the camp area we can see the planes landing and taking off ... [and] the airfield lighting at night is beautiful."[34] She told him that some of the Thai laborers were beginning to leave. By spring, Harbert supervisory personnel were closing down or shifting to another Harbert Mideast project nearby.[35] John received a letter from the commanding general who was overseeing the Ovda project. Writing on the day when the bases were to be turned over to the Israeli military, he congratulated Harbert on creating this "air base miracle in the desert," a project many people said could not be done in time. Brigadier General John F. Wall wrote that "the bases are the best in the world," and he commended John "on the great team effort" that made them so.[36]

Before the Ovda project was completed, Harbert received another contract to construct two camps in the Sinai to house the multinational

When Jay visited Cairo with his father in the late 1980s, he had an opportunity to try out the local transportation—a camel.

peace-keeping troops that would be stationed in the Egyptian desert. Harbert signed the contract on August 21, 1981, and agreed to have the bases ready for occupancy when the troops were scheduled to arrive on March 24, 1982. The first camp was in the north and was a contract to renovate one of the old Israeli air bases. But the camp in the south was a new base—complete with barracks, offices, kitchen and dining hall, water, sewage, electricity, and a communications system that reached 350 miles to the northern peace-keeping camp. The campsite in the southern Sinai near the Gulf of Aqaba was so remote that food had to be flown in for the workers. John was even more interested and involved in this project, especially because Harbert had full responsibility for the job.[37]

Harbert's success in its Mideast projects led to a number of contracts for extensive and challenging jobs, especially in Egypt: a tallow, oils, and fats terminal in Alexandria; a grain storage and shipping facility on the Red Sea at Safaga; and an upgrading and extension of the sewage treatment plants, pumping stations, and pipelines in the cities of Ismalia, Suez, and Port Said. Some of this collection of jobs, worth $300 million, was sponsored by the U.S. Agency for International Development for the Arab Republic of Egypt.[38]

One of the "John Harbert stories," about which he was often teased, occurred at about this time in February 1978 and illustrates how quickly John and Wita could react and how totally unflappable they both were. They were returning from Europe and were staying over in New York City to meet Jack and Annis Bowen. Bowen, a fine watercolorist as well as John's friend and business associate on the Florida gas line project, had been invited to exhibit his work in the Cafe des Artistes gallery. John went along to help him, and the maitre d' served them drinks while they were hanging paintings. Then they had lunch at the Gloucester. Somewhere along the way something John ate or drank was to make him suddenly and violently ill.

After lunch the group called on the daughter of a deceased New York art dealer who was selling the remainder of her father's paintings from her apartment on Park Avenue. As Jack Bowen tells the story: "Just as Mr. Chappelier's daughter opened the door, I said `hello' and started to introduce the others. As I was about to introduce John, he removed his new felt hat, which he had just purchased in London, and immediately threw up in it. We were naturally all stunned, but Wita, the gracious southern lady she is, said, `We are so glad to meet you—may we use your bathroom?'"

Wita escorted John to the bathroom, and when they returned he was feeling better. John purchased two paintings, had them sent to Alabama, and the group left. One of these works was the 1895 Hermann Herzog *Pines in the Mountains* painting that the Harberts donated to the Birmingham Museum of Art in February 1978. As they were catching a cab to the hotel, John took his new fedora and plunged it deep into a snowbank.[39]

In May 1980, soon after communist China opened its doors, *Construction News*, a London-based magazine, sponsored a two-week trip to China for Western engineers and construction people interested in doing work in China. John and Wita went, along with the head of Harbert's London office, Roy Anderson, and his wife, Mae, who had been born in China. Mae was the daughter of prominent supporters of General Chiang Kai-shek, and as a child she had escaped with her parents to Taiwan, where she grew up. She spoke several dialects of Chinese, and although Mae was anxious to visit China, she was also apprehensive. Her presence enriched the experience for John and Wita because she was able to explain many things and translate John's constant questions and the answers he received.

The flight to Beijing from London's Heathrow

Airport took twenty-three hours.[40] John was especially interested in seeing China's coal fields and construction sites, and he hoped to make contacts that might lead to opportunities for Harbert work in China. John was impressed by Beijing's underground city, which served as an air raid shelter. After visiting the coal areas, John recognized that "China needs to develop its coal reserves. We can be a help to them in surface mining, if they will let us."[41] He invited the Chinese to visit his coal operations, and in July he escorted a Chinese delegation around the Kentucky mines and entertained them in Birmingham.[42]

Although John was hesitant about operating in a communist country and Harbert never entered the Chinese market, in 1981 Harbert did move into the Far East with an $18 million job in Bangkok, Thailand. There were jobs in Gabon, West Africa, in the Sudan, in Chile, and in the Congo. Harbert had contracts from the U.S. government for work in Bahrain, Thailand, Burma, and Korea, projects involving installation of stronger security in U.S. embassies.

Harbert's involvement in the Middle East was the reason that in the spring of 1980 John became involved in a campaign to convince the Alabama Education Television Commission not to carry a national showing of *The Death of a Princess*. This docudrama of the 1977 execution of a Saudi princess for defying Islamic law by eloping with a commoner, instead of marrying "the man her family had selected for her," had been financed by a Boston television station and the British Associated Television Corporation. The film had already aired in Britain. John was joined by

During John and Wita's trip to China in 1980, John visited a Chinese construction site. John was especially interested in the unusual construction hats worn on Chinese jobs. Although John had some initial interest in bidding on projects in China, he determined that the problems and risks would be too great.

officials of Blount Corporation in demanding the blackout in the state because they questioned the safety of American workers in Saudi Arabia, given the extreme opposition of the Saudi family to the portrayal of Saudi culture in the film. Harbert had a contract for the water system for Jidda, and Blount was in contention for the multi-billion-dollar contract to build a university in Riyadh.[43] Dozens of telephone calls from business and civic leaders were made to the Alabama Educational Television Network to protest the scheduled program, and on May 11 the network announced that it would not air the film. Seven days later Harbert took out a full-page advertisement in the Sunday *Birmingham News* justifying its position. The episode did not injure either Harbert or Blount operations in the Arab country. By the end of the year Blount was awarded a $2 billion contract to construct King Saud University in Riyadh.[44]

John Harbert was eager to enter the international construction market because he perceived that opportunities were there for profits. This was the bottom line. But he also plainly enjoyed the occasions to travel and learn about countries and cultures of the world, although he never was gone as much as his brother, who had responsibility for supervising Harbert's international operations. John recognized that Harbert's foreign involvement would effectively push it into a position in world trade. Harbert's international operations promoted jobs for Alabamians and poured money into the state's economy, not only through Harbert's work but also from companies from which Harbert purchased materials, supplies, and equipment. Idealistically, John believed that the bow-legged green and yellow "H" promoted to the world the best that the Unted States had to offer and also promoted peace. In his words, "Those who are involved in world trade seek every means at their command to induce, promote, and maintain peaceful existence between the nations of the world."[45]

10

CANOE CREEK AND PINEBLOOM

"rainbows on a light fly rod"

In 1968 John decided to sell the 420-acre Green Hill Farm in Talladega County that he had purchased from Oliver Hicks in 1951 for $16,800. The sale was complicated because John wished to negotiate a swap real estate deal in order to avoid the tax consequences of a straight sale. After lengthy and difficult negotiations, he sold the farm to Dr. Thomas O. Paul for $150,000 and was able to acquire property in Saint Clair County that belonged to Dr. Griff Harsh. This land, approximately 1,067 acres, was located on Canoe Creek, and John acquired it for $255,000, which included the sale price of Green Hill Farm. In the next fourteen years John purchased and swapped land with his neighbors, so that eventually the Canoe Creek farm was just under 2,000 acres.[1]

At Canoe Creek John raised cattle and hay and had a lake stocked with trout. On Saturday mornings he would drive up to the farm, sometimes taking the whole family, often just Margie or perhaps only Jay and Raymond with him. Margie remembers those times when she was alone with her father. He would let her steer the car, and on the trip he would cut, core, and share huge Red Delicious apples. Invariably, she recalled, her father would be stopped by a policeman who reminded him he was driving too fast. But her father was so polite that he usually talked the official out of giving him a ticket. Margie observed that her father "had the spirit of a young boy" and was fun to be around.[2]

He taught the children to fish, and after 1970 when Neville Palmer came from Jamaica to work for the family, he taught Neville to fish, too. Neville recalls that he went to the farm "at least once a week with Mr. Harbert, usually on Saturday." They would ride around, "checking all the property," and just before they left, Jack Ward, the farm manager, would "dip up some rainbow trout for them to take home and eat." Neville would smoke the fish for supper.[3] The farm was used for picnics, barbecues, and parties, and local garden clubs occasionally held spring meetings there. A visitor described the farm as a parklike showplace with fresh air, clean water, and well-manicured pastures in the shadow of Blount

Mountain.[4] Hall Thompson went trout fishing with John at Canoe Creek once and was impressed with the progress John was making with the farm. With its "abundance of spring water" and "fertile land and rugged mountains to protect it," Hall thought it was a "gorgeous piece of farm land."[5]

John and Wita enjoyed shooting quail and other wild game. Wita had shot with her father, and she and John went bird hunting at Canoe Creek. John entertained his clients at Canoe Creek with dove and quail shoots in season, but the location and number of birds were frequently not very dependable. So John experimented with raising birds to add to the wild ones. Billy Land, one of the most devoted bird shooters at Harbert, tells his favorite story about John and a shoot at Canoe Creek. There was a certain public official whom John wanted to impress and who loved to shoot birds; so John invited him to Canoe Creek. To make certain there were birds for him to shoot, John instructed his farm manager and his helper to put some farm-raised quail in several places. On the hunt the dogs eagerly went to work, but they could not seem to find any birds. Finally, John offhandedly said to the worker, "I wonder where all the birds are?" To which the man responded honestly: "I don't know, Mr. Harbert. I put them right there."[6]

The Harberts' friends came to Canoe Creek to enjoy the fishing, which was one of John's personal pleasures. Through the years he became an expert at tying flies and usually carried a fly rod and small tackle box in the trunk of his car. He was known to be speeding down a country road, see a likely creek or stream, and bring his car to a screeching halt. He would fish for a while, then get back in the car and press on at his usual fast pace.[7] In the early 1970s, John decided to try to raise rainbow trout and salmon in the cool waters of a large spring that spilled into Canoe Creek. He remembered how much he had enjoyed fly fishing for rainbow trout during World War II when he was stationed in Colorado; he and his cousin's husband would seek trout in the

In February 1969, Kirk Bailey and Margie and Raymond Harbert spent the day with John at the Canoe Creek farm in Springville.

John usually scheduled a quail hunting trip to Rolling Rock, Pennsylvania, each fall. In November 1976, John and Wita were joined by Mary Samford (next to John) and (in front) her husband, Yetta Samford, of Opelika, and Boots DeBardeleben. Wellie DeBardeleben, who was with her husband, probably took this photograph.

John and his three buddies—Charlie Arendall, Bobby Radcliff, and Jack Bowen—were ready for fishing at the Illiamna Fishing Lodge in Alaska in September 1978.

John and Wita took several trips to Alaska to fish. This photograph was taken in September 1978 when they visited the Iliamna Fishing Lodge.

cold clear streams pouring from the Rocky Mountains. John would have agreed with fellow Alabamian Howell Raines, who has said that "fly fishing is the most beautiful way to catch a fish."[8] John once observed that "rainbows on a light fly rod are not only terrific fighters, but delicious eating."[9] Local people told him that it was impossible to raise rainbows in Alabama—and that was just the challenge John needed to prove he could. Rainbows require clean, cool water with high oxygen, so John built a dam and created a pond from the spring water. He hired a biologist from Madison, Wisconsin, to come to Canoe Creek and advise him, and the scientist told him he could do it. John purchased some breeder trout and began to raise rainbows on the farm. They did well.

Unfortunately, John's program ran into trouble. The rainbows at Canoe Creek attracted intruders from Coach Bucky Waid's Springville High School football team. Four players slipped into the farm and "speared" some of John's breeder-size trout. The boys were caught, but instead of turning them over to the law, John put them to work in the hayfields to pay off the cost of the fish. But the real disaster came when heavy rains and floods broke the dam, releasing ten to twelve thousand rainbow trout to go swimming down Canoe Creek. Coach Waid remembers that for several days after the dam broke, he went fishing in the creek below the dam and caught fifty rainbows every day using yellow hominy on a simple hook and cane pole. John had told him what bait to use.[10]

In 1986, John explored the prospect of raising Australian crawfish at Canoe Creek and worked with the Auburn University

Department of Fisheries and Allied Aquacultures to locate a supply and to see if the crawfish could survive in Alabama and if raising them was economically feasible. Auburn researchers tried various techniques, but they found it difficult to keep the crawfish alive in the fifty-nine-degree water from John's spring. They thought they might mix the warmer surface waters of the lake with the spring water, but experiments proved it was not practical, and John dropped the idea.[11]

John loved to turkey hunt. In the spring of 1981, he shot this bird in Marengo County. He is standing behind Warwick, Bill Spencer's Marengo County home.

Besides Canoe Creek, John and Wita sometimes hunted in other places, especially with Tom and Mary Bradford at their Marengo County preserve, Turkey Trot. Tom and John were old friends and worked together on many Birmingham civic projects. He taught John to turkey hunt. Tom soon learned that in the woods "you could never walk ahead of John—he's in the lead." Within a few years turkey hunting was a passion of John's life, and Wita enjoyed it, too. John was good enough to hunt alone and do his own calling with the aid of a caller. He was never able to use his voice to call the turkeys.

One morning Tom and John had been hunting in different places, and John was late getting back. At about eleven o'clock, he finally returned, all scratched up. It seems that John found a large gobbler, shot him once, then twice. The turkey went into heavy brush, and John went in after him. He emptied all his shells into the bird, but it still would not die, so he threw his shotgun at the creature and finally killed him—an example of John's persistence.

On another hunt Tom and John rose before dawn to find a turkey they had located late the day before. They heard the bird gobble and quietly moved off the road, creating a blind of sorts, and sat down at 5:00 to wait. At 8:15, they killed the turkey. When Tom first told the story, a mutual friend commented, "No way John Harbert would sit still for three hours!" Tom insisted that John had developed the ability to sit quietly and wait to kill a turkey. Tom went fishing and duck hunting with John in Louisiana and recalls the astrology lesson John gave him one night when the sky was clear and the stars bright. John told him about that night in Germany during the war when his Boy Scout training saved his life by helping him find his way back to American lines.[12]

In the late 1960s John and Wita made their first trip to south Georgia to hunt birds. One of Wita's golfing friends in Highlands, Richard Tift, was a real estate executive from Albany, Georgia. He invited Wita and John to his plantation, The Oaks, during the fall hunting season. For many years Tift had been involved in putting together some of the hunting plantations in the area south of Albany, which is considered one of the best locations in the nation for birds and wildlife. Large hunting preserves cover much of Dougherty and Baker Counties, and although John was not in the market to purchase land at this time, he was keeping an eye open for just the right property. On one visit to south Georgia, Tift took the Harberts to see a 10,000-acre preserve then owned by the U.S. Steel Corporation. The plantation, called Pinebloom, was located north of Newton in Baker County and had giant oak trees dripping with Spanish moss, flat sandy fields, tall pine groves, picturesque sinkhole lakes, swamps, and a historic antebellum home. John immediately fell in love with the place and the land.[13]

In the following months John was able to negotiate an option to purchase the property if the U.S. Steel Corporation decided to sell it. At the time U.S. Steel management was under pressure because of a decline in profits, due partly to the national recession in the late 1970s. There was also a restless feeling among stockholders, and the steel corporation's executives were being criticized for their lavish hunting trips to Georgia. In 1980 the management of U.S. Steel decided to sell Pinebloom, and John finalized a contract. This sale was made initially to the Harbert Corporation; John later transferred ownership to the Pinebloom Corporation, which he and Wita jointly owned. Because of U.S. Steel's commitments for the hunting season, the Harberts agreed to take control of the property early in 1981.[14]

Pinebloom is located not far from the Flint River in a region of fertile soils, pine forests, and a good water supply. The area is attractive to a variety of wild game, especially turkey, quail, dove, ducks, and deer. Fish are abundant in the natural lakes. The region was once inhabited by prehistoric Indians. In the 1730s Native Americans of the Chiaha (or Chehaw) tribe of the Lower Creeks were living in the area. Evidences of these bygone cultures are found on Pinebloom today when newly plowed ground or soft sand after a heavy rain yields projectile points and Indian relics. The U.S. government acquired title to the land in the 1820s, and Baker County was organized in 1825 with Newton as the county seat. As the Indians were pushed westward, farmers settled the region. Two portions of the Pinebloom property, land lots 204 and 205, were drawn in the Georgia land lottery, and

In February 1977 John and Wita traveled to south Georgia to attend a picnic at Richard Tift's plantation in honor of Prince Faisel of Saudi Arabia.

these plots were eventually claimed and were being farmed by 1836 when Albany, located on the headwaters of the Flint River, was established.

One of the founders of the town, Hartwell Tarver, had extensive land holdings in south Georgia and acquired the area of Pinebloom, eighteen miles south of Albany. From "swamps, pine trees, and scrub oak thickets," he carved "a private empire" that remained in his family for three generations.[15] Tarver gave lots 204 and 205 and other contiguous lands to his daughter, Dorothy, as a wedding present when she married Alfred Holt Colquitt of Columbus, Georgia, in May 1848.[16] Tarver used his slaves to build his daughter a classic one-story Greek Revival house on lot 204. The house, with its hip roof and wide porches that wrap around the front, faces what came to be known as the Tarva Road.[17] Alfred Colquitt fought in the Mexican War, became a U.S. congressman, served in the Confederate army, and in 1876 was elected governor of Georgia, serving from January 1877 until November 1882. Afterward he was a Georgia U.S. senator for two terms. The Colquitt plantation has been referred to as Pinebloom at least since 1868 when the name appeared on the wedding invitations of Colquitt's daughter, Ann Lane. The plantation yielded Colquitt "a princely income," and there Colquitt offered "hospitality almost boundless."[18] The house itself is known as the Governor's Mansion.[19] It seems appropriate that John and Wita's plantation was once the home of a Bourbon, the name for postwar conservative southern politicians who supported a New South. Governor Colquitt was a "business-oriented Democrat who favored sectional reconciliation, industrialization, low taxes, and frugal government." He reorganized Georgia's fiscal affairs, reduced government, and lowered the state's expenditures. John would have approved of Colquitt's politics.[20]

Following Alfred Colquitt's death in 1894, the house and farm fell into disrepair, and tenants and sharecroppers lived there; however, much of the property remained in the family's hands until 1923, when Colquitt's grandson deeded the land to a developer. The Pinebloom property went though several owners, and in 1938 the house was restored by Winthrop Bancroft of Boston and more acreage was added to encourage wild game. The property was developed as a hunting preserve. In 1946 Kentucky horse breeder Hal Price acquired the farm and made improvements. He designed a system of roads through the property and named them for New York City streets, and he designated certain sites on the plantation by Manhattan placenames. In 1964 Rockwell International acquired title to Pinebloom, holding it for a decade before deeding the plantation to the U.S. Steel Corporation in 1974.[21]

When John and Wita Harbert came to Pinebloom in 1981, it was a working farm, producing corn, grains, pecans, soybeans, and peanuts. It was a site for agricultural research on fungicides and fertilizers and for experiments with products produced by the Agri-Chemicals Division of U.S. Steel. However, its main function was to serve as a hunting preserve and vacation place for U.S. Steel executives and their clients, family, and friends. The Harberts intended to continue operating the farm and to strengthen the hunting operations. Despite the large white-tailed deer population, they decided not to allow open deer hunting on Pinebloom, although the Pinebloom staff have annual drives to control the deer population so the deer will not eat all the quail food.

John's appreciation for history made him especially proud of the antebellum Colquitt home, which he wanted to restore. There were several other small bungalows on the property and a farm office. On Long Pond there was a large guest lodge, which was called the Swamp House. Pinebloom came with a collection of dog pens and runs, bird dogs,

During a February house party in the 1980s, guests gathered around an open fire at Pinebloom. From the left, John McKinley, Eugenie and Joe Nickerson, Helen McKinley, Gene Torbert, Wita, and Bo Torbert. One friend reminisced that he ran into John in a hotel in New York City one Thursday and John stopped him to say: "I'm going to Pinebloom tomorrow. Can you meet me there for the weekend?"

horses, mules, barns, tractors, and its own well-lighted airstrip, 5,700 feet long, where corporate jets could land and drop off hunters and their gear.

John hired a farm manager and brought in Larry Moon from Virginia to direct quail shoots and train the dogs. Moon was experienced in running hunting operations and in game management. He was a "top trainer, handler, and judge" who had won major victories and was well known in eastern circles for his field trial champions. Moon at first declined John's offer and refused even to look at the property. But John was persistent, tracking Moon down at an Illinois field trial and eventually convincing him to come for a visit. Seeing Pinebloom was all Moon needed to convince him to accept John's offer.[22]

Two thousand acres of Pinebloom's fields were irrigated, and John, who loved farming and "raising things and driving a tractor," worked the land for a while; however, financially it was always a "losing proposition." At one point John determined to raise watermelons, and although everyone tried to talk him out of it, he insisted on clearing land for the melons. His sister-in-law, Acky, recalls that John once took her out and showed her "this beautiful piece of land where all the watermelons would grow." John had the entire operation worked out in his head. He planned to hire Mexicans to come in and pick the melons. When Larry Moon was finally able to convince him to run the figures on the watermelons, John determined he would have a hard time breaking even in good weather and with bad weather he could lose $700,000. Once during this time the family was giving thanks around the table at Pinebloom. At his turn, son Raymond prayed: "And God bless the watermelons, and God bless the Mexicans." John eventually gave up on his watermelons—one of the few times in his life that he ever gave up on anything. He eventually wrote off his watermelon adventure at $100,000 for clearing and preparing the land for cultivation, and he leased the acreage to a local farmer. The watermelons became a story the family enjoyed telling, at John's expense, but he never minded—he invariably took teasing well.[23]

In June 1993 John wrote President Bill

Muse of Auburn to inquire about how small farmers had benefited from all the agricultural research the university had done over its history. In a tone depressing for John, he wrote:

> I am aware of the substantial progress made since World War II in improving fertilizers, developing hybrid, disease-resistant seeds, and eradicating the screw worm and boll weevil. Nevertheless, the average individual farmer cannot make any money, or at least not commensurate with the investment of time, sweat, knowledge, and finances. If any profit is made, it apparently goes to a "middleman," unless a farmer is part of a huge conglomerate. I don't think farmers should be subsidized, nor do I believe that they should have to purchase goods and equipment from industries that have been subsidized, such as manufactured steel equipment.

Calling himself a "part-time farmer," John said that he had "stopped planting crops on non-irrigated land. On all dry land, or land without irrigation, I am planting longleaf or slash pine." And he asked, "What are the best crops for irrigated land in Alabama and Georgia?" He confessed to Dr. Muse that answering these questions did not "fall under the category of a university president's duties," but he asked Muse to refer his questions to a person who could answer them.[24] Muse responded with a long letter drafted by a committee of agricultural researchers that surveyed the extent and impact of agricultural research in Alabama; however, the letter probably did not address John's immediate problems.[25] Eventually, John abandoned farming altogether and leased more than 2,400 acres of Pinebloom land to a large farmer. The lease arrangement has proved profitable without costly management and investments.

John took special pride in the Governor's Mansion. He enjoyed history (when he was in the army in World War II he had requested that his mother send his history books). Throughout his life, he read history and biography, and he was fascinated with the history of the American South. He wanted the antebellum Greek cottage restored properly but with the conveniences of modern life, such as heating and air conditioning. He had been pleased with what Robert Hiden had designed and acquired for his office, so he asked Wita to see if Hiden would take on the project and turned over the decorations to her. Hiden spent several weeks at Pinebloom, measuring every inch of the Colquitt house, taking inventory of items that could be used, observing how light came through certain windows, and making sketches and copious notes of his ideas.

Going into this project Hiden felt John did not appreciate style. While that may have been true in 1951 and even in 1961, by the 1980s John was very interested in art, antiques, silver, and sculpture, and he was knowledgeable about all of them. The decorator's plan for the Governor's Mansion came mostly from the Georgian (1760-1811) and Regency (1811-20) periods, more elegant styles than the heavy Victorian designs that predominated in the mid-nineteenth century in the South. Wita and John were pleased with Hiden's work and the overall restoration of the house.

Although Wita was in charge of working directly with Hiden and making all final decisions, John took more interest in the decoration of the Governor's Mansion than he had in any other such project. He and Wita made trips to England to give final approval on furniture and artwork. On one occasion, John, Wita, and Hiden were touring an art gallery to look at some paintings; when they left, with John strongly in the lead, Hiden turned to Wita and whispered, "I have never *run* through an art gallery before!"[26] John was

The classic one-story Greek Revival house built by Hartwell Tarver for his daughter when she married Alfred Holt Colquitt in 1848 has been called the Governor's Mansion since Colquitt was elected governor of Georgia in 1877.

especially proud of the hand-blocked Hindustani scenic wallpaper (ca. 1807) that Wita picked out for the foyer. For the floor, Hiden designed and had made a hand-loomed Portuguese rug that repeats some of the eighty-five colors of the wallpaper. In the rug's center is a medallion rendering of the Governor's Mansion.[27] After collecting items in Europe, Hiden spent months living at Pinebloom overseeing painting and installation of wallpaper and drapes and putting the final decorative touches on the Governor's Mansion.[28] Wita had the drapery and some upholstery work done in Birmingham, and she would often fly over for the day to deliver pieces and check on the progress of the decorations. The result is one of south Georgia's finest treasures.

The Pinebloom staff members were always notified of John and Wita's arrival time, and they would appear at the runway when the plane taxied to a stop. John would greet each one by name, stopping to ask a question about something at the plantation or to make a personal inquiry, perhaps asking about a family member who he knew had been sick.[29] John and Wita nearly always flew to Pinebloom and while there drove one of the farm vehicles. John invariably selected one of the old trucks. Knowing what a fast driver he was, staff members were very careful when "Mr. Harbert" was in residence to drive slowly and stay far to the right side of the dirt roads that crisscrossed the plantation.[30] Wendell Hines, who had worked at Pinebloom for years before the Harberts came to own the property, observed that "Mr.

The Harbert machine shop restored this fire truck to its original glory, and John placed the truck at Pinebloom. John enjoyed passing out helmets and driving his guests around the plantation with the siren on.

Harbert was a man who would not beat around the bush. He could do everything in a minute."[31]

John was always inviting people to Pinebloom, sometimes on short notice. Wita frequently was hostess to total strangers, a duty she performed with grace even when she felt put upon. John once invited a couple from a distant state, giving Wita their names and remarking that he was an elderly man in his mid-eighties. Wita's southern upbringing required that she call the man's wife, invite her personally, and answer any questions she might have, especially about appropriate clothing. Because her husband was elderly, Wita was reluctant to address the woman by her first name since she had never met her, but she did. Wita called and asked for "Joan" and identified herself and the reason for her call. When the answering voice responded, "Glad you got me. I've just come in from my five-mile run," Wita knew she was not speaking with the first wife.[32]

The Governor's Mansion has a staff to care for it and a housekeeper to direct and supervise when the Harberts are away and when they are in residence. The first housekeeper was Dottie Huff, and then Deanna Paisley took over responsibility for making sure the Governor's Mansion is kept in good order, also supervising the care of guest rooms at the Swamp House and providing meals for the Harberts and their guests. She works closely with Wita, collecting recipes and planning menus. She soon learned that "Mr. Harbert liked plain foods" and disliked casseroles. He hated leftovers and would not eat dried beans. Fresh foods pleased him most. Mrs. Paisley maintained for Wita a complete computer list of all visitors to Pinebloom. She could determine when a particular guest came, what foods were served, and what Wita had used on his or her place card.[33]

Wita was known for her witty comments on place cards, all written in verse, and she never used names. One would have to read them all to discover one's place. A few of her favorites are

This very chic lady,
An Annie Oakley no doubt,
We know the sweethearts are flocking
And we want to find out.

Just let him whisper in your ear.
Then go invest & never fear.
And if by chance you deal the cards,
Be sure that you and he are pards.

A yankee lady now our own.
She loves her grits, greens & corn pone.

From Tennessee he came our way
A Banker of renown they say.
The ladies like him—there's a reason.
He's the one that always is in season.

A philanthropist—all know his name
Fund raisers—Boards—they are his game,
He also fishes—shoots—he's regal
High in his booth—A true War Eagle.[34]

Visitors usually arrived at three o'clock on Thursday afternoons, and Wita often knew nothing about her guests. She would visit with them at the Swamp House and later over drinks at the Governor's Mansion. Then she would excuse herself and go to the kitchen to write the place cards for dinner.

Gentlemen always wore coats for dinner at the Governor's Mansion, and John enjoyed wearing his yellow linen or plaid jackets. The food was served by Will Rudolph, the butler. John presided at the dinner table and began each meal with his special "Prayer for Pinebloom," giving "thanks and praise for the glories of nature, the beauty of water, field, and sky," asking God's blessings upon "this fair place and all who come to it seeking companionship with one another and communion with Thee."

Will is a special fixture of Pinebloom, where by 1997 he had worked for three decades. A master at barbecuing and grilling steaks and chicken, he is especially renowned for his secret basting sauce. Will is fondly remembered by guests, so much so that the portrait artist Everett Raymond Kinstler, who painted John's portrait at Pinebloom in hunting clothes in 1987, also painted a double portrait of Will that now hangs in the bar in the Governor's Mansion.[35]

On Thanksgiving morning all the Harbert children join in the hunt. Margie, holding Marguerite, with cousin Reynolds Herlong, Wita holding John, Mary Kathryn standing, with Raymond, Jr., riding shotgun with J. L. Jackson.

John enjoyed the Pinebloom lakes, prime fishing sites made even finer after John invited the Auburn University Department of Fisheries and Allied Aquacultures to do research on the lakes, especially on Long Pond, Liar's Lake, and Chance Pond. Researchers made recommendations about surface weed control, stocking, and fertilization and feeding programs. Professors Wayne Shell and William Davies had never had an opportunity to study such an unusual lake as Long Pond, a 280-acre limestone sinkhole lake, rather shallow and with a unique style of fish biology and food base. They began regular visits to Long Pond, keeping records of water levels, the density of fish population, and fertilization programs. They stocked the lake with fat-head minnows and tried, unsuccessfully, to introduce grass shrimp as another food source for the wide variety of fish in the lake. The condition of Long Pond remained a concern of John's, and despite some problems with water levels and surface grasses, the fish population thrived. In February 1994 John reported that "everything is in good shape" and "Long Pond maintains its reputation." He had "caught 46 pounds of bass" one weekend, and seventy-five pounds the next weekend, when he and Wita were fishing with friends in two boats for two hours.[36]

Will Rudolph helps Bubbles Brungart and Bamie Williams in May 1985 with their morning catch from Long Pond.

John never tired of having company at the plantation and never worried about the weather. He once wrote his good friend Jack Bowen in Houston that "Pinebloom is a wonderful place to be even in bad weather."[37] Bowen recalled that John "loved to drive his guests all over the place and show them where he was reclaiming the land, planting crops and trees, raising and training dogs, catching bobcats and cultivating a bumper crop of quail."[38] John had a Jeep Cherokee on the plantation that had a horn that played dozens of tunes—from college fight songs to lullabies—and he would fill it with children and ride around pushing the buttons on the horn.

John loved to make excursions at night at breakneck speed to catch deer and other animals in the car headlights. He particularly disliked raccoons because they would eat the quail eggs. Once he, Wita, Margie, and Margie's husband, Sam, went looking for raccoons. Wita was sitting in the car with her fur coat over her nightgown, and Margie was holding the light, while Sam and John argued over the gun and who was going to shoot next. At the end of the evening, they had an ice chest full of raccoons that they gave to Will.[39]

John wanted his guests to enjoy themselves and never be idle, and he kept up a hectic pace. One evening at Pinebloom when John was taking numbers for the early morning hunt scheduled for the next day, he asked: "How many of you want to ride in the wagon? How many of you want to ride horses?" And Wita piped in with "and how many of you want to stay home and sleep?" Wita usually ran one wagon and John the other and often neither of them shot.

John enjoyed taking his guests on tours of Pinebloom. Jack Biddle, who was in the Alabama legislature and knew John in Birmingham and also worked closely with a Georgia plantation six miles from Pinebloom, recalled that "when John was on that farm, he was not a corporate executive, he was just John."[40] Because John loved the land so much himself, he understood why a former president of U.S. Steel, Ed Spears, had requested that he be buried at Pinebloom. Deep in Pinebloom's woods is a small white picket fence that marks Ed Spears's grave.[41]

Neville Palmer enjoys fishing at Long Pond. He recalled that once when he returned to Jamaica, "Mr. Harbert bought me a new suit, drove me to the airport, and insisted on carrying my bag to the check-in counter."

In January 1993, soon after Bill Muse became president of Auburn University, he and his wife, Marlene, visited Pinebloom. They recalled the stimulating dinner table conversation about "politics, literature, history, and interesting people." After the other guests left, John took the Auburn president on a trip around Pinebloom in his truck, showing Muse his "prize-winning bird dogs" and his forest land and ponds, and detailing how Auburn faculty and staff had provided him with advice and assistance for his farm's operation.[42]

There are two visitors the Pinebloom staff remember most. One is Jane Fonda, who came with her husband when Pinebloom hosted the Georgia-Florida Field Trial Club in 1994. The other visitor is Bonnie Swearingen, the blonde, vivacious, and totally unpredictable

Wita, John, and Tasca admire one of Pinebloom's finest turkeys.

The Georgia-Florida Field Trial Club was hosted at Pinebloom on February 20, 1994. Wendell Hines had the Pinebloom dogs ready to hunt, and Rollie Etchells and Cole Turner had the Pinebloom woods prepared for a good day's hunting. Hundreds of people, dogs, horses, cars, trucks, and horse trailers came to Pinebloom for the day.

On May 16, 1987, Wita and John were hosts to the Albany Junior League's Plantation Party fund raiser. Quilts with baskets of food and flowers were scattered across the lawn.

wife of Amoco president John Swearingen. When the Swearingens arrived for a long weekend, Bonnie came not with suitcases but with trunks. To one dinner she wore "a Scarlett O'Hara dress" with a hoop skirt.[43] Staff members also recall the Albany Junior League charity picnic that Wita and John hosted at Pinebloom. For this event blankets were spread over the grounds under the huge oak trees and food was packed in lovely baskets. Horse-drawn carriage rides were offered to tour the plantation.[44]

John insisted upon strong safety rules for hunts at Pinebloom, and visitors were provided a flyer that listed guidelines and safety precautions. Shooters were warned to unload their guns before placing them in a saddle scabbard or on the hunting wagon, and they were reminded that they were to aim only at birds flying in front of them or to their side. Each guide was "to perceive unsafe situations and rectify them."[45] Sometimes this meant unusual action. John once invited two elderly Atlanta men to come to Pinebloom for a weekend of hunting. Although they were a bit shaky on their feet, slow of movement, and had never been in the field or on a quail shoot before, they were eager to participate. When the dogs pointed, John got out of the wagon to help one guest with his shotgun. Wita walked over to Larry Moon and whispered, "Larry, where do you think the birds are?" The plantation manager responded: "Mrs. Harbert, forget about the birds. If that man lifts his gun to his shoulder, we are both hitting the ground."[46]

Occasionally a new visitor ignored the safety rules. Once a hunter from Texas forgot to unload his gun as he started to board the wagon. Wita reminded him to unload his gun, and the man stopped, took his shotgun, and fired two shots into the ground six inches from the foot of Pinebloom guide Rolly Etchells. One time there was surprise and embarrassment when a gentleman hunter aimed and fired his shotgun and his pants dropped to the ground.

J. L. Jackson, a longtime Pinebloom employee, drives the hunting wagons, takes care of the mules, and works with the retrievers. He makes certain that his riders are comfortable and return uninjured. Once Jackson noticed that a man who was riding with him was intoxicated. After the man left the wagon to shoot, Jackson was able to get John's attention, telling him, "Mr. Harbert, that man is drunk." As soon as John was able to reclaim the gun and secure it, J. L. made sure that the man never got to touch it again. At lunch at the Skeet House, Will Rudolph served him martinis until he asked to be taken back to the Swamp House for a nap.[47] Jackson is responsible for the retrievers, including John's favorite dog, Tasca, a yellow Labrador retriever who was born and trained in England. Tasca went everywhere with John while he was at Pinebloom, and he often took him home to Birmingham or Wita carried him with her to Highlands in the summer. Tasca stayed inside as much as he did outside. John once remarked that he always appreciated the fact that Wita never minded him having his dogs in the house.[48]

When he was working on a business deal, John invited the men involved to Pinebloom. Many of his most significant agreements were either partially negotiated at Pinebloom or the parties to the arrangement had previously enjoyed Wita and John's hospitality at the south Georgia plantation. Once when John had a coal deal going, he invited the prospect to Pinebloom for a hunt. In the woods the dog pointed, the birds flew, shots rang out, and a bird fell. John was so excited he immediately congratulated the man, "Good shot!" But the gentleman had never fired his gun. It was Wita's bird.[49]

Although people have been killed in south Georgia while on organized hunts, at Pinebloom there has been no accident from a gun, although there have been close calls when people were excited as birds flew and shot over the wagon. But horses are a different story. John fractured his back when a horse reared as he was remounting after retrieving his hat, and a horse once fell on Jay, causing Jay and Wita to have a wild ride in the back of an ambulance to an Albany hospital. Luckily, Jay was not seriously injured.

Pinebloom was the place John loved most

and where he was happiest. He loved to drive around the farm with the staff to see what improvements had been made since he last visited and, when he was farming, to check on how the crops were doing. Wita called it "his domain," but Pinebloom was also special to Wita, providing a certain calmness in her busy life and a place where she had John's attention and more of his time. In May 1983 she wrote in her journal: "I walked alone down to the Swamp House and sat at the dock in the boat for a while. The night noises were wonderful—mystical—and the night was lovely—soft and overcast. I walked back to the main house and to bed." The next day Wita wrote that she rode out with John to see the property: "I saw the new corn coming up. Also the soy beans, peanuts, and rape seed—beautiful planting."[50]

Each May, Wita and John would come to Pinebloom for their last visit before fall unless John needed to return on business. Neither could stand the hot south Georgia summer weather. They would usually fish Long Pond after breakfast, and when they saw the Harbert plane dip over the lake and fly toward the landing field, they would head for the Governor's Mansion. On May 2, 1983, Wita packed, took the dogs, Rob Roy and Tobo, for a long walk early in the morning, fished with John at Long Pond, then flew home, not planning to return to Pinebloom "before fall—it is getting so hot."[51]

Jack Bowen believed that "John was at his best at dinner, with fires roaring at the Governor's Mansion and Will supplying the drinks." He reminisced that "at the dinner table, John was as good as any country preacher with a blessing, and after dinner, there was always some good port and more discussions about the heritage of Pinebloom and the day's hunting. He was never happier than when he was at Pinebloom."[52] In 1986 John wrote to a friend in England inviting him to the plantation: "Pinebloom is like going into another era of the past, when life was simple, yet elegant."[53] His family and friends agree that regardless of where he was, a part of John's heart was always at Pinebloom.

John with his dogs at Pinebloom's Skeet House following a good morning hunt. He often told people how much he appreciated Wita, who loved dogs as much as he did, letting him bring his dogs into the house. When hunting season was over, John brought Tasca home with him to Birmingham. After John's death, Tasca fell ill. Wita sent him to Pinebloom, hoping he would recover, but three months after John died, Tasca died also. Pinebloom manager Larry Moon feels that Tasca died from a broken heart.

11

THE GALLERIA AND AMSOUTH/HARBERT PLAZA

"I do care about Birmingham"

The decade of the 1980s would see perhaps John Harbert's most significant civic leadership and his most meaningful philanthropic contributions to his hometown, as well as important business decisions he made that would have long-range positive impact upon the city and the metropolitan area of Birmingham. Continued development of Riverchase and the construction of the Galleria shopping mall, the completion of the thirty-two-story AmSouth/Harbert Plaza in the downtown business district, the donation of a major classroom building to Birmingham-Southern College, and a leadership role in the creation of the Harbert Center on Fourth Avenue highlighted these years. In writing to an old friend about the Harbert Center, John reiterated his commitment to the city: "I do care about Birmingham."[1] On the eve of the opening of the AmSouth/Harbert Plaza, John addressed the Redstone Club and traced the history of the project, saying that "going through the ups and downs, problems and solutions of AmSouth/Harbert Plaza has been difficult for me, yet exciting and challenging. I would have walked away and turned my attention to something else had it been in any city other than Birmingham."[2]

The 1980s were years of great change for John and Wita and their children. The children were off at school, and the family expanded with marriages and the birth of grandchildren and decreased with the loss of John's mother, Mae, in 1986 and Wita's mother, Marguerite Jones, in 1987. Jay went to school in Florida and Massachusetts and returned to work with Harbert Equipment, a division of Harbert Corporation. Raymond attended Auburn University, where he met and, after his graduation in 1982, married Kathryn Dunn, a dark-haired beauty from Greenville, South Carolina, whom he first met on a blind date. A political science major still remembered by her professors for her solid academic performance, Kathryn enjoyed fishing with Raymond during their courtship. In the 1980s Raymond and Kathryn became the parents of three children. Raymond, Jr., was born in 1984 and in the next few years was followed by Mary Kathryn and John M. Harbert II.[3]

John Harbert with his family—his mother, Mae, seated with Margie and Jay, John with Wita and Raymond.

Wita and Acky honored their mother, Marguerite Jones, nicknamed "Benny," with a party on her eighty-fifth birthday. Surrounded by her grandchildren, seated, left to right: Margie Harbert (Gray), Meg McGriff (North), Benny, Addie McGriff (Walters), Jane McGriff (Herlong). In the rear, Raymond Harbert, Lee McGriff, and Jay Harbert.

Raymond joined Harbert Corporation following his graduation from Auburn University.

Margie attended the University of the South at Sewanee, Tennessee. Midway through her college years, she received her first car, but only because her father was concerned about the mechanical condition of the automobiles and some of the drivers with whom she was catching rides going to and from Sewanee. In February 1982, Margie was crowned queen of the Krewe at the Beaux Arts Ball, and in 1983 she graduated from Sewanee with a major in art history. Following graduation she went to work at AmSouth Bank and later was an assistant curator with the Birmingham Museum of Art. In 1987 she married Sam Gray, an obstetrician who grew up in Athens, Alabama. Margie and Sam's three children, Sam, Marguerite, and Caroline, made six grandchildren for "Paw Paw" and "Nanny," which is what the children called John and Wita.

John took special delight in the grandchildren, always making sure he had some little surprise for them in his pocket when he dropped by to visit with them. Often it was a small sack of jelly beans. When the grandchildren came to his office at Harbert, he would find something in his desk to give them, and when they visited Wita and him at home, John would go up to his office where he stored his "treasures" to find a toy or trinket they would like. When she was a child,

In February 1982 Margie Harbert (Gray) was crowned queen of the Krewe at the Beaux Arts Ball, shown here with her king, Gene Moore, and her attendants.

In 1982 Raymond Harbert married Kathryn Dunn in her hometown of Greenville, South Carolina. They met as students at Auburn.

John and Wita were the proud parents at daughter Margie's marriage to Dr. Samuel Gray at Saint Mary's Episcopal Church in 1987.

Margie remembered, her father had called this his "store," and she had wondered when and where he accumulated the goodies that magically appeared. Her father had, Margie noted, "an understanding of the simple things that make children happy."[4]

John and Wita acquired Pinebloom Plantation in the 1980s, and family Thanksgivings in south Georgia became a tradition. Wita planned special decorations and holiday foods. The grandchildren would ride in the wagons or on horses, or they would fish, and the adults would shoot birds and enjoy the brisk fall weather. As the decade progressed, John and Wita began spending more time in Georgia and more time traveling.

When the 1980s opened, the Harbert Construction Corporation was overextended and in a cash flow bind as it had been so often in its history. International jobs were profitable, but domestic construction struggled to stay out of the red. What has sometimes been called "the Carter recession" was causing havoc in the American economy, and many small residential contractors and businesses were selling out or closing their doors. However, the sale of the coal mines in 1981 made the Harbert company flush, and there were some who suggested John should just retire. Harbert had sold its coal mines, limestone quarrying, and barging businesses. For almost a decade these operations had produced almost 65 percent of Harbert's total revenues and 75 percent of its profits. But John enjoyed the challenge of business and decided to stay on and find a new course for the company. Harbert looked for opportunities in areas that would complement the company's "knowledge and experience" and would "stabilize cash flow and lower [Harbert's] overall risk profile."[5]

In 1982 Harbert moved into oil and gas by forming Harbert Energy Corporation and purchasing two companies to begin drilling wells both offshore and onshore. Oil exploration is risky and requires large amounts of investment capital and depends upon future—sometimes long-term—returns for profits. Harbert Cogen was organized in 1986 to invest in independent power production on the cutting edge of energy technology. But this operation, too, required enormous capital before profits could flow back into the company.

Harbert Properties Corporation was formed in 1983 to direct investments in real estate development and management. Carefully selected properties were acquired from the eastern seaboard across the South to Texas. John believed this was a relatively easy area to move into and that Harbert's experience in construction would make it a logical step. Domestic and international construction branched from civil and pipe-laying jobs to commercial and industrial construction.

The Harbert Construction Corporation that began the decade in 1980 was very different from the holding corporation that existed at the end of those ten years. There was a changing of the guard, and the company was transformed in many ways. In January 1985, Ted Randolph was the first of the old management team to retire, and when he left, Harbert lost what many people recognized as a true technical genius. He had the knowledge, the experience, and the creativity to solve the most complex problems and to extricate the company from technical difficulties. John had depended on Ted to decipher the new water purification system and its automatic controls at Fort Payne, to design the underpinning for the Highland Avenue apartment buildings in the Red Mountain interstate construction, and to solve the problems at Ovda in Israel and dozens more. A mentor to many of the younger engineers at Harbert, "Ted could," according to John, "always figure out a solution and get on with the program."[6]

Bill Rossman retired four months later, and Harbert Corporation lost its financial genius, the man whose fiscal judgments John trusted most and the one who had pulled rabbits out of hats during hard times and monetary crises. "His word," John once said, was "gold," and John called him a man with the ability "to spot a problem on a project or development long before the engineers or superintendents have any idea they are in trouble."[7] Although he led Harbert into the computer age with instant printouts, job-specific figures, and management information, according to Rossman's long-time secretary, Van Hoover, he also "kept the books by hand and his eye on everything."[8] With Rossman's departure no one knew or understood the bottom line so well, and no one had the clout to communicate what they did know to John with the same frankness and credibility that Rossman's long years of friendship allowed him to do.

In November 1986, Ed Dixon retired. For more than forty years he had been John's close friend and detail man, the one who made sure the paperwork was right and the company was protected. This quiet and gentle man made hard-nosed personnel decisions when needed for the good of Harbert. Meticulous and careful, the marine engineer had spent his life's work far from the sea and ended his career at Harbert in charge of the corporation's stock investments. At his retirement dinner John expressed his gratitude to Ed and said how much he "depended on his level-headedness and his unwavering support."[9]

The corporation had no understudies ready to succeed these men, and none, even if ready, could replace the confidence John had in them. John's brother, Bill, was made president of Harbert and became the chief operating officer, and John continued as chairman of the board. Two months before the sale of the coal mines, John celebrated his sixtieth birthday. Bill was only two years younger, and Raymond was still in college. Ever the optimist with his vision on the future, John realized, however, that the time would come when he would have to make some decisions about the future of his company. Bill's main interest continued to be on international jobs, while Billy Land focused on civil and domestic construction.

Time was needed to develop younger people and to test the leadership ability of others. There were Harbert employees in management positions who had been with the company for some time and who shouldered responsibilities that often shifted during this decade of transition. As Harbert Corporation moved into new and cutting-edge areas, many in brand-new territory, and as new companies were purchased, new people were brought on board. But they came from different corporate backgrounds and different experiences, and they could not appreciate the rich heritage of Harbert. Besides John, Bill, Don Cook, Van Hoover, and Walter Rowe, few of the old-timers were left. Not only was Harbert losing its longtime people, but there was a sense that it was also losing its identity, its sense of company tradition.

By 1987, much of the esprit de corps of the old Harbert Construction Company, Inc. had vanished in diversification and the transformation into the holding company. To help restore and strengthen the old feeling of family and to give new employees a sense of the past, the company newsletter was given a fresh look and a new name, *On Site*. It began to include a regular column called "Legends," in which various chapters of Harbert's history were highlighted. In 1988 John commissioned Charlotte Gafford to write a history of the Harbert Construction Corporation. John worked with her through several drafts of the early chapters, rewriting some material in pencil on yellow legal pads and making comments or corrections in the margins of his copy of her manuscript.

In 1989, *On Site* began the year with a special fortieth anniversary issue highlighting the activities of the company through four decades. John understood the importance of history, once telling Birmingham historian Hill Ferguson that "a good knowledge of history"

John not only took a leadership role in the development of Riverchase but also pushed the construction of the Galleria shopping mall.

helps one "appreciate the present."[10] He no doubt believed that narrating the remarkable story of Harbert Construction Corporation would give everyone a shared memory. For several reasons, but probably because he clearly recognized that changes were inevitably coming to the corporation, he never pushed the project to completion. John was never afraid of change, for his eyes were always focused on the future.

In 1981, at the same time that the secret negotiations for the sale of the Kentucky mines to Standard Oil were proceeding, John was meditating on another challenge. He had been invited to deliver an address before the Newcomen Society in North America, an organization established to promote the study of business history. His speech would be published as part of the Newcomen Society addresses on company histories. John appreciated the importance of the occasion. He began in late spring writing drafts on a yellow legal pad that his secretary, Sandi Falkenhagen, typed and retyped as he edited and rewrote, and Wita read and made suggestions. For months he worked and solicited critiques from several people he trusted. He sent a draft to Charlotte Gafford, who had edited some of John's previous speeches. She was then teaching English at a college in Vermont. Gafford responded that she had "*many* suggestions," that in his draft he was far too modest and "humorously understated" about his own accomplishments. He had neglected to speak about his striving, always, for the very best. This goal was, she wrote, "the major asset of this country. You, my dear John, are an aristocrat in rumpled khakis. Nothing is more American. And nothing is better business."[11]

John responded to her letter with appreciation for her honest assessment despite Gafford's "severe criticism," but he insisted that "I do not want to be boastful and bombastic, but I do want to express the pride I have in this company and in the people who have made it great. We have done things that amaze even me. I look back and wonder how in the hell we made it over this or that hurdle. Maybe this is a story that should be told after I'm out of the picture." He assured Gafford that he was continuing to work on the speech. He intended to practice on his delivery, and he planned "to video-tape it to concentrate on gestures, voice projection, and enunciation."[12] The commitment to perfection that John gave to this address was typical of his efforts in both his personal and his business life.

On the evening of October 7, 1981, only weeks after John had sealed his deal with Standard Oil (a transaction that made headlines in newspapers and business journals across the country), Hall Thompson introduced John to a gathering of the Newcomen Society in Birmingham. His friend presented him as "farmer, fish breeder, sportsman, art collector, linguist, world traveler, horticulturist, philanthropist, and humanitarian," as well as successful businessman and builder. The pressure was on, and John performed well. When he reached the place in his speech where he said that Harbert had been "flat broke and owed millions" but that fortunately his creditors and bankers "were never completely aware of the seriousness of our condition," his friend, Hall, who had sold Harbert much of its heavy equipment during this time period, tugged John's coattail. In a loud stage whisper, he said, "John, we knew it," and chuckles rippled across the room.[13] In the end John was pleased with his address, *Harbert: A Story of Continuous Beginnings*, and he was duly complimented by his audience.

Despite the excitement of the Newcomen evening, John and Wita really had their minds elsewhere. About ten days before the dinner, John had received a letter from a friend in London, the noted Italian sculptor Enzo Plazzotta. He wrote John: "First things first: I'm slowly dying with cancer of the pancreas, so this may very well be my last letter to you." Plazzotta wanted John to know that he would not be able to continue one of their projects—a sculpture of Leonardo da Vinci's famous drawing, *The Vitruvian Man*. The first-century Roman architect and engineer Marcus Vitruvius Pollio had described the perfect proportion of the human body within a circle. Thirteen centuries later da Vinci had drawn it. Plazzotta wanted to create a sculpture of the drawing, something no one had ever done. He and John discussed this idea over a game of chess one evening, and John agreed to finance it. They believed it sad there was no monument in Leonardo's hometown, so they agreed to place the sculpture in the town of Vinci, Italy.

Enzo completed a maquette, and in the spring of 1981, John, Wita, Enzo, and his wife, Gillian, traveled to Italy and visited Vinci. But the town officials were not receptive. The two couples discussed the possibility that the sculpture could be erected in France, where da Vinci is buried. But Plazzotta on his return to London made arrangements through the Italian ambassador to place the nine-foot statue in London's Belgrave Square opposite the Italian Institute of Culture.

Now, Plazzotta had learned he was dying, and he wanted John to know he would not

Enzo and Gilly Plazzotta with Wita in Vinci, Italy, in May 1981, coming from the house where Leonardo da Vinci was born. John and Wita and the Plazzottas were visiting Italy to locate a proper site for a sculpture Enzo was proposing to create of da Vinci's The Vitruvian Man.

When Enzo Plazzotta told John he was dying, John and Wita rushed to London to be with him. Plazzotta wanted to see Wita "only if she would not weep."

live to complete the sculpture. He hoped John would carry on with the project, for he was certain his assistant, Mark Holloway, could complete it. To Plazzotta, it was "my life's dream. I want to see it through." John immediately placed a trans-Atlantic call to assure him the project would continue and he would see him soon. Plazzotta told John he wished to see Wita, but "only if she would not weep."[14]

The morning after the Newcomen address, Wita and John were on the early morning Concorde flight to London. They went to Claridges, rested briefly, then took a cab to Westminster Hospital. At Plazzotta's bedside they visited and talked about the good times they had shared and about the Vitruvian man. The sculptor asked, "John, I wonder where we'll finish our chess game?" Then, with a thumbs-up sign, he whispered, "Maybe in heaven." He had clung to life just long enough to see his friends. Within twenty-four hours, he was gone.

There were two castings of Mark Holloway's *Homage to Leonardo: The Vitruvian Man*. One arrived in Birmingham in spring 1983, and the other was placed in London's Belgrave Square. John and Wita donated the first sculpture to the Birmingham Museum of Art "in honor of the many contributions of the Italian community to Birmingham's development," and on December 15, 1984, it was unveiled on a plinth on the western side of the museum overlooking the garden walk. John wanted it placed so it could be viewed from the street. When the museum expanded, a large glass window prevented the sculpture from remaining in its original location. Later it was placed in front of Birmingham's Medical Forum, and *The Vitruvian Man* was adopted as the forum's symbol.[15]

On May 21, 1983, the Harberts went to Sewanee for Margie's graduation the next day from the University of the South. Wita drove and John worked from his briefcase stuffed with papers because they planned to leave the country later in the week. It was not unusual for John to work while traveling. When he and Wita boarded the Harbert plane, John would carry three briefcases with him. He would work through all the papers in one, signing letters and making notes, and then leave this briefcase with the Harbert pilots to deliver to his secretary. Two cases then continued with him on the trip.

On May 24, 1983, Wita was sixty years old, and John arranged for a surprise dinner party for her at Shoal Creek. The next morning they flew to Chicago to join a group of Standard Oil of Indiana (soon to be called Amoco) leaders for a business trip to Europe and Saudi Arabia. John Swearingen was planning to retire in June as CEO of Standard Oil, and it was to be his farewell visit to the company's European organizations. This became one of Wita's most memorable trips. When the G-2 Standard Oil plane took off for Rome at 5 P.M., most of the top brass of the corporation were on board and so was Swearingen's vivacious wife, Bonnie, who slept through the night on a couch at the rear of the plane. Wita recalled that just before they landed at every stop, Bonnie would disappear into the bathroom and change from her hand-painted jumpsuit into "some Adolfo suit, complete with hat or turban, neatly pressed, looking as though it had come right out of a band box," and she was ready to be greeted by the local dignitaries.[16]

On May 28 the Standard Oil party was received by Sheikh Sultan in a gold and red room with "large ornate gold gilt armchairs all around the walls." The Arabs were dressed in robes, and the men talked about oil prices and speculated on when the conflict between Iraq and Iran might end. Although the women were supposed to be excused before the luncheon, Bonnie persisted and the American ladies were allowed to stay. The party drove to Abu Dhabi through the desert, then flew to Cairo.The trip included some interesting experiences, but Wita was tense because her mother was quite ill in Birmingham; however,

During his visit to Abu Dhabi in 1983 John renewed his friendship with three Arabs who had been associated with earlier Harbert projects.

One of John and Wita's favorite restaurants was Alfredo's in Rome. During the Standard Oil trip abroad in May 1983, Bonnie and John Swearingen joined the Harberts for dinner at Alfredo's.

Benny improved somewhat by the time Wita returned from Europe.[17]

John was able to keep much of his financial activities private; however, the sale of the coal mines was a publicly recorded stock transfer and resulted in his being named to the *Forbes* list of wealthy Americans. John first made the ranking in 1984 with an estimated fortune of $500 million, and he appeared every year thereafter.[18] He knew the figures were grossly exaggerated, and although he tried, he was not able to prevent his name from being listed. Each year this publicity caused a large and rather outrageous correspondence. Letters came from people all over the world asking him for money—gifts and investments—often for bizarre reasons, from people who wrote claiming they were unemployed, temporarily "down-and-out," and needed operations and food to the obvious con artists who offered him the opportunity to invest in gold mines, inventions, film productions, and art works. Some letters came from people who were obviously deranged. Perhaps the most interesting letter was sent by the U.S. agent of a nonreigning titled prince, a duke, sovereign grandmaster, and royal highness of an eastern European country who offered John a hereditary title of nobility—with a donation suggested. Many of the letters were carefully retained under "kook files."

During the 1980s John and Wita made numerous trips and tried to visit Rolling Rock in the Pocono Mountains of Pennsylvania each October. They traveled abroad, especially to England. In early August 1983, after their May trip with Standard Oil, John and Wita flew to London, where John met with his Egyptian contact man and discussed Harbert jobs and Wita had lunch with Mae Anderson, whose husband was head of the London office of Harbert International Establishment. Wita and John visited Belgrave Square to see the bronze sculpture of *Homage to Leonardo: The Vitruvian Man,* which they had donated, and then began a trip to the north of England. They had been invited by Lady Eugenie and Sir Joe Nickerson for a weekend of grouse shooting. The Nickersons were at Middleton House, built in 1820 near Teesdale.

Also visiting at the time were Lady Celia and Sir Viscount Lord Willie Whitelaw, deputy prime minister of Great Britain and head of the House of Lords, and several other distinguished and titled couples. And, as Wita recorded in her journal, "plain old John Harbert and wife."[19]

John had never shot grouse before, and he and Wita were anxious to see how the hunt would be organized. There were many beaters to push the birds toward the hunters, and fifty-three birds were shot. The guests were served lunch under tents in the field. Wita had been told before they left home that ladies did not shoot, and she came with that understanding; but Lady Nickerson's daughter, young Eugenia, was shooting, so that evening Lord Nickerson invited Wita to shoot the next day and gave her a 20-gauge shotgun. He placed her in a creek bottom with a loader, a retired British army veteran. Wita shot fourteen birds. The next day John and Wita left Middleton House and drove to the Lake District. They found small English hotels like Castle Combe and visited Blenheim Castle, where they enjoyed walking the grounds and discussing Capability Brown's landscape designs. Then they flew home from Gatwick.[20]

The next year John and Wita returned to England to visit the Nickersons, and it proved to be a trip they would never forget. On this occasion in August 1984, Viscount Whitelaw and his wife were again guests of the Nickersons along with several other couples, including Amelia and Pepe Fanjal and the duke of Marlborough, who was called Sonny. John and Wita arrived at Middleton House on August 23 after visiting the Roche Abbey ruins on the trip north from London. Wita recorded in her journal that she was worried about John

John and Wita enjoyed grouse hunting at Middleton-in-Teesdale, England, on September 19, 1986, as guests of Sir Joseph Nickerson and his wife, Eugenie. Ian Yates, Anthony Carlbom, John, Diana Yates (in front), Gunilla Carlbom, Eugenie Nickerson (in back), Sir Joe Nickerson, Wita, and Mareur Edmondson pause for a photograph outside Middleton House.

because of the stress he was under from his "deal with Boone."[21] After a black-tie dinner of grouse, the Harberts retired. At breakfast Wita wrote in her journal that "we've really come a long way lately—to be mixing with the top people in the British government—knights, lords, and dukes and these plain old Alabama Harberts."[22]

The next morning in the middle of the third drive Wita heard "a scream from the top of the hill." It was "barely discernible" to her because of all the firing and her earplugs. Lord Willie Whitelaw had accidently shot Lord Nickerson in the stomach and Nickerson's loader in the arm. Wita wrote that "it was all so bad—Willie weeping and unable to talk. Celia also. All to pieces." There was a flurry of security men, and Joe and his loader were taken to the local hospital amid great secrecy. No one wanted the news to leak out and find its way to the newspapers.

The guests remained in the field, were served lunch under tents, and then retired for a nap as though nothing had happened. At tea they were asked again not to divulge the shooting accident. By evening Lord Nickerson had returned from the hospital, and "to everyone's amazement," despite his pain, he came down for drinks wearing a pink dinner jacket to host his guests at dinner. He had been X-rayed, and the doctors counted twenty-eight shot in his abdomen. The doctors

During the last week of August 1984, John and Wita were grouse shooting at Middleton, England. Among the party were Lady Celia Whitelaw, Joe and Eugenie Nickerson, Sally Shillington, Wita and John, Sonny, the duke of Marlborough, Pepe Fanjal, and Sir Willie Whitelaw, head of the House of Lords.

determined that the bird shot, "barring complications ... would work their way out." The British secret police had taken Lord Whitelaw directly from the moor to his home. John and Wita left Middleton House early the next morning, and with John driving, they went north through Carlisle into Scotland and had lunch at Lockerbie, a sleepy little Scottish town that in later years would be associated with a major plane crash.[23]

On their visits to England John and Wita frequently visited the Richard Walgates, who lived at Cuxwald Hall in Lincolnshire. The hunts were smaller at the Walgate estate, and there was no help, but the Walgates were delightful hosts and the countryside was beautiful. One visit is particularly memorable for Wita. On the Walgate property there is a small parish church dedicated to Saint Nicholas. The Anglican priest came only occasionally for communion. When he was not scheduled, Dick Walgate and the local men conducted a service. On this Sunday, Dick asked John to join him. John had been raised a Presbyterian, but some years after their marriage he had asked Wita to meet him for lunch at the Birmingham Country Club and had surprised her with a gift of a Book of Common Prayer. He had secretly been taking lessons from David Cady Wright, minister at Saint Mary's, and had joined the Episcopal Church. Wita and John attended Saint Mary's regularly when they were in town and especially when the children were young. John sometimes took notes during the service. Once the minister stopped in the middle of his sermon to say, "John Harbert, I'd appreciate it if you would stop writing."[24]

Still, John was not well versed on the rituals of the Anglican Church, and Wita wondered what he would do at Saint Nicholas. When the Harberts and the Walgates walked down to the tiny church, it was festooned with vegetables and fruits for the Harvest Festival. John sat on the far side of the front row, and when his time came, he rose, read his assigned selection from Corinthians, closed the book, stepped out into the altar, and genuflected as though he had done it all his life.[25]

In May 1984, Wita and John made a memorable trip to Greece with the Ben Hardaways, the Roy Greenes, and the Cason Callaways. They flew to Athens and visited the Acropolis. John had been there in 1970, but he enjoyed showing Wita the architecture and explaining how the Greek columns were designed for maximum strength and beauty. After a few days they boarded a small ship, the *Illyris*, for a trip through the Corinthian Canal and were eventually to end their trip at Venice. Along the way they enjoyed beautiful scenery, saw historic sites, and walked through lovely small towns. The first thing John wanted to do when he visited a town was to find the markets and to engage in conversations with the local residents.

Although the scenery was fine, the ship was not proving satisfactory. There were plumbing problems, and the ship had no telephone or television. Then the weather turned foul. John and Wita had decided to take the trip because they were especially interested in seeing the Dalmatian coastline of the Adriatic Sea, but at Corfu the captain informed his passengers that he would have to turn back because his boat could not carry enough fuel to make it from Corfu to Venice, and stopping to refuel in communist Albania or Yugoslavia was not possible. John and Wita had cruised the Greek Isles before, so they decided to leave the boat at Corfu and fly to Paris. They rented a car and drove through the French wine country, then flew to London to rejoin the others for the Chelsea Flower Show.[26]

The next year, on June 23, 1985, John and Wita were in London and attended the tennis championship matches at Wimbledon. It was hot, and while Wita was able to sit in the shade, John was in the sun. He had gone off without a hat, and when the sun came out, he took his handkerchief and placed it on the top of his head. Only after his return to

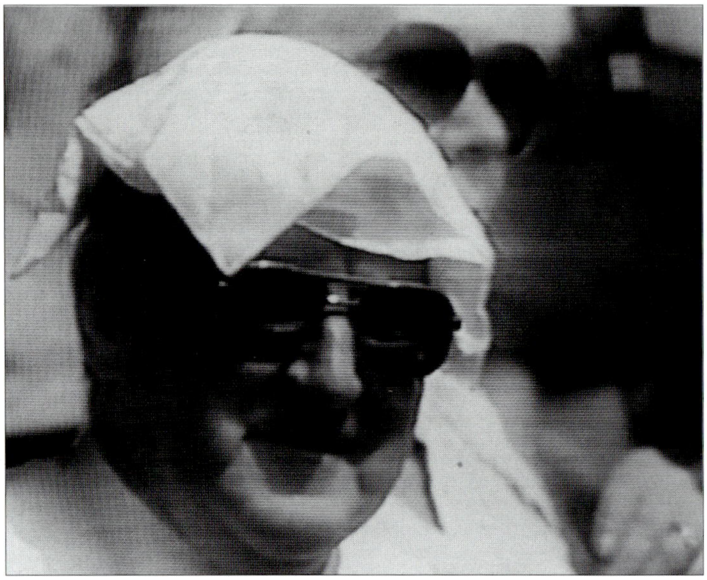

When John and Wita attended the tennis championships at Wimbledon, England, in June 1985, John forgot his hat and made do with his handkerchief. Miles and Mary Pollard shared with John this photograph, taken from television coverage of the match.

Celebrating their thirty-fifth wedding anniversary in June 1986, John and Wita joined Evalina and Bill Spencer for a cruise through the Norwegian fjords to the Arctic seas. Cooped up on a ship, John walked more than thirty miles on the deck track and won second prize for the most miles; Wita won third prize for walking more than twenty miles.

Birmingham did he learn that the television camera had focused on him during breaks in play for such an extended time that every friend who was watching saw him at Wimbledon with a handkerchief hat![27]

On June 30, 1986, Wita and John celebrated their wedding anniversary in London, and John gave her a lovely sapphire and diamond pin and earring set. They flew to Hamburg to have lunch with Margie and a friend who were touring Europe, then they met Bill and Evalina "Brownie" Spencer and boarded the

John and T. Boone Pickens head for the Swamp House at Pinebloom after a morning of fishing on Long Pond in February 1986.

Vista Fiorde for a cruise through the fjords. During the runs through the North Sea the winds were high and the seas had twenty-foot waves. Most of the passengers clung to life in their cabins, but John, undaunted, exercised by walking the decks. Wita wrote that "only John went to dinner," and he was "fit as a fiddle." The ship sailed north to the ice barrier beyond Spitzbergen but could not land at Mageroy Bay because of the rough seas. The Harberts went ashore at Hammerfest, which had been a German naval base in World War II, and visited the local museum. At Bergen John walked to the market to see the fruits and vegetables, and he and Wita shopped for sweaters and gifts. Before leaving the ship at Hamburg, John was awarded second prize for walking more than thirty miles on the deck track; Wita won third prize for walking more than twenty miles. They flew to London for a few days, then home on the Concorde, which was delayed by a bomb scare.[28]

When John traveled, he liked to be close to a telephone and would call the office to check in and receive his messages. In fact, one of those things friends most often recalled about John was that he seemed always to be talking on the telephone. In the 1980s he had so many business deals in various stages that it was difficult for him to arrange travel plans long in advance. This was especially true when he was involved in the stock deals. The sale of the Kentucky coal mines to Standard Oil in 1981 made the corporation a major player in the stock market. The decade of the 1980s was a particularly volatile time for American corporations. Wall Street stockbrokers and investment bankers were wheeling and dealing through corporate mergers, takeovers, and leveraged buyouts, and terms such as pacman defense, poison pill, golden parachute, scorched earth, and bear hugs were sprinkled through conversations in $500-a-day hotel suites where strategies were planned. Acquisitions and mergers increased in the United States fivefold between 1980 and 1988.[29] John

Harbert entered this tumultuous world of wheeling-dealing corporate executives and raiders and white knights through his acquaintanceship with T. Boone Pickens, a native of Holdenville, Oklahoma, and the president of Mesa Petroleum, a large independent Texas oil company. One writer has described Pickens as having "two normally opposing strains—wealth and idealism,"[30] a combination that would appeal to John Harbert.

Pickens first contacted John in the spring of 1982 when he flew into Pinebloom on his way to New York with some of his financial advisers. Wita recalled that she was "coming in on horseback from a hunt when suddenly out of the sunset came a jet that settled down on our landing strip." She described Pickens as "a very disciplined man ... not a typical westerner," for he wears conservative suits and no ten-gallon hat but "has 10-gallon ambitions."[31] Pickens was searching for money and partners in his move against Cities Service Oil Company, which was much larger than Mesa but in Pickens's opinion had been "unusually sluggish" for fifty years. He believed its management was not as effective as it should be. In New York Pickens rented an extra suite at the Waldorf to explain the deal to his potential partners; John was there. After some tense weeks of purchasing Cities Service stock, some quick moves and many negotiations, Pickens and his supporters gave up and accepted a tender, selling the stock they had accumulated in Cities Service to the oil company for a pretax profit of $30 million.[32]

John's next involvement with Pickens came when the Texas oilman moved against corporate giant Gulf Oil, the sixth largest company of the "fabled Seven Sisters" (large oil companies). Gulf Oil was an old company that originated in Pittsburgh in 1901 and was financed by T. Mellon and Sons Bank. The Mellons came to own large amounts of Gulf stock.[33] Gulf had toyed with playing white knight to Cities Service, but after Pickens sold his stock back to Cities, Gulf then backed out and caused Cities' stock to plummet.[34] Pickens recognized "undervalued assets in Gulf's annual reports" and went after the large oil company.[35]

The Gulf fight was longer, more involved, and more acrimonious than the Cities Service bout; but in contrast to the Cities deal, there was never a goal to take over Gulf and the risk was small because the stake was in Gulf stock, a sound investment in itself. The only questions were: What was the true value of Gulf stock? What was the selling price? What should the selling price be? Although Gulf stock had risen as high as $53 in the pseudoboom of 1980-81, by 1983 it seemed "anchored" in the high $30s. Pickens wanted Gulf to place part of its oil and gas reserves in a royalty trust, which he believed would have positive tax savings for the corporation and for the stockholders and would increase the price of Gulf stock.[36] Pickens invited John and seven men to meet with him to discuss forming a partnership. They gathered at the Meridian Hotel in Houston in October 1983 under cloak-and-dagger rules, fearing Wall Street "spotters" might find them together. Food was delivered to the meeting rooms, and no time was spent in the lobby. John loved the intrigue, which was in operation during all their subsequent meetings across the country.

In Houston Pickens's Mesa team presented a complete review of Gulf Oil and its assets and proposed a plan. Pickens recalled John responding that "if a big stockholder came to me with an idea like this, I'd sure sit down and listen to him." The Texan explained to the group that he had been accumulating Gulf stock for some time and that on August 11 he had started buying large blocks through Alan "Ace" Greenberg, chairman at Bear Stearns and Company in New York. The *Wall Street Journal* had reported that Gulf shares had "been traded at an unusually heavy pace since August" and that Gulf Oil Corporation was bolstering "its defenses against a still-unidentified purchaser." There was speculation Boone Pickens could be behind the "hostile accumulation of its stock," but an Arab nation and a Canadian consortium were also mentioned as possibilities. No one would know for sure who the party was until its holdings reached 5 percent. At that time, according to Securities and Exchange Commission regulations, the party had ten days before a report had to be filed notifying the SEC that 5 percent of the stock had been acquired.[37] The Gulf stock that the Mesa CEO had already purchased had gone up two points, and if the deal were struck, John and the other potential partners had a share of this profit. Pickens had stopped purchasing Gulf shares when his ownership amounted to 4.9 percent, because he was not yet ready to file with the SEC that he owned 5 percent. He did not wish to reveal any of his cards until his associates were committed.

By late afternoon Pickens had his partners. He, John, and seven men formed the Gulf Investors Group (GIG). Pickens owned two-thirds of the partnership and John had 9 percent. GIG was in business. The members agreed that if there were a hostile move on Mesa and it was taken over, "it wouldn't stop things, because the voting rights of the group's Gulf stock would shift to Harbert International." Pickens commented that his "partners gave us such financial strength that Gulf would never know for sure how much money we could come up with."[38] With a "$1.1 billion war chest," Pickens and his partners began buying Gulf stock in earnest. They were in the "run-up period," the ten-day window before they were required to file with the SEC. By October 17, GIG owned 9 percent of Gulf stock, 14.5 million shares, and had spent $638 million. They filed with the SEC showing 5 percent, then amended the report seven days later indicating 11 per cent.[39]

John's participation with Pickens in the Gulf Oil deal was headline news for the morning paper in Birmingham. Although John could not be reached for comment, Bill Harbert explained that "it's strictly an investment," and he preferred that his brother comment on the stock purchase.[40] In December the *Pittsburgh Press* ran a story about Pickens's partners, and John insisted that we are "just little fellows," that he had "no interest in running the Gulf Oil company," and that his friend Pickens "is a very alert, careful individual—a man of great integrity" and "not a gambler."[41] There were fierce disagreements in the press between Pickens and Gulf CEO James E. Lee, who insisted that Pickens was wrong and that "a royalty trust cannot work at a major oil company."[42] Lee refused to talk directly to Pickens, but because he was a good friend of John's from past years, John became the go-between. Wita recalled that twice at Pinebloom John was "summoned to the telephone from the hunting fields to transmit a message. Suddenly I would be left with dogs, wagons, and guests way out in the hinterlands, and he would be gone."[43]

In recalling John's involvement through these months, Pickens noted that "John was a strong personality, and he was quick to give advice, mostly good advice."[44] GIG kept buying Gulf stock and the price continued to rise. Pickens announced the GIG Gulf acquisitions in separate press releases, and although the partnership held just 12.9 percent of Gulf stock by early December, the public perception was that its holdings were much larger.[45] After GIG lost a proxy fight with the Gulf stockholders, John asked Pickens during a secret GIG meeting in Los Angeles about "taking some profits now"; but after a long discussion John agreed to "keep moving." Pickens believed at the time that John was "testing" him to determine whether he "had the resolve to see it through." Pickens wrote that "John and I have gained a great deal of respect for each other, and this was one of those key exchanges."[46] During a bitter part of the fight, Wita and John ran into Gulf CEO Lee and his wife at John's Island in Florida. Lee and John left to talk, and Wita remembered that "John returned to our table visibly shaken," for Mrs. Lee had burst into tears telling John that he "was ruining her husband and she'd never forgive him."[47]

The stock battle that ensued was highly public and closely followed by Gulf stockholders, corporate executives, investment bankers, and the media. Not all the publicity was positive, and the fight involved Gulf's attempt to restructure its incorporation and a congressional effort triggered by Gulf's supporters to pass legislation to curb oil company mergers for six months.[48] As the pressure rose, Gulf management offered GIG a tender at $70 a share, but because other stockholders were not included, Pickens declined. Meanwhile, unknown to John and his partners, many of Gulf's top management had secretly sold their stock, some for as low as $47 a share, such was their confidence in the company. On June 15, 1984, the great battle for Gulf was over when Socal proposed a merger with Gulf and its offer of $80 a share was approved, making this the largest corporate merger to that time. John and the Gulf Investors Group made $760 million before taxes, while other Gulf stockholders chalked up $6.5 billion in profits. As a result of all the profit taking, the U.S. government made headway in balancing the

In February 1986, John and Wita entertained Boone and Bea Pickens (on John's right) and Libby and Jack Shannon (on his left) at the Governor's Mansion at Pinebloom.

national debt when, as John said, "Uncle Sam got a billion dollars worth of taxes."[49]

John was involved with Pickens in other stock deals, such as the move on Diamond Shamrock, a Texas-based oil and gas company that used a restructuring plan and a defensive spin-off to counter Pickens.[50] Although the deal made money, Pickens's "Lucky Strike" partners were not successful in taking over Diamond Shamrock, and the news was relegated to the "back pages of the *Wall Street Journal*."[51] The Newmont Mining deal with Pickens lost money for Harbert, but it was small when compared to previous profits. Neither of these stock battles was so well covered by the media or had the excitement and profits that the Gulf deal did.[52] *Time* magazine concluded that the result of all this was a lesson to executives of American firms: if they "do not manage their companies skillfully, they could find themselves in the middle of a takeover fight with the gambler from Amarillo, or someone like him"[53]— perhaps John Harbert, who believed that "there are a lot of company managements that are not the entrepreneurs who founded the company. They are in there as hired hands, and often they're not all that good."[54]

In 1983 Harbert organized a commercial construction division to build the Riverchase Galleria. This giant shopping mall with parking decks, a hotel, department stores, and an office building was developed by Harbert, Jim Wilson and Associates, and 150 Mall Associates. Ground preparation was a massive undertaking because Harbert had to create a level space among the hills off Interstate 459 at the Hoover exit. It was at the time the largest construction project in the nation. Divisions of Harbert Corporation also were involved with the construction of the SouthTrust Tower with Brice Company; the Hoover Metropolitan Stadium; the spectacular and graceful "trumpet" interchange bridge over the Gulf of Mexico at Biloxi, Mississippi; the Auburn University Draughon Library expansion and parking deck; the UAB Convocation Center and multiuse arena; the complicated I-75 and I-595 interchange in Fort Lauderdale, and many other projects.

In the early 1980s Harbert Properties became interested in acquiring a well-located piece of Birmingham property in the new banking district near Fifth Avenue and Twentieth Street to construct a high-rise office building. Such an acquisition was seen as a good investment, as well as a contribution to the revitalization of the Birmingham business district. Block 47 was targeted since the Masonic Temple had been demolished in 1970; only the old YMCA building, which faced Twentieth Street, remained.[55] The lot was owned by AmSouth and Southern Natural Gas, and although a three-way partnership failed to materialize, Harbert and AmSouth did negotiate a partnership and a joint venture to build the office tower. Because of a running controversy over the value of Block 60, property values in downtown Birmingham had skyrocketed, and Harbert made what John later described as "a mistake—a costly financial decision" to purchase all of Southern Natural Gas's interest and half of AmSouth's ownership for $165 per square foot—what John believed to be "the highest price paid for any real estate in the State of Alabama."[56]

The joint venture with AmSouth was executed on April 25, 1986. Gyo Obata of Hellmuth, Obata, and Kassabaum, of Saint Louis, was selected as architect, with Gresham, Smith and Partners of Birmingham collaborating. John insisted that he did not want just another building, but one with style that would blend with the historic structures of Birmingham and make a contribution to the city's architecture. Harbert would build the building with Brasfield-Gorrie General Contractor, and it was decided to begin on a "fast-track design/construct" schedule. When ground-breaking ceremonies were held on

March 2, 1987, with excavation to begin the next day, there was only "a one-sheet drawing of tentative foundation plans." The plans and detailed specifications grew as the building progressed.[57]

At the ground-breaking celebration John noted that "shortly after Mayor [Richard] Arrington was elected, he called me with a request that my company make an investment in a downtown project." Although John had agreed, he had never found just the right investment until the present project.[58] Throughout planning and construction, John's main concern was safety, something he always worried about. Part of the prayer that the Very Reverend Laurence Gipson from the Church of the Advent gave at the dedication helped soothe his anxiety: "Keep from harm's way all who will labor here to lift up this complex."[59]

The architects and designers of the building were determined "to make this building as contextual as we can make it, to work with a fabric of design that is already in the city." The architects created a modern building with "a great deal of romance about it." William P. Lacey, a chief designer with Hellmuth, Obata, and Kassabaum, noted that "we used a lot of the same detail, textures, and colors as the historical buildings [in downtown Birmingham]. Certainly spheres, pyramids, and pointy roofs were something that's been there for a long time."[60] The building has "a curtain wall of golden Carioca granite" and a darker green stone called Ubatuba, both of which were mined in Brazil, shipped to Italy to be cut, polished, numbered for placement, and then sent to Birmingham.[61] As the building design materialized, it was the major topic of conversation throughout the city. Mitch Mendelson, a *Birmingham Post-Herald* reporter, noted, "In a city not known for wide public interest in contemporary building design, AmSouth/Harbert has put the kettle on to boil."[62] When Paul Goldberger, architecture critic for the *New York Times*, visited Birmingham in 1989 and presented the Robert Graves Hiden lecture at the Birmingham Museum of Art, he discussed cities and postmodern architecture. When his lecture was published, photographs of the AmSouth/Harbert Plaza illustrated the historical precedents revived in the architecture of the building.[63]

The construction of the SouthTrust Tower and the AmSouth/Harbert Plaza, shown here, changed the skyline of Birmingham and confirmed the move of the city's financial center to the north.

Every day that John was in town, he came by the construction site to check on progress. Always every inch the builder, John told *Business First* magazine that "it's my baby and I'm proud of it."[64] In his "topping out" speech on October 13, 1988, John announced that construction was six months ahead of schedule. He praised the workers and supervisory personnel for the project and said that "I have a reputation for exaggerating now and then, but I don't need to on this one," drawing chuckles from his friends.[65] In the city there was a great deal of speculation on which building—AmSouth/Harbert Plaza or SouthTrust Tower—was the tallest in the city. *On Site* commented that "depending upon whether the buildings are measured by numbers of floors or numbers of feet above street level, either of the two can claim title to Birmingham's tallest."[66] The Summit Club was located on the top floor of the AmSouth/Harbert Plaza and provided an elegant setting for business lunches and formal dining occasions. Wita took an active role in approving the decor for the club.[67]

A month before the formal opening of the building, Harbert and AmSouth announced that Harbert Corporation was buying AmSouth's share of the tower. AmSouth Bank chairman John W. Woods stated that the bank wanted Block 47 developed "to its fullest potential" and that "the joint venture's primary goal had been successfully accomplished," so the bank could now direct its "resources back into bank-related activities."[68] However, the bank maintained "a strong presence in the landmark building bearing the AmSouth name."[69]

By 1988 Harbert's commercial construction had twenty-one projects in ten cities, but construction of all sorts represented only one of the four divisions of Harbert. The other three were resource recovery and electrical energy generation, gas and oil exploration and production, and real estate development.[70] Making acceptable margins of profit for the risks and capital invested continued to be difficult in areas that were highly competitive. The stock market crash on October 19, 1987, hurt Harbert as it did all investors. There were cash flow problems and concerns within Harbert's top management that perhaps the corporation was overextended in some areas. Close supervision was recommended. In November 1988, the *Birmingham Business Journal* ranked Harbert Corporation second behind the Drummond Company on a list of the top one hundred private companies in Birmingham.[71]

John was also mindful in the late 1980s that Harbert traditions were being lost. At a Harbert business strategy meeting in the summer of 1988, John praised the "many young and capable executives within the company who are developing and maturing rapidly" and said he had confidence that the future leadership of the company could come from this group. But he warned his audience that it was essential for these young people to concentrate "on working together for the good of the organization, rather than focusing on individual achievement. That is the test for true leadership." John believed that "many attributes are necessary for leadership, but the most important one is the skill of working with people, all kinds of people at all levels of the organization." He told his audience that he was looking forward to the company's fortieth anniversary, which would occur in January 1989. John took this opportunity to discuss Harbert's reputation for integrity, noting with pride that throughout its history Harbert had "steered clear of any shenanigans that would damage our name," and he never wanted anything to "reflect negatively on our honor and integrity."[72]

In mid-1988 John was still physically strong and healthy but concerned about the long-term future leadership of the corporation, especially since he was sixty-seven and his son was only twenty-nine years old. Raymond Harbert had spent the last few years building Harbert Properties Corporation, to which he was named president in 1986. John was pleased and, as he sometimes said, even surprised with the development of his son's business acumen. His mother was not surprised. Wita had confidence that Raymond, given time, would be ready to shoulder whatever responsibilities he needed to assume. In May 1988 Raymond was elected to the board of directors of Harbert Corporation, and although John was observing him closely, he did not at that time anticipate that Raymond would be ready to assume the responsibilities of CEO before he was ready to retire.

Later in 1988 Raymond was caught off guard when his father told him he wanted him to leave Harbert's real estate branch and come to the holding company. Raymond asked for six months to plan the transition and decide on someone to replace him. His father agreed; however, in a matter of weeks John told him to "come now."[73] During these months father and son grew close. In 1989 Raymond was elected vice-president of Harbert Corporation and was given responsibility for subsidiaries, corporate mergers and acquisitions, and evaluation of all venture capital investments. From this position John and Raymond worked on the acquisition of Birmingham Steel, a local company that was a recent reorganization of the old Birmingham Bolt Company. John was a member of the board of directors of

Birmingham Steel, had watched the growth of the company, and believed it had unlimited potential. For several years he had been impressed with its operations and its management team.

Raymond negotiated with New York investment bankers to secure funding commitments for the planned leveraged buyout. Continental Bank agreed to $350 million, Bear Stearns and Company committed $100 million, and Harbert Corporation would put up $75 million. In September 1989 John offered a $30-per-share buyout for Birmingham Steel stock, which was then selling in the low $20s. John had hoped to secure the deal by October 1, but Birmingham Steel requested First Boston Corporation to analyze the Harbert bid and felt it necessary to secure the approval of its stockholders.[74] After the offer was deemed a fair price, Birmingham Steel management scheduled a vote at the annual stockholders meeting in January 1990.[75] Although John's commitment to purchase the company remained firm, Birmingham Steel's stock began to move downward in early January. The general slump in the steel industry nationwide and a poor earnings report from Birmingham Steel caused the financing to collapse. It was impossible to underwrite the transaction at the current numbers when the earnings dropped, and the deal fell through.[76] Despite the failure of the takeover bid, John was impressed with the way Raymond handled the negotiations and put together an acquisition agreement with the banks, something that Birmingham Steel president James A. Todd, Jr., praised the next year.[77] But besides all of this, John was enjoying working with his son.

On July 25, 1990, at the North River Yacht Club in Tuscaloosa at a conference of Harbert Corporation's top management, John announced that he was retiring immediately and that his son Raymond was becoming the new CEO of the company. Following the meeting, father and son posed for photographs and John wished Raymond good luck, promising to stick around to help him for a while.

On Christmas Day 1989 John penned Wita a note and attached it to her present. He acknowledged that the gift "may be a small token compared to what I realize you really desire. I understand what your wishes are, and I concur that it is time for me to seriously initiate the slowing down process so we can enjoy more leisure together. So my major gift is a promise to do so in 1990!" Over his signature he affirmed his "love for this day and forever more—John."[78]

In the summer of 1990 Raymond was again surprised when his father told him he wanted him to assume the position of chief executive officer of Harbert Corporation. John "had agonized for more than two years" on who should succeed him when he was ready to retire. He was pleased that despite "having grown up fully aware of the demands of the job," Raymond was "willing to make the commitment," which would involve "many sleepless nights for him and sacrifices for his family."[79] The first announcement was made on July 25 at a conference of Harbert officers and top management at the Tuscaloosa North River Yacht Club. For those who had observed the closeness with which father and son were working together and the maturity of their relationship, it came as no surprise. In his announcement John noted that "construction was a young man's game," and his choice for CEO was young and energetic with "leadership qualities necessary to direct an organization as diverse as this one." He commended Raymond's "lively and entrepreneurial nature" and his ability to work long hours and to earn "the respect of fellow employees, investment houses, local and international bankers." John ended by confiding that "it means a *great* deal to me that he is capable and willing to look after *my* interest as well as *yours*."[80]

John remained chairman of the board but, although he was involved in major corporate decisions, it is remarkable how willingly he turned over the reigns of the corporation that had been his very life for forty-one years. On the other hand, this move was also typical of John Harbert. One of his finest attributes as a corporate leader had been his willingness to give young people responsibility and to step back and let them make decisions. It was no less so with his son. For Harbert Corporation there were some challenges ahead and problems to solve that had origins before Raymond's watch. There were fresh tests to the corporation's future that he tackled head-on. For John a personal health problem that no one could have anticipated in the summer of 1990 loomed three years down the road. How John reacted to a diagnosis of cancer is another example of the strength of the man. It has often been said that John's timing was excellent, that he had over-the-horizon vision. Nothing illustrates this vision better than his decision to step down in July 1990 from the CEO responsibilities of Harbert Corporation.

12

RETIREMENT

"the game's not over"

When John gave up the day-to-day operation of the Harbert Corporation and its various companies in mid summer 1990, he did not really retire. Hall Thompson recalled that in these years, although John "didn't stop to smell the roses, he slowed."[1] Raymond Harbert observed that his father never had the pangs of adjusting to retirement as some men did because he still had his office and his secretary and he remained chairman of the board. John relished playing the role of elder statesman to the young men whom Raymond began to gather around him at Harbert.[2] Although John was kept informed and remained very interested and involved in the business, he was able to step back and let Raymond lead, a difficult task for any parent and a hard one for many retiring executives. When the young men of Harbert decided to reduce operational expenses by cutting off the air conditioner in the building on weekends and Sandi Falkenhagen worried about the wilting condition of the ferns and greenery in the Harbert gardens, John refused to get involved. He told her, "Honey, when you give it up, you give it up."[3]

In the next years John stayed busy. He spent more time at Pinebloom and more time traveling with Wita, and he became involved with new causes. In 1994 when *Alabama Construction News* interviewed John on the occasion of presenting him with its first Cornerstone Award for lifetime excellence in the construction industry, John observed that he had never thought of himself as "successful," for "I always think there's something else I've got to do. The game's not over."[4] In the summer of 1990 John was looking forward to the rest of his life.

The announcement of John's retirement as CEO of Harbert Corporation made headlines in state newspapers. In a front-page story the *Birmingham News* called John an "Alabama business giant" and quoted him as saying that he was stepping down because "age is creeping up on me. It's been an interesting and fun job, and I wish I could repeat it all over again."[5] *Post-Herald* reporter Patrick Rupinski noted that John's retirement "marked the end of the reign of one of Alabama's most powerful and successful industrialists," a man whose "construction company reshaped the physical face of Birmingham and points beyond."[6]

On September 26, 1990, John introduced Raymond to the Birmingham Rotary Club. The invitation to speak had been tendered and accepted in May and had no relation to the executive changes made at Harbert Corporation during July. Raymond's talk was essentially an update on Harbert corporate history since John had addressed the Newcomen Society in 1981. After Harbert had sold its coal interests, the corporation had invested in four areas: the traditional heavy civil and commercial construction, plus energy, real estate, and power plants. Wita and Kathryn were in the audience when Raymond traced the successes and admitted the failures of the past decade. The risk, he said, was worth the challenge to take the "unproven path of leadership." Raymond pledged that the Harbert Corporation of the future would "continue to be entrepreneurial, continue to push the proverbial edge of the envelope, continue to be a leader and risk-taker in business as well as in the community." John was a very proud father.[7]

On October 25, 1990, John went to the University of Florida to give the Gregory Distinguished Lecture address to a group of engineering students. He looked back on his career somewhat nostalgically and observed that the Harbert team "experienced camaraderie at its best and most productive. We knew each other's abilities and each other's weaknesses; we praised the abilities publicly and protected the weaknesses from outsiders. We supported each other to the maximum, and collectively, we never gave up."[8] The young team that Raymond was putting in place at Harbert during fall 1990 and early 1991 adopted the same philosophy as its members met their special challenges. The most important one was to improve the profit margin of the Harbert enterprises by cutting those companies or ventures that were requiring extensive amounts of risk capital and that seemed unlikely to provide an acceptable return on investment. Whereas John was uncomfortable about closing down an operation or firing anyone, Raymond was more willing to make hard personnel decisions with bottom-line figures in mind. He felt a heavy responsibility following in his father's footsteps.

John realized that the corporation had to be changed and restructured and that it needed a new and more focused vision of what it wanted to do. A coherent strategy was needed. John's generation was fading fast from the scene. Construction had changed, and federal legislation and regulations had made it a much less profitable endeavor. At age sixty-nine, John realized that his company was too far-flung for his close management and control, and he made decisions to get things straightened out. Raymond observed that at the time "our business needed to be rationalized."[9]

The financial constraints that the company faced in the fall of 1990 continued patterns common in the history of Harbert. Yet there were significant differences: the Harbert corporate investments and companies were more widely diversified, not just confined to construction, and they were geographically dispersed; Harbert Corporation had a stronger profile in the 1990s; there was a wider public perception of Harbert strength and invulnerability, so the significance of any downsizing would be overemphasized; the corporation had more assets than ever before, but they were fixed and not liquid; and the baton of leadership had passed to a younger generation. Any selling or leveraging of resources or reorganization would be closely observed as banks and the corporate world vigilantly watched the new Harbert leadership.

The construction divisions of Harbert had been struggling during the past few years. Construction was soft nationwide. Harbert attempted to consolidate its various

John enjoyed checking on Harbert's jobs, especially its bridges, but he was uneasy about taking over construction of the complicated cable-stayed new Cochrane Bridge over the Mobile River after the first contractor defaulted.

construction entities and to focus the talents of management personnel so that profits could be maximized. In September 1990, Harbert seemed to be doing well, bucking the national downturn in the construction industry, and a decision was made to divide the construction branches.[10] Then in November Harbert laid off forty workers in its construction companies in order to streamline operations and tighten up. Nationally, construction continued in decline. In Montgomery, Blount International also announced layoffs from its construction divisions because of a decrease in new business. In his autobiography, Red Blount discussed the difficulty the company was having at this time playing "catch-up in a weak domestic market" after making good profits in the Middle East, a situation that he said was "disastrous" for Blount. "We got the contracts, all right," he wrote. "But our bids were so low they left little room for surprises or errors, or for profits, resulting in a string of losses."[11] In 1992, Blount decided to phase out bidding on all fixed-price projects, and although it was unannounced at the time, this action "represented a conscious decision to phase out of construction."[12]

Harbert Construction and Harbert International had decreases in the number of new jobs, but they remained busy laying oil pipelines in South America, building facilities on Kwajalein Atoll in the Marshall Islands, working on or completing various commercial projects in Florida, building prisons in Texas and a convention center in Mobile, and finishing three major civil projects: the mammoth interstate interchange near Fort Lauderdale, Florida, which included thirty bridges; I-565 in Huntsville; and the Cochrane Bridge in Mobile. Harbert had been encouraged by the state of Alabama to bid on the completion of this complicated cable-stayed structure over the Mobile River after the original contractor defaulted. John advised against the bid because of the new design and because dealing with the state had become so difficult, but the state was in a bind and Harbert had an excellent track record in solving challenging construction problems.[13] The civil division of Harbert planned to begin the complicated I-20 and I-40 interchange near Shreveport, Louisiana, early in 1991. On both the Louisiana and the Cochrane Bridge projects there

Harbert Corporation advanced from John's simple 1947-48 Autauga County bridge to stately structures such as the new Highway 280 bridge over the Coosa River at Childersburg and complicated projects such as the thirty-bridge interstate interchange at Fort Lauderdale, Florida, shown here in a model.

were disputes over retainage and final compensation between Harbert and the two states' highway departments after the projects were completed. John made many calls and trips to Louisiana and Montgomery to try to resolve the issues. His displeasure at being treated unfairly on these projects made it easier for him to agree to move Harbert away from its original construction base when that issue was being decided in late 1992.

In a long interview in the January/February 1992 issue of *On Site*, Raymond stated that in discussions during the summer of 1990 about the transfer of leadership, he and his father "recognized that some difficult decisions had to be made about the direction of the company, some major changes had to come about." Raymond's new Harbert team evolved from the time he moved to the holding company in 1988. Michael White had joined Harbert in 1983; Charlie Miller came to Harbert in 1985; Swift Barnes was in place as chief financial officer by December 1989; Tom Hough arrived in December 1990 from Ernst Young; David Boutwell became controller in June 1991; Will Brooke joined the team in August 1991. This management team developed a plan and decided to narrow the focus of the business and divest red-ink companies and investments. In order to reorganize its assets, provide needed cash flow for construction projects, and meet current obligations, Harbert Corporation negotiated a $288 million loan from six banks in March 1991. The collateral for the loan included the corporate headquarters, stock, airplanes, and construction equipment. Although the amount of the loan was large, in relative figures Harbert was probably less leveraged at this time than it had been in fiscal crises years before when Bill Rossman worked miracles.

The plan to pay back the loan anticipated the selling of several assets as soon as possible in order to reduce the loan by about half. Harbert Energy Corporation was targeted; however, the energy market was depressed and the timing was unfortunate. Furthermore, John and Raymond discovered to their dismay that the Harbert book value of HEC was inflated. In June 1991, Raymond was informed that the sale of HEC would not bring in the cash the team had planned. This setback forced the young leaders to regroup. July was spent in meetings. They drafted a new business strategy and on July 15, 1991, began to implement the second generation plan.

On October 10, 1991, John welcomed a group of Harbert bankers to a meeting at the Riverchase headquarters of the corporation. He assured them that Harbert had the resources to repay its loan and had a plan to do it. Various members of the Harbert management team then explained to the bankers how this would be accomplished.[14] All but two of the six banks were satisfied. For some time it was touch-and-go regarding whether the reluctant two would go along. Finally they did. All the while John watched, asked questions, gave advice, but generally stood back and let Raymond take the lead.

During spring 1992 Harbert sold stock and carefully selected assets. In May the *Birmingham News* published a story by staff writer Robin DeMonia that was based upon public documents, reports of stock and real estate sales, and records at the Shelby County Courthouse and Alabama Secretary of State's office. Anticipating the negative article, Harbert issued a press release on May 14 that noted that because Harbert was a private company "without the regulatory disclosures required of publicly traded firms," a true picture of the corporation could not be made only from matters of public record. Headlined "Hard times for Harbert," the tone of the front-page DeMonia story offended both John and Raymond, as did the photograph of John that showed him with a pained expression.[15]

In November 1990, as the sorting out of Harbert's fiscal position was ongoing, John wrote Raymond a personal letter. He wanted to put into words how he felt about certain things. He told Raymond that he believed he would live longer with "a life without undue stress. My life," he wrote, "has been one of stress, and I have learned to live well with the stress factor." He talked about the stress of his sixteen-year-old sister's tragic death and the impact it had upon his entire family. He said his college experience "was not as pleasant as yours," for "there was never enough money to pay for clothes, required textbooks, tuition. To this day, I dream about going to classes without the necessary books and proper clothes." John hinted that he did not feel socially accepted in college and that fraternity life was not a positive experience for him. "Then," he wrote, "came the war years and stress of an entirely different character. I feared failure in combat, which I learned to overcome with the first few battle engagements. I also learned to be a survivor. And although, through it all, I was mentally and physically gutted, I do know that I made a positive contribution to many minor situations."

Then John turned to the future and his concern for Raymond and the "many business problems not of your doing, but caused by others." He second-guessed himself, saying he should have quit when he was ahead instead of continuing "to gamble and provide others with wealth." John told Raymond that he was "particularly concerned about your mother and how unfair the present pressures are on her. She has spent most of her married life under the constant pressure of stress of one kind or another." He said he was concerned about Margie and especially Jay when he and Wita were not available to protect and sustain him.

John told his younger son that he was "pleased in how I perceive you are handling the responsibilities of leadership, particularly by your selection of talented individuals to support your efforts." He told Raymond that he wanted "to be completely retired, out of the limelight and no longer burdened by decision-making responsibilities." But at this time, John wrote, he did not feel it "possible or feasible" and "it would be completely unfair to you and to your new associates." John promised he would "be available to provide support and contribute whatever knowledge" he could. He was not glossing over the situation. He knew "of the problems ahead of us," for he saw "the pitfalls clearer than anyone, but I also know that a winning attitude—a refusal to give up and quit—can produce success. Conditions change. Timing is often the difference between success and failure."[16]

In December the Harberts enjoyed a good Christmas. As he was in the habit of doing, John took up his ink pen in 1990 and wrote Wita a personal note for her Christmas present. This year he affirmed his love for her and observed that "we have come through a great deal in our life together—It is my desire and hope to make our remaining years the *best* of our lives. We have much to be thankful for—probably more than we deserve. ... Sharing most of my life with you has been a wonderful experience. Let's look forward to the good years we have left."[17]

In January 1991, John was concerned about the beginning of war in the Persian Gulf, considering "the work and people we have in the area." He supported U.S. efforts in the region because he distrusted Saddam Hussein, and he guessed that the war would be over soon. In mid-January while hunting quail at Pinebloom, John was "knocked off" his horse and suffered a fractured vertebra in his lower back, which "was painful but not serious," and he anticipated that the "fracture would be healed in eight weeks or so." Doctors ordered him to lie flat and get plenty of rest—instructions John had "a hard time following."[18]

John considered his health excellent when he turned the reigns of his company over to his son, and he reasonably expected to live into his eighties. He was bothered by a blur in his left eye when reading at close distances, but Dr. Callahan at the Eye Foundation Hospital had helped with that. He knew he was overweight—Wita worried him about it—but it was hard for him to give up candy bars and ice cream. He knew he needed to be getting more exercise, and he was not playing enough tennis. In December 1991, he was not feeling as chipper as he usually did, so he decided it was time for a physical. He visited his internist, who put him through a battery of tests, then he and Wita waited for the results.[19]

On December 20 at the Harbert Christmas party John addressed the employees to thank them for their commitment to Harbert. He noted that the company had "survived major adversities by adapting to change, although never in our history have we experienced as many changes as we have been through the past year or so." John observed that some of these changes were "imperative to our survival, and some were dictated by the passage

During a house party at Pinebloom in December 1994, John rides his favorite horse while Anne Keresey and Annis and Jack Bowen ride in the wagon being driven by Willie James. Dan Burns rides in front with Willie. John's yellow Labrador retriever, Tasca, waits for the order to fetch the birds.

of time, including the replacement of senior officers with bright, energetic young leaders." John wished he were "thirty years younger and able to work" with the new generation of Harbert executives, but he knew that opportunities would evolve "which will take Harbert Corporation to new heights and exciting adventures in the years ahead." He planned "to be around a while longer to offer advice and support when needed—and probably some not wanted."[20]

John and Wita flew to Pinebloom for the annual staff Christmas party. Wita had toys and gifts of clothing for the children, and John had bonus checks for the employees. The large tree was beautiful, but it was difficult for John and Wita to feel the Christmas spirit because they were so concerned about his test results. While they were in Georgia, John received a call from his doctor that all was fine except that his PSA count was 138 when it should have been about 4. Wita recalled that "John sort of expected it." A second test made to verify the count showed a rise to 144 PSA. John had prostate cancer.[21] The doctor ordered a series of X-rays of his back and spine, and the radiologist reported a spot on his back. At first there was concern that the cancer had spread. Then Wita reminded John that this spot was exactly the place where he had hurt his back when he fell off the horse at Pinebloom in January 1991. She asked him to get a copy of the old X-rays to see if the spots matched. This was indeed what had happened. The cancer had not metastasized.

John reacted to the diagnosis of cancer just

as he did to every problem of his life—he first read everything he could find, collecting books, pamphlets, and articles on prostate cancer. He consulted experts at Sloan-Kettering Cancer Center in New York and M. D. Anderson Cancer Center in Houston. Then he and his doctor devised a plan of attack. He would take a series of radiation treatments beginning January 1 and continuing to March. John scheduled the treatments at Saint Vincent's Hospital early in the morning. Every day he would be at the hospital by 6:00 A.M., take his treatments, come home, eat breakfast, and head for the office. Once he flew to Seattle for a Birmingham Steel meeting right after a radiation treatment. Wita recalled that all during this time "he was tough."[22] On April 30 John wrote a friend in California that he had "completed just over eight weeks of radiation without missing a day of work or a weekend of hunting, usually on horseback. Toward the end," he wrote, "I experienced some fatigue, but that was the worst of it except for the restraints on my time."[23] By late spring John's PSA count was down to 8. He felt the battle was won, but he was not at all sure the war was over.

John became such an expert on prostate cancer that friends and strangers alike called and asked him for information. He was almost obsessed with sharing his knowledge, and he went about providing support for prostate cancer victims with virtually missionary zeal. He would call, write, or visit those with the diagnosis to reassure them. Sometimes he contacted men he did not know but whom friends had told him about. Sometimes strangers called him and apologetically said that someone had urged them to talk to John Harbert. These men remembered John as being warm and caring and providing them with knowledge that was valuable to them. John's office became such a clearinghouse for materials and information on the latest research on prostate cancer that his secretary teased him about practicing medicine without a license. Once when John and Wita were at Highlands, Wita came home from a golf game and told John that a friend's husband had just been told he had prostate cancer. John immediately drove over to the man's house, where he spent more than an hour talking to him.[24]

In 1990 the Smithsonian Institution had invited John to become a member of its national board. John took his duties seriously and planned his schedule so he would not miss a board meeting. He was especially interested in the Smithsonian's plans for a major traveling exhibition that would include a representative sampling of the nation's heritage. John immediately began to advocate Birmingham as the southern venue for the exhibition. The Smithsonian arranged a number of trips for its board members, and John and Wita took Smithsonian trips to Russia and Turkey; but the wildlife safari to Africa in June 1992 was their most memorable trip. It could easily have been the last journey for the Harberts.

John and Wita checked their luggage through to Africa and took the British Airways Concorde flight to London. On arrival they carried their hand luggage and went to a London hotel to sleep and rest up for the evening flight to Zimbabwe. But after only a short rest, John hired a driver and went to lunch and to see *The Vitruvian Man* at Belgrave Square. He stopped by Foyles to find a book. At 10 P.M. he and Wita boarded their flight to Africa and in the morning arrived at Salisbury, then traveled to the Pamuzinda Safari Lodge. Cocktails were followed by a dinner of crocodile tails.

At 5:30 the next morning, Wita and John went for a walk with guide John Stephens, considered one of the finest white hunters in Africa. They saw animal tracks and three cape buffalo, which approached and followed the group back toward the lodge. John wrote that Stephens, who carried a high-powered rifle, got between them and the buffalo and told them "to walk fast, not run, and we did exactly as we were told. The buffalo followed

A thatched-roof hut was one of the many types of accommodations John and Wita had during their African tour. Wild animals, like this rhinoceros, moved freely in the camp sites, and one rhino chased Wita and forced her to seek refuge in another hut.

us for almost a mile, matching our pace exactly. I think they were just curious, but I didn't stop to ask."[25] Wita recorded in her journal that it was "very frightening." Most of the travel, John recalled, "was not in protected vehicles, and we spent a great deal of time walking or hiking through the jungle. Almost every day was a ten-mile hike."

John and Wita visited an aviary to see African birds and then had lunch with one of the country's leaders. That night a rhino came close to the thatch-roof cottage complex and charged Wita when she was walking to the main cottage. She dashed into the nearest hut and into the arms of total strangers. The party divided into several groups and flew in small planes to land "on a dirt runway in the middle of nowhere." Here in the bush they observed baboons, monkeys, impalas, and elephants and then traveled by Land Rover to a rustic campsite. The Harbert quarters had an open shower with a concrete floor and a small double bed with mosquito netting. Wita wrote that now "the situation was far wilder."[26]

They were near the banks of the Zambezi River. John and Wita watched the crocodiles and the sunset over the river. The next morning some of the group left early to travel by land up the river to take canoes for the trip back down the Zambezi River to their campsite. The group in four canoes paddled and floated down the river, passing wildlife. They watched several pods of hippopotamuses bathing in the shallow water, and although they saw no crocodiles, they knew they were in the river. When they were almost back to camp, the group silently paddled between fourteen hippopotamuses about fifty feet from the riverbank.

John noticed that one of hippos bellowed, then disappeared under the water. The first three canoes went by without incident, but suddenly John and Wita's canoe jerked with tremendous force. Wita "thought we had hit a stump" but soon realized that "a hippo had attacked our canoe." A large hole appeared in the bottom of the canoe, water gushed in, and then the canoe was thrown up

The Smithsonian trip to Africa in June 1992 was strenuous and exciting. Accommodations were often primitive, and Wita and John endured cold-water showers and rough camping conditions.

Taken in June 1992 by fellow Smithsonian travelers, this photograph shows John and Wita with their guide canoeing on the Zambezi River just before their canoe was attacked by a hippopotamus.

One highlight of the Africa trip was the visit to Victoria Falls.

The occupants in the other canoes looked on in horror and quickly paddled back for them. Wita was bleeding through her sock and on her elbow. John had lost his camera and ruined his watch and binoculars. Soaking wet and freezing cold, they were just happy to be alive. The short trip back to camp was uneventful. The guides came to Wita's hut and dressed her wounds. After hot showers, a shot of gin, dinner, and a good night's sleep, John and Wita were ready to go again in the morning.

The next day's itinerary called for finding lions and leopards. Wita confessed in her journal that she stayed very close to the guide, who carried a gun. In the afternoon they flew from the dirt-strip airport to Bumi Hills Safari Lodge. They traveled by Land Rover through open plains, watching zebras and elephants and that night taking flashlights to look for leopards. They visited aborigine villages and schools and enjoyed the dancing presentations, and along the way John took a photograph of a native bridge. They went cruising on Lake Kapenta, enjoyed the sunset, and then flew to Kariba to see Victoria Falls. Before the Smithsonian group departed Africa, Wita was voted the best camper on the trip by the group, and John bought her a small silver hippopotamus. The trip home took thirty hours.[29]

and capsized. Wita and John were hurled into the air, and she grabbed his belt as they hit the water together. Wita wrote in her journal that night that she "went under, hitting the bottom with some force. It was terrifying."[27] The water was more than five feet deep, and she was able to struggle to shore, while John was thrown into water just over his head, and it was with difficulty that he made it to the riverbank. Not knowing what could be under the muddy water, John later wrote that he "had plenty of encouragement to reach the shore in a hurry."[28] John had completed his radiation only ten weeks before, and Wita was immediately concerned about an injury that would be more serious because of his recent treatment.

As early as 1975 John had considered getting out of construction. The coal operations were going well, and when he was interviewed that year by the *Engineering News-Record* he noted that diversifying investments had allowed the company to be selective and freed it from taking jobs just to make the overhead. He observed that Harbert had "done a lot of charitable work I didn't like doing—providing the U.S. Government and the state of Alabama and other owners with projects we lost a pile of money on." He insisted that he was "trying to change the type of business" he was in so "we're not taking any big risks. The contracting industry is geared for a man who is willing to pit his energy and his brawn and really doesn't have anything to lose. Once you've got a lot to lose, you'd better think about it."[30]

Quietly, as part of the long-range plan, Harbert first left the international construction market, selling its South and Central American division of Harbert International and its interest in Harbert International Establishment to John's brother, Bill, in December 1991. Bill incorporated Bill Harbert International as a Delaware corporation in September 1992 and organized Bill Harbert Construction as a domestic construction corporation.[31] But Harbert Construction Corporation was still operating in domestic construction. In late 1992 the Moles, a group of heavy and civil contractors, notified John that the national organization was awarding him its nonmember Outstanding Achievement in Construction Award at a January banquet at the New York Hilton. By the time John was introduced at the gala occasion on January 27, 1993, he knew Harbert was leaving the construction business entirely. Knowing it was the right thing to do did not make the decision any easier for him.

John took the opportunity of the Moles' address to testify to the importance of the construction business to the nation—for jobs, for its effect upon vendors and suppliers, and for the creation of the country's infrastructure and its commercial buildings. He warned of the troubles he saw in the industry—low profit margins in a high-risk business, the loss of net worth in the industry over the past

Karen and Joel Piassick, Anne Kinder, Barbara and Bobby Shook, John and Wita, Rick Kinder, and Ace and Kathy Greenberg gather in the hall at the Governor's Mansion during a house party in December 1994.

decade, an increase in lawsuits and "contentious claims," and excessive government regulations. He urged the contractors to become involved in the political process before the industry was "buried even deeper in a morass of laws that compete and conflict with each other for constant attention." Much of the talk had a pessimistic tone, but in the end John was forever the optimist, anticipating that the future would hold exciting changes. For his own life, he said, he would not change places unless he "could be 50 years younger."[32]

In late 1992 Harbert began secret negotiations to sell its domestic construction unit. This sale was completed to Raytheon Engineers and Contractors International of Lexington, Massachusetts, on June 17, 1993. Harbert Construction Corporation, the largest of Harbert's construction companies, was to become part of Yeargin, Inc. of Greenville, South Carolina, and would operate as Harbert-Yeargin, Inc., with the Harbert portion to be headquartered in Birmingham. John was to serve on the board of directors of the new corporation.[33] Despite the sale, Harbert still held a number of significant assets: Harbert Cogen, which operated eight alternative electrical plants in California; Harbert Realty Service, which owned and managed commercial properties; and Harbert Machine Company, a steel fabricating plant. The divestiture of its construction operations would allow Harbert Corporation to concentrate on other investment opportunities.[34]

In January 1995, John called Hall Thompson and asked him to fly to Washington, D.C., with him and Harold Apolinsky, a Birmingham attorney who was heading up a national effort to repeal the federal inheritance tax. Hall agreed and they went in his plane. They were to testify before a congressional committee on Tuesday, January 31, so they flew up on Monday. John had a cellular telephone and a new tiny computer Rolodex that Hall had given him for Christmas. When the three were in a taxi headed for town, John started making calls. Before they reached the hotel John had contacted half of Alabama's congressional delegation and had luncheon and dinner dates with Senators Howell Heflin and Richard Shelby. John also made arrangements for the three of them to meet the president of Heritage Foundation, the executive director of the Smithsonian Institution, and the chairman of the Republican Party. Apolinsky was amazed, for he thought he could have "worked for six months and not been able to make appointments and see all the people we saw in eight hours."[35]

Throughout 1993 and 1994, Harbert Corporation continued to pay down the March 1991 loan. Harbert Power Corporation put a number of new power plants into operation, and the San Francisco Bay area plants, in which so much was invested, began to produce income. During this time Wita took John to a California spa to relax, but he did not enjoy the experience. In November 1994 John was honored by the *Alabama Construction News*. It presented him with its first annual Cornerstone Award for his lifetime achievements in the construction industry. During his speech, John quoted from his 1975 interview in the *Engineering News-Record* when he had contemplated leaving construction; he also talked about how gratifying and exciting his work had been, and he paid tribute to all his employees and associates who made the success of Harbert possible.[36]

On February 16, 1995, Harbert Corporation made the final payment on its loan. To celebrate and express his appreciation, Raymond planned a dinner at the Summit Club for the management team that had worked so hard. He called the March 7 affair the "Sheep Dip Dinner" from a cheap brand of single malt Scotch whiskey they would share before the meal. Joining Raymond and John were the team that made the celebration possible: Will Brooke, Charlie Miller, and David Boutwell from Harbert. Swift Barnes flew in from San

On March 7, 1995, just weeks before his death, John joined son Raymond and the young management team of Harbert Corporation for dinner at the Summit Club to celebrate a successful restructuring period. Seated: Tom Hough, Raymond, John, Swift Barnes. Standing: Will Brooke, David Boutwell, Charlie Miller, and Joel B. Piassick.

Francisco and Tom Hough from New York, where they were currently working. Joel B. Piassick, who had helped with restructuring the corporation, flew over from Atlanta. Raymond had whiskey glasses etched with the event and the date, and he passed out enlargements of a drawing that had inspired them, a cartoon that said: "It ain't over 'til it's over." Each man passed around his copy and the others autographed it with words of wisdom. John wrote the same inscription on every one: "Problems create opportunities. Winners solve problems. John M. Harbert III." John had witnessed every entrepreneur's hope and every father's dream—that of seeing his business passed on to another generation and watching a son succeed.

Despite the celebration of the evening, John was not feeling his best because his PSA count had risen again, but this time only to 20. The Birmingham doctors were convinced that all was fine, for they could not find cancer any other place in John's body, but John wanted to be checked at M. D. Anderson Cancer Center. So on Monday, March 13, 1995, six days after the "Sheep Dip Dinner," John and Wita flew to Houston, Texas, where they were guests of Jack and Annis Bowen. John went to the hospital with his records. He was checked from head to toe, and some tests were made. By late afternoon John met with Dr. Andrew von Eschenbach and was given a clear report: although the cancer was still present, it had not spread. John called his office at about 4:30 and told Sandi to spread the good news: "They say I've got the body of a fifty-five-year old man, and I'm going to die of something, but it ain't gonna be prostate cancer. Go have a drink and celebrate."[37] It would be the last time John called the office.

That night the Bowens and Harberts went to Maxim's for dinner. But as the salad course was being served, John suddenly felt ill and excused himself but insisted that Wita and the Bowens finish eating. He would take a taxi to the Bowens' condo. When they returned home, Wita found John in great pain. Jack called his internist, and they rushed John to Methodist Hospital.[38] Wita remembers that at the time she was "very concerned, but had no real thought he would not live."[39] The next morning John seemed to be better. The doctors diagnosed acute pancreatitis but told Wita she could take him home to Birmingham on Wednesday by Medjet. It was all arranged. The Harbert plane had remained in Houston. The Medjet, with nurse and doctor, was to take John to UAB. However, early Wednesday John took a sudden turn for the worse and was rushed into intensive care. Although everything was done to save his life, his organs were not able to fight the poison pouring from his pancreas. Margie, remembering the agony of those days and how all the family suffered at watching their husband and father suffer, said, "Daddy had such a strong will and such a strong heart, it took him eighteen days to die." John Harbert died in Houston, Texas, on March 31, 1995.[40]

Two days later the Birmingham airport was especially busy for a Sunday morning as an unusually large number of private planes flew into the city. In the early afternoon, Saint Mary's Church was overflowing with dignitaries, friends, and family. The service was according to the Episcopal ritual for the dead, and there was no eulogy. No words could possibly do justice to John's life. He was buried at Elmwood Cemetery in Birmingham in Wita's family plot.

13

A LIFE OF CONTINUOUS BEGINNINGS

"some of us are born to build"

John M. Harbert III was very much a man of his generation. He was born in the Roaring Twenties, grew up a Boy Scout in the Great Depression, earned his manhood on the battlefields of a world war, and founded his corporation during the economic boom of postwar America. He had come up the hard way, suffering from the effects of the depression when his family never had enough money. Very early in his life he learned that to get what he needed and wanted he would have to work for it. When he was a boy, John made a commitment to live by the scout creed, and when he became a man, he never forgot it. He always tried to do his best, to do his duty as he saw it to God and country, to be honest, help other people, and stay morally straight. From scout to college student to engineer to soldier, John's early life was one of continuous changes and expanding horizons.

World War II affected John's life in untold ways. During stateside training he became fascinated with the concepts of leadership and how to direct men and accomplish goals. The examples of poor leadership that he witnessed in the army helped him become a skilled leader with the ability to instill in his workers an esprit de corps that had much to do with his company's success. His army experiences brought him into contact with diverse people and honed his skill for getting along, but it also convinced him that he did not like being under the direction and orders of others. He much preferred to work from his own initiative, directing himself. Combat and his months in Europe gave him a deeper appreciation for life and an understanding of suffering and hunger. Home and country became ever dear to him.

His ASTP experiences at the University of Illinois made John aware of the limitations in his own education, and as the years passed, John realized that his civil engineering education was incomplete. He expanded his knowledge through reading, study, and travel. In 1986 when Birmingham-Southern College awarded him an honorary degree, John said in his acceptance speech that he recognized "the importance of a strong liberal arts background" and that his own college courses in

On February 11, 1987, John and Wita joined their close friends Hall and Lucy Thompson when Hall's portrait was dedicated at the Center for Advanced Medical Studies at the University of Alabama in Birmingham.

children to be comfortable in different cultures.

Growing up in the shadow of Birmingham's elite suburb, John was close to but never felt part of the city's inner social circle, and he had an uneasy relationship with established Birmingham money. He was never invited to join the Redstone Club, one of the city's oldest and most prestigious social organizations, although he was put up for membership three times and on several occasions spoke to the group. Wita's friends were her Mountain Brook Grammar School classmates, neighbors, and relatives. They were, through Wita, John's friends, too, but some of his closest personal friends were men not originally from Birmingham: Hall Thompson; at Harbert, Ed Dixon and Bill Rossman; and men from other places—Jack Bowen of Houston and Bobby Radcliff of Mobile. Feeling not quite accepted only worked to John's advantage, increasing his incredible drive to succeed and to prove himself.

math and science were not enough. The humanities, the fine arts, and communication skills were areas John explored and studied on his own. He observed that "in today's world, there is scarcely time for such self-tutelage." John supported "a broad liberal arts experience," which he believed was "essential for young people who hope to succeed in business or a profession."[1] He always regretted that he was not fluent in several languages, and he advocated a foreign language requirement for students. Once when the family was dining at La Tour d'Argent in Paris, John was impatient with Margie because she would not use her French to speak with the waiter.[2] He wanted his

John was proud of his financial success because he had earned it the hard way. He enjoyed the fruits of his labors. Although in his later years he enjoyed dressing in the finest black tie, handmade English shoes, and clothes from Savile Row, he was never vain and he was usually more comfortable in khaki pants and boots. He could be as polished as he wanted to be, but when relaxed or when the occasion demanded it, that soldier's vocabulary he learned in the war years peppered his conversation.

He was, as the men of his generation mostly were, something of a chauvinist, and he was the patriarch of his family. Although he was

The Thanksgiving weekend was set aside for the family to gather at Pinebloom. In 1994 a professional photographer came from Albany to take pictures.

generous and always provided what his wife and children needed, he still controlled the purse strings; they had to ask, and he sometimes said no. Margie once observed that "Daddy let us know that it was his money, not ours."[3] He expected his sons to work hard, just as he did. John did not establish trust funds for his children when they were young because he wanted them not to live their lives dependent upon what he had earned but to understand that they must make their own way in life.

Some of John's friends perceived that his usual optimism faded in his last years; however, for most of his life John was an unfailing optimist with a strong faith in humanity. Even when those whom he trusted most let him down, he was not cynical about people. When Hall Thompson unveiled the statue of John at the Harbert Plaza on February 24, 1997, he stressed John's empathy for human beings. Thompson pointed out that although the public realized what an astute businessman John was, "what really isn't known generally is how deeply John cared about people and certainly about those less fortunate than himself."[4]

When Raymond was asked about the

Nothing pleased John more than wrestling with his grandchildren. To have time with them was one of the main reasons he retired.

All three John Harberts pose with their birds in the fall of 1994.

essence of his father's life, he observed that "some people take energy, and others, like my father, give energy to people and leave them feeling better about themselves." He thought his father was "one of those people who were capable of reaching out and touching people." He believed that his father "lived life to its absolute fullest, and consequently, he was full, he was vibrant."[5] Jay remembered a father who was hard on him, demanding as much perfection as he could master, and he misses the time he spent with his father traveling to the coal mines and job sites and the excitement of construction and heavy equipment. Margie noted that her father always "had the spirit of a young boy" and "was so much fun to be with." She remarked that "Daddy was not around a lot, but his ability to make his love last during his absences was remarkable to me."[6]

Wita observed that John was "the most industrious man I ever knew," and he had "the most overwhelming desire to understand everything—the land, farming, old silver, birds, the stars, rivers, art, sculpture, topography. His search for knowledge was constant and his interests were catholic." She looked back on their long years of marriage and nostalgically reflected that "when John woke up in the morning each new day was a new adventure for him." He was, she believes, the quintessential philanthropist. He enjoyed "doing things for people less fortunate than he was," and he wanted "to make the world a better place."[7]

In his Newcomen speech in October 1981, John described the Harbert Corporation history "as one of continuous beginnings, an ever-expanding middle, and so far, no end."[8] John had prepared his company well for the time when he would no longer be around, and he had supported Raymond in initiating a new beginning. But John's sudden death in 1995 following such hopeful news about his prostate cancer caught his family and friends completely by surprise. For Wita it was difficult to realize that John would not be coming home again. For almost forty-four years he may have missed dinner or been on the other side of the world, but he would always be coming home. He was to his children, especially to his daughter, Margie, a special father and a hero. Soon after his father's death, Raymond observed his son, John, whose personality so much mirrors that of his grandfather, as the child watched Disney's *The Lion King*. The death of the old king, Mufasa, and Simba, his son, taking his own place in the circle of life suddenly had a deeper meaning for Raymond.[9]

For himself, John Harbert once said that the source of his greatest satisfaction was "to realize that we have helped provide jobs and a better way of life for thousands of families associated with Harbert," and "if I am to be remembered for anything, this accomplishment means the most to me."[10] Beyond the creation of jobs, he was proud of the good roads and bridges he built so people could travel more conveniently; the water, gas, and sewer lines that his company buried so that the quality of life for a town's citizens was improved; the higher standards of living he brought to his coal mining families in eastern Kentucky; the natural forests of Riverchase's landscape; the Harbert Center that adds so much to the civic spirit of his city; and the AmSouth/Harbert Plaza addition to Birmingham's skyline.

Hall Thompson said that "John Harbert *was* a special man, and history will prove him to be among the greatest of all Alabamians."[11] James R. Nelson, who, as director of the Alabama School for Fine Arts, had a twenty-two-year friendship with John, believed that John was "an artist in every best sense of the word" whose "accomplishments will long outlive the opinion of his critics." "The artist," Nelson wrote, "changes the face of his time with works of lasting, transcendent value. John Harbert built things that will outlast his generation and serve generations to come. He changed the landscape of his beloved Alabama and affected every part of the world he touched."[12]

Neal Berte noted that John "was a builder, not only in a literal sense, but figuratively as well," a man who "personified the spirit, values, and rewards of American free enterprise."[13] John was satisfied and happy being a builder. In accepting the Moles' Outstanding Achievement in Construction Award at the New York Hilton Hotel on January 27, 1993, John expressed appreciation for the award but said that his "true reward is having the opportunity to be a builder, to create structures that will last long after we are gone. If I had my life to live over, I would be what I am today. Some of us are born to build."[14]

While John was serving on the Board of Regents of the Smithsonian Institution, he lobbied for Birmingham to be the southern city to host the 150th anniversary Smithsonian touring exhibition planned for 1997. After his death in 1995, Wita took his place on the board and continued to support Birmingham as a tour site. When the America's Smithsonian *exhibition opened in Birmingham, May 29, 1997, it was dedicated to John.*
At the gala the night before Wita celebrated with Winton "Red" Blount and his wife, Carolyn, and the secretary of the Smithsonian, Michael Heyman (far right).

NOTES

Introduction

1 Interview with Hall Thompson, February 26, 1997.
2 Ethel Armes, "The Spirit of the Founders," *Survey*, January 6, 1912, 1453.
3 Bill French, "First, one must learn," *Birmingham News*, January 22, 1989.
4 James Saxon Childers, *Erskine Ramsay: His Life and Achievements* (New York: Cartwright and Ewing, 1942), 281.
5 *Birmingham News*, December 3, 1976.
6 French, "First, one must learn."
7 Interview with Ed Dixon, October 10, 1996.
8 John M. Harbert III, *Acceptance Remarks: The Cornerstone Award, Associated Builders and Contractors of Alabama*, November 4, 1994, 10.
9 Although John's Newcomen speech was copyrighted in 1982, the Harbert Corporation also copyrighted the phrase "continuous beginnings" in 1994.

Chapter 1

1 John's father compiled a genealogy that traces through his grandfather's Crockett and Drake lines to Sir Francis Drake and through his grandmother's Cash and Robertson lines to General James Robertson, a well-known Tennessee frontiersman. Harbert Ancestry Chart, original courtesy of Margie Harbert Gray and duplication courtesy of Ann Harbert Moulton.
2 Although the information his father used was based upon family records and the Daughters of the American Revolution papers, which his grandmother and aunts had filed in the early part of the century (however, with no dates and no documentation), this line has been challenged by recent genealogical studies.
Sarah Foster Kelley, *Children of Nashville: Lineages from James Robertson* (Nashville: Blue and Gray Press, 1973), 189, questions whether "John Robertson, son of McNairy [the youngest son of General James Robertson], married Elizabeth Williamson, as declared in DAR papers #37493, #34993, #8182, and #47385." (See *DAR Lineage Book*, vols. 9, 35, 38, and 48.) These are John Harbert's great-grandmother's and great-aunt's DAR papers. Kelley cites the fact that John McNairy Robertson was born April 26, 1792, and would have been only seventeen years old when the man who was supposed to be his *son*, John Robertson, was married to Elizabeth Williamson in Wilson County, Tennessee, on March 9, 1809. (Edythe Rucker Whitley, *Marriages of Wilson County, Tennessee* [Baltimore: Genealogical Publishing Company, 1981], 9.) Kelley believes that the John Robertson who married Elizabeth Williamson was more likely the son of Hugh Robertson, who died in 1805. She believes that Captain John Robertson was killed in the Creek War. Telephone conversation with Kelley, August 4, 1997, and Sarah Foster Kelley to Leah Atkins, August 14, 1997. Evidence indicates that Ms. Kelley is correct.
3 Ramsey is sometimes spelled Ramsay. Harbert Ancestry Chart; Thomas Perkins Abernethy, *From Frontier to Plantation in Tennessee* (1932; reprint, University: University of Alabama Press, 1967), 3-15, 22, 27-32, 117, 129; DAR work sheet of Virginia Daday, Denver, Colorado, courtesy of Virginia Daday.
4 Janie Preston Collup French, *Notable Southern Families*, vol. 5, *The Crockett Family and Connecting Lines* (Bristol, Tennessee: King Printing Company, 1928), 101; Janice L. Abercrombie and Richard Slatten, comps., *Virginia Revolutionary Publick Claims* (Athens, Georgia: Iberian Publishing,

1992), 1:339; Lewis Preston Summers, *Annals of Southwest Virginia, 1769-1800* (Abingdon, Virginia: Lewis Preston Summers, 1929), 672, 710.

5 Virginia Gorin Daday, DAR membership papers #483665. French, *Notable Southern Families*, 5:101-02, 104-05. The John Harbert in Richmond County may be John's ancestor. U.S. Census, 1810, 1820, North Carolina Index and Cumberland County; U.S. Census, 1850, Madison County, Tennessee; *History of Tennessee from the Earliest Time* (Nashville: Goodspeed, 1887), 818, 845, 889. The Murchison family was still living in Madison County at the end of the nineteenth century. William Murdoch Murchison's son, who had been born in North Carolina in 1828, was a doctor who served in the Confederate army's Fifty-second Regiment. He provided information that he came from North Carolina with his father and his mother, Isabella Reid Murchison, who bore her husband ten children. The doctor reported that his father "was a man of more than ordinary mental force, and served in the North Carolina Senate for about twenty years, acquiring a State reputation for legislative work" (889). A list of North Carolina state legislators, however, indicates that Murchison served Cumberland County in the General Assembly as a senator for only one year in 1830. See John H. Wheeler, *Historical Sketches of North Carolina from 1584 to 1851* (1851; reprint, New York: Frederick H. Hancock, 1925), 132.

6 U.S. Census, 1850 and 1860, for Madison County, Tennessee, lists John Harbert as age fifty-three in 1850 and sixty-three in 1860, which would put his birth year as 1797 instead of 1790, which is the year given on the Harbert Ancestry Chart. The census gives his place of birth as Virginia and his wife's place of birth as Tennessee. U.S. Census 1850, 263; U.S. Census 1860, Madison County, 90.

7 *History of Tennessee from the Earliest Time*, 889.

8 Carlisle Page to John M. Harbert III, October 6, 1986, in John M. Harbert III Scrapbook, Personal, October 1986-August 1990; scrapbook hereafter abbreviated SB. Unless otherwise noted all Harbert citations are from materials located in the corporate archives of Harbert Corporation. *Memphis Commercial Appeal*, October 4, 1911; Harbert Genealogy Notebook compiled and written by John M. Harbert II, copy courtesy of Ann Harbert Moulton; May Keyes, *Belvedere and Other Places* (Memphis, Tennessee, 1992), 37-38a.

9 Clipping from *Memphis Commercial Appeal*, April 30, 1995, courtesy of Ann Harbert Moulton; Harbert Genealogy Notebook.

10 Interview with Virginia Daday, November 24, 1997.

11 Virginia Gorin Daday, "Harbert History," a collection of notes on family history and genealogy, courtesy of Virginia Daday; photograph of house on Popular Street taken in 1899 or 1900 with notations on back, in Harbert SB, Personal, 1937-78.

12 John M. Harbert III, handwritten memoir (hereafter cited as Harbert Memoir), n.d., no page numbers, but written for Charlotte Gafford in the late 1980s when she was writing a history of Harbert Corporation.

13 John William Leonard, *Who's Who in Engineering: A Biographical Dictionary of Contemporaries, 1922-1923* (New York: John W. Leonard, 1922), 555.

14 Harbert Memoir.

15 Leonard, *Who's Who in Engineering*, 555.

16 Interview with Bill Harbert, February 25, 1997.

17 John M. Harbert II to Mr. Brown, n.d., copy of letter in Harbert SB, Personal, 1937-78.

18 Western Union telegram, Jno. Harbert to Mrs. E. L. Schooling, Seattle, July 19, 1921; John M. Harbert III, birth announcement.

19 Rex Barrington, Memoir, 2. Rex served as John's secretary from 1950 to 1962 and wrote a recollection of those years for the author.

20 Irving Beiman, "Fast-moving John Harbert," *Birmingham News*, October 6, 1974; *Polk's Birmingham City Directory* (1924), 780; (1925), 602. No Harbert was listed in the 1923 *Birmingham City Directory*.

21 Corporation Records, Probate Court, Jefferson County, 29: 593. The company was incorporated with equipment worth $19,800 owned by Harbert Engineering Company. Incorporation records do not show what assets Cargile brought to the partnership.

22 Harbert Memoir.

23 Corporation Records, Probate Court, 33:450; 34:519; 36:477; 37:325.

24 Interview with Wita Harbert, October 17, 1996.

25 Jeff Hardy, "Corporate executive presented award," *Birmingham Post-Herald*, March 26, 1982. Mrs. Harbert had accepted on behalf of her son an Outstanding Philanthropist Award from the Alabama Society of Fund Raising Executives.

26 Phil Shook, "John M. Harbert," *Birmingham News*, June 24, 1979; John M. Harbert III, "Acceptance Remarks, Alabama Academy of Honor," August 18, 1980.

27 Magazine article, n.id., copy in Harbert SB,

Personal, 1937-78. Internal evidence indicates the year is 1967.

28 Interviews with Wita Harbert, May 23, August 3, 1996; interview with Fay Belt Ireland, September 12, 1996; interview with Wayne Peake, August 15, 1996; John M. Harbert III, *An Unpaid Debt: Reflections of a Boy Scout*, an address before Troop 5, Birmingham Area Council, Boy Scouts of America, February 7, 1994, 9.

29 Interview with Bill Harbert, February 25, 1997.

30 Beiman, "Fast-moving John Harbert"; Harbert, *An Unpaid Debt*, 4.

31 Interview with Bill Harbert, February 25, 1997; interview with Joy Harbert, February 25, 1997.

32 Ann Moulton has the certificate for the school year 1932-33. Although her father remembers the year as 1934, he also said that he was in fourth grade and John was in sixth grade. The school year 1932-33 fits these grades; John Harbert, Seattle Junior Safety Patrol Merit Medal, 1932-33, 1934, courtesy of Bill Harbert.

33 Interview with Bill Harbert, February 25, 1997.

34 Polk's 1928 *Birmingham City Directory* lists Mr. Harbert's home address as 200 Bonita Drive, Homewood, under his downtown company listing in 1928, but the directory excludes Homewood until the late 1940s. From 1932 to 1934 there is no Harbert listed in the *Birmingham City Directory*.

35 It was during this time that John met Bobby Radcliff, who became a close friend for the rest of his life. Interview with R. H. "Bobby" Radcliff, Jr., June 4, 1997.

36 Interview with Wayne Peake, August 15, 1996; John M. Harbert III to B. Wayne Peake, October 22, 1984.

37 Harbert, *An Unpaid Debt*, 4.

38 Ibid., 5.

39 Ibid., 6-7; John M. Harbert III, "Stuffed Crows, Credit Buying and Star Gazing," *Scouting*, October 1977, 56.

40 John M. Harbert III, *Making the Most of What You've Got and Having Fun Doing It*, a presentation to the University of Alabama in Birmingham School of Engineering, February 20, 1976, 2.

41 Typed Court of Honor document that could be a press release, April 30, 1937, copy courtesy of Wayne Peake.

42 James E. West to John M. Harbert, May 10, 1937, in Harbert SB, Personal, 1937-78.

43 Harbert, *An Unpaid Debt*, 4-5, 8-9.

44 Copies of *Jamboree Journal*, June 29, 30, July 3, 6, 1937; Ken Spear, "The 1937 Jamboree," 4-5, in *Now & Then*, n.d., but probably a 1986 issue, in Harbert SB, Personal, 1937-78.

45 Clipping from the *Birmingham News*, n.d., in Harbert SB, Personal, October 1986-August 1990.

46 Interview with Ed Dixon, September 26, 1996.

47 Beiman, "Fast-moving John Harbert."

48 *Alabama Magazine*, September 1982, 11.

49 Interview with Bill Harbert, August 15, 1996. A picture of young Billy and Betty appears with the eighth grade in a photograph in Marilyn Davis Barefield, *A History of Mountain Brook, Alabama, & Incidentally of Shades Valley* (Birmingham: Southern University Press, 1989), 67.

50 John M. Harbert III to Dad, February 19, 1944. John M. Harbert III's original World War II letters are courtesy of Margie Harbert Gray.

51 Interview with Fay Ireland, September 12, 1996.

52 John M. Harbert II to sister Bessie, September 2, 1940.

53 Charlotte Gafford, "Harbert: The History of a Corporation," typescript, copyright 1989 by Harbert Corporation, revised copy of chap. one, 2-3. At least two typed versions of this history exist, and there is an error in the page numbering on the copy in the Harbert Corporation files.

54 Interview with Wita Harbert, May 23, 1996.

55 John M. Harbert III to Principal, Gulfport High School, April 20, 1970, Margaret Evans file, Miscellaneous Correspondence.

56 Harbert, *Making the Most*, 8. John M. Harbert III to Principal, Gulfport High School, April 20, 1970; E. M. Keith to John M. Harbert III, April 23, 1970; John M. Harbert III to Mrs. Houston Evans, August 19, 1974; Margaret Evans to John M. Harbert III, September 3, 1974, all in Margaret Evans file, Miscellaneous Correspondence.

57 John M. Harbert III to Mrs. Houston Evans, January 30, 1981, and Margaret Evans to John M. Harbert III, February 10, 1981. This series of letters was prompted when John spoke with Dr. Otis Singletary, president of the University of Kentucky. Singletary reminded John that they had been classmates at Gulfport High School and had been in Mrs. Evans's English class together. Singletary said he knew John would be successful because he "made it out" of Mrs. Evans's class; in Margaret Evans file, Miscellaneous Correspondence.

58 Interview with Wayne Peake, August 15, 1996.

59 Draft of a letter by Wayne Peake to John and Bill Harbert following their mother's death in September 1986, original in possession of Wayne Peake; interview with Bill Harbert, February 25, 1997.

Chapter 2

1 John M. Harbert III, *A Student's Reflections: Opening Remarks, Auburn University School of Business, 1980 Executive-in-Residence Program*, 2.
2 Gafford, "Harbert Corporation," 3.
3 Harbert, *A Student's Reflections*, 2. For background and other details about Harbert's API experiences see student directories, API *Bulletins*, the student newspaper the *Plainsman*, and the college annual the *Glomerata*.
4 Harbert, *A Student's Reflections*, 2.
5 Jim Killian, "Not a Scholar while at Auburn, Harbert Supports Education with Money & Time," *Auburn Alumnews*, April 1985.
6 Harbert, *A Student's Reflections*, 2; interview with Wayne Peake, August 15, 1996.
7 Interview with Wayne Peake, August 15, 1996.
8 Killian, "Not a Scholar," 16.
9 John M. Harbert III, *From Boarding House to Board Room—and Lessons I Learned Along the Way*, Executive-in-Residence, University of South Alabama, Mobile, November 15, 1977, 6.
10 Harbert, *Acceptance Remarks: Cornerstone Award*, 3.
11 John M. Harbert III to Dad, February 19, 1944.
12 John M. Harbert III, "Risk: Key to Fulfillment," the Harbert S. Gregory Distinguished Lecture Series, School of Engineering, the University of Florida, October 25, 1990, 2.
13 *Alabama Polytechnic Institute Bulletin* 35 (February 1940): 328.
14 Harbert, *A Student's Reflections*, 2-3.
15 Interview with Wayne Peake, August 15, 1996.
16 Interview with Fred Hopton-Jones, December 19, 1996; interview with Charlie Shewmake, Sr., December 19, 1996; Allen Cronenberg, *Forth to the Mighty Conflict: Alabama and World War II* (Tuscaloosa: University of Alabama Press, 1995), 51; and Harbert, *Acceptance Remarks: Cornerstone Award*, 6-7.
17 John M. Harbert III, "John Harbert stresses importance of study of English," a reprint of part of a May address to the University of Montevallo student body, *Auburn Alumnews*, July-August 1979, 1.
18 Ibid.
19 John M. Harbert II to sister Bessie, September 2, 1940.
20 State of Mississippi, Death Certificate #14222, courtesy of Bill Harbert.
21 *Elmwood: Charter, Rules, Regulations and By-Laws of Elmwood Cemetery Association of Memphis* (Memphis: Boyle and Chapman, 1874), 13, 195. (When this cemetery history was published in 1874, John Harbert had been buried there on Chapel Hill Circle, Lots 20 and 21. Betty Harbert was buried in the Harbert plot in Elmwood Cemetery on August 30, 1940.) Marian Frye to Leah Atkins, December 19, 1996.
22 John M. Harbert II to sister Bessie, September 2, 1940.
23 John M. Harbert III to Raymond Harbert, November 1990; interview with Wita Harbert, August 3, 1996.
24 Interview with Wita Harbert, June 5, 1996; interview with Wayne Peake, August 15, 1996. When the author talked to the third student in August 1996, he related that all three were equally guilty but that at the time he took responsibility because he was leaving Auburn for air corps training.
25 Harbert, *Acceptance Remarks: Cornerstone Award*, 4.
26 Ibid.
27 Harbert, *A Student's Reflections*, 3-4.
28 David E. Alsobrook, "Auburn in 'The Good War,'" *Auburn Alumnews*, July-August 1991, 6.
29 John M. Harbert III to Mother, Sunday night, but undated letter in envelope postmarked from Auburn, March 1, 1943. February 28 was a Sunday, and John probably wrote the letter this day. The *Alabama Polytechnic Institute Bulletin, 1942-43*, gives final examination dates as March 3-5; however, because of wartime conditions during 1942-44, classes were often doubled-up and exams given early.
30 Harbert, *Acceptance Remarks: Cornerstone Award*, 3.
31 John M. Harbert III to Mother, March 1, 1943.
32 John M. Harbert III, *The Civil Engineer: His Life and Times Have Changed*, an address before the South African Institution of Civil Engineers, 1982, 4-5.
33 Harbert, *A Student's Reflections*, 4.
34 Army Service Forces, Headquarters Fourth Service Command, Atlanta, Georgia, Special Order No. 146, 19 June 1943, copy in Harbert SB, Personal, 1937-78.

Chapter 3

1 John M. Harbert III to Mother and Dad, Thursday night, July 8, 1943. John always put the day of the week on his letters, but he never put the date; however, most of his letters were saved in the original envelope with postmark. By using a calendar for the year, the correct date can be determined. Decades after the war when John made an inventory of his letters, he assigned dates to most of his letters. With only a few exceptions, the date he designated is used for note citations. The original letters are courtesy of Margie Harbert Gray.
2 John M. Harbert III to Mother, July 13, 1943.
3 Ibid., July 18, 1943.
4 Ibid., July 20, 1943.
5 John M. Harbert III to Mother and Dad, July 25, 1943.
6 John M. Harbert III to Mother, n.d., no envelope; interview with Wita Harbert, June 5, 1996.
7 John M. Harbert III to Dad, September 28, 1943; Harbert to Mother, October 20, 1943; John M. Harbert III, notes on his inventory of letters.
8 Outgoing Troop Movement Memorandum, Fort McClellan, October 19, 1943, Harbert SB, Personal, 1937-78.
9 John M. Harbert III to Mother, October 23, 1943; postcard (with photograph of the Alpha Delta Phi house) to Mother, November 10, 1943.
10 John's initial appointment was made official in 13th Co ASTP SEC 3652nd SU, Company Order No.1, December 1, 1943, in Harbert SB, Personal, 1937-78.
11 John M. Harbert III to Mother, November 7, 15, 1943.
12 John M. Harbert III to Mother and Dad, November 17, 1943.
13 John M. Harbert III to Mother, November 21, 23, 1943.
14 John M. Harbert III to Mother and Dad, November 27, 1943.
15 Ibid., December 5, 1943.
16 Ibid., December 7, 1943.
17 John M. Harbert III to Mother, December 11, 1943.
18 Ibid., January 1, 9, 15, 1944.
19 Ibid., January 14, 1944.
20 John M. Harbert III to Mother and Dad, January 30, 1944.
21 Ibid., February 3, 1944.
22 John M. Harbert III to Mother, February 6, 1944.
23 John M. Harbert III to Mother and Dad, no envelope, but probably February 7, 1944; Harbert to Dad, February 5, 1944.
24 John M. Harbert III to Mother and Dad, February 14, 1944; Wayne Peake to John M. Harbert III, February 21, 1944.
25 John M. Harbert III to Mother and Dad, February 16, 1944.
26 Ibid., February 18, 1944.
27 John M. Harbert III to Dad, February 19, 1944.
28 Ibid.
29 John M. Harbert III to Mother, February 22, 1944; undated letter but before February 25, 1944.
30 John M. Harbert III to Mother (postcard, San Antonio, Texas), February 25, 1944.
31 John Risen Jones wrote a recollection especially for the author (hereafter cited as Recollection) of his war years with John Harbert; see Recollection, 4.
32 John M. Harbert III to Mother (postcard, Niland, California), February 28, 1944.
33 Jones, Recollection, 1.
34 John M. Harbert III to Mother, February 28, 1944.
35 Ibid.
36 Leo A. Hoegh and Howard J. Doyle, *Timberwolf Tracks: The History of the 104th Infantry Division, 1942-1945* (Washington, D.C.: Infantry Journal Press, 1946), 8-9, 23.
37 John M. Harbert III to Mother, February 28, 1944.
38 Hoegh and Doyle, *Timberwolf Tracks*, 23-24.
39 John M. Harbert III to Mother and Dad, March 1, 5, 18, 1943; Hoegh and Doyle, *Timberwolf Tracks*, 28; the *Timberwolf* (104th Division newspaper), March 2, 1944.
40 John M. Harbert III to Mother, March 1, 1944.
41 Ibid., March 5, 1944.
42 John M. Harbert III to Mrs. James Shook, March 9, 1944.
43 Ibid.
44 John M. Harbert III to Mother, mailed March 21, 1944, from Albuquerque, New Mexico.
45 Ibid., March 24, 1944; Harbert to Mother and Dad, March 24, 1944.
46 John Risen Jones recalled that the "majority of the 104th was made up of men from Washington and Oregon" who were, "for the most part, uneducated." Jones, Recollection, 1.

47 John M. Harbert III to Dad, March 25, 1944.
48 John M. Harbert III to Mother, March 28, 1944.
49 John M. Harbert III to Dad, March 25, 1944.
50 Ibid., April 14, May 1, 7, 1944; Harbert to Mother, April 15, 17, 21, 24, 1944; Harbert to Mother and Dad, April 21, May 6, June 22, 27, 1944.
51 John M. Harbert III to Mother, April 8, 1944.
52 Ibid., April 17, 1944.
53 Ibid., May 25, 1944.
54 John M. Harbert III to Mother and Dad, June 14, 1944.
55 John M. Harbert III to Mrs. James Shook, June 17, 1944.
56 John M. Harbert III to Folks, June 27, 1994; John Risen Jones to John M. Harbert III, July 22, 1944.
57 John M. Harbert III to Mother, July 29, 1944.
58 Interview with Wita Harbert, June 5, 1996.
59 John M. Harbert III to Mother, July 8, 1944.
60 John M. Harbert III to Bill Harbert, July 5, 1944.
61 Jones, Recollection, 4.
62 John M. Harbert III to Bill Harbert, July 5, 1944.
63 John M. Harbert III to Mother, July 31, 1944.
64 Ibid., August 12, 1944.
65 Jones, Recollection, 1.
66 John M. Harbert III to Mother and Dad, somewhere on East Coast, August 19, 1944.
67 Interview with Fay Ireland, September 12, 1996.
68 Hoegh and Doyle, *Timberwolf Tracks*, 35; interview with John Risen Jones, September 2, 1996.
69 Shelby L. Stanton, *Order of Battle, U.S. Army, World War II* (Novato, California: Presidio, 1984), 182; Hoegh and Doyle, *Timberwolf Tracks*, 25-39; Jones, Recollection, 1.
70 Jones, Recollection, 2; John Risen Jones to Leah Atkins, October 16, 1996; U.S. Army, *Timberwolves: The Story of the 104th Infantry Division* (Paris: Curial-Archereau, 1945), 21-22; Hoegh and Doyle, *Timberwolf Tracks*, 39-42; John A. Mehlhop, *The Memoirs of a Maverick Major in World War II* (Roswell, New Mexico: Old-Time Publications, 1990), 217.
71 *Order of Battle [of the] United States Army, World War II: European Theater of Operations, Divisions* (Paris, 1945), 415, copy from U.S. Army Military History Institute, Carlisle Barracks, Carlisle, Pennsylvania.
72 U.S. Army, *Timberwolves*, 23; clipping, *Evening Standard* (London), October 18, 1944, Harbert SB, Personal, 1937-78.
73 Hoegh and Doyle, *Timberwolf Tracks*, 47, 55, 61; clipping, n.id., Associated Press, September 30, [1945], in Harbert SB, Personal, 1937-78; U.S. Army, *Trail of the Timberwolves*, 104th Infantry Division, Camp San Luis Obispo, California, 1945, 2-3.
74 Major General Terry Allen, *Night Attacks*, lecture based upon original pamphlet published by the 104th Division for combat use in Europe, [1944], 1952, 1-4, copy from U.S. Army Military History Institute.
75 Department of the Army, Historical Division, *Combat Chronicle, 104th Division*, 89, copy from U.S. Army Military History Institute.
76 U.S. Army, *Trail of the Timberwolves*, 3-5.
77 John M. Harbert III to Aunt Bess, from somewhere in Germany, November 19, 1944.
78 Jones, Recollection, 2-3; interview with Wita Harbert, June 5, 1996.
79 Jones, Recollection, 2-3; interview with Wita Harbert, October 17, 1996; clipping, *Sunday Graphics* (London), December 1, 1994, in Harbert SB, Personal, 1937-78.
80 Hugh M. Cole, *The European Theater of Operations, The Ardennes: Battle of the Bulge* (Washington, D.C.: U.S. Department of the Army, 1965), 334, 520; Hoegh and Doyle, *Timberwolf Tracks*, 195.
81 *Birmingham News*, December 17, 1984.
82 John to Wita, Christmas Day, 1990.
83 Clipping, Associated Press report by Don Whitehead, February 25, 1945, in Harbert SB, Personal, 1937-78; Hoegh and Doyle, *Timberwolf Tracks*, 144, 195.
84 Clipping, unidentified, February 25, 1945, in Harbert SB, Personal, 1937-78.
85 John M. Harbert III to B. Wayne Peake, February 19, 1993, copy courtesy of Wayne Peake.
86 Harbert, *An Unpaid Debt*, 7-8. John first wrote this story for an Eagle Scout awards banquet on February 19, 1975, twenty years before he rewrote the speech and published it as *An Unpaid Debt*.
87 *Rocky Mountain News*, February 26, 1944, clipping in Harbert SB, Personal, 1937-78.
88 Hoegh and Doyle, *Timberwolf Tracks*, 144, 195, 203, 269; clipping, United Press release, March 5, [1945], Paris, in Harbert SB, Personal, 1937-78.
89 Interview with Wita Harbert, September 25, 1996.
90 Mehlhop, *Memoirs of a Maverick Major*, 281-89. John Risen Jones recalled that Nordhausen was taken April 10 and that "John got word to

me to get into the city, and with Bill Meinz, my Sgt., we saw and photographed that horror." Jones, Recollection, 2-3.

91 John M. Harbert III to Parents, April 12, 1945. John's letter was printed in the *Shades Valley Sun*, clipping, n.d., in Harbert SB, Personal, 1937-78.

92 Hoegh and Doyle, *Timberwolf Tracks*, 320; Stanton, *Order of Battle*, 183.

93 William O. Jones to Mrs. John Harbert, May 16, 1945.

94 Hoegh and Doyle, *Timberwolf Tracks*, 376, 377-79.

95 Interview with Robert Jones, June 25, 1997; Jones, Recollection, 3.

96 Hoegh and Doyle, *Timberwolf Tracks*, 380-81; interview with Bill Harbert, August 15, 1996.

97 John M. Harbert to Fay Belt [Ireland], August 29, 1945.

98 Beiman, "Fast-moving John Harbert."

99 Hoegh and Doyle, *Timberwolf Tracks*, 379-80.

100 Interview with Sandi Falkenhagen, May 20, 1997.

Chapter 4

1 Harbert, *A Student's Reflections*, 4-5; interview with Bill Harbert, October 10, 1996.

2 Wayne Peake to John M. Harbert III, February 7, 11, 21, 1944. Unfortunately John's letters to Wayne have not been preserved. Wayne's original letters are with John's World War II letters in possession of Margie Harbert Gray. Permission to quote granted by Mildred Noland Peake.

3 Wayne Peake to John M. Harbert III, March 22, 1944.

4 Wayne Peake to John M. Harbert III, November 29, 1944. John recalled the discussion from "many, many years ago" following a visit to the MIT campus where he gave a speech at a construction industry summit. In a letter to Wayne, John noted that "looking back, I don't believe either of us missed a thing by not pursuing that MIT education. Still, one wonders what turn our lives might have taken." John M. Harbert III to B. Wayne Peake, September 10, 1993.

5 Harbert, *A Student's Reflections*, 4-5.

6 Interview with R. H. "Bobby" Radcliff, Jr., June 4, 1997.

7 Wayne Peake to John M. Harbert III, December 4, 1945; clipping, "Letter to a Seventeen-Year-Old Son," *Harper's*, August 1945, 167-74.

8 Wayne Peak to John M. Harbert III, December 8, 20, 1945.

9 Kaye Lovvorn, "A Success Story," *Auburn Alumnews*, April 1986, 4. When the John M. Harbert III civil engineering building was dedicated on April 4, 1986, John had Professor Honour's widow, Frances, as one of his guests.

10 John M. Harbert III, 1946 Federal Tax Return, and John M. Harbert III, "Fact and Dates on Some Personal Background," September 8, 1986.

11 *Forbes*, March 26, 1984, 48.

12 Killian, "Not a Scholar," 16; Harbert, *A Student's Reflections*, 5. John would have received his diploma earlier had he paid his fee.

13 John M. Harbert III, *Acceptance Remarks: Cornerstone Award*, 4.

14 Harbert, *A Student's Reflections*, 5; Gafford, "Harbert Corporation," 5-6; John M. Harbert III, 1946 Federal Tax Return; Drawings Coloma-Centre Rd., Proj. FAS 110-(1), Harbert SB, Jobs, 1971. On a concrete bridge the temporary underpinnings that support the concrete until it hardens are called the bridge's false work.

15 Harbert, *A Student's Reflections*, 5; John M. Harbert III, 1947 Federal Tax Return; Gafford, "Harbert Corporation," 5-6.

16 Harbert, "Fact and Dates."

17 John M. Harbert III, *Harbert: "A Story of Continuous Beginnings"* (New York: Newcomen Society in North America, 1982), 10.

18 Beiman, "Fast-moving John Harbert."

19 John M. Harbert III, *Appalachia: Its People, Its Coal, Its Future*, 1980, 1-2; John M. Harbert III to Joe H. Brady, April 12, 1966, Harbert SB, Jobs, 1971.

20 Gafford, "Harbert Corporation," 5.

21 Harbert, *Continuous Beginnings*, 10.

22 Ibid., 10-11.

23 Ibid., 12-13.

24 Bill French, "Desire to Survive," *Birmingham News*, January 22, 1989.

25 Harbert, *From Boarding House to Board Room*, 3; Harbert, 1946 and 1947 Federal Tax Returns; *Harbert Newsletter*, no. 2, 1961, 1.

26 Interview with Belton Y. Cooper, November 20, 1996; John M. Harbert III, "Remarks at Retirement Dinner Honoring Edwin M. Dixon," April 7, 1987, 2.

27 Harbert, "Remarks Honoring Dixon," 2-3; interviews with Ed Dixon, September 26, October 10, 1996.

28 John M. Harbert III, *The Individual: Industry's*

Greatest Asset, a presentation to the National Management Association, Birmingham Chapter, April 21, 1977, 7; Harbert, "Remarks Honoring Dixon," 3-5; "Rooster Bridge" in Helen Morgan Akens and Virginia Pounds Brown, *Alabama Mounds to Missiles* (Huntsville: Strode, 1966), 191-95.

29 Harbert, "Remarks Honoring Dixon," 6; Harbert, *From Boarding House to Board Room*, 3-4.

30 Interview with Belton Y. Cooper, November 20, 1996.

31 Gafford, "Harbert Corporation," 8; interviews with Ed Dixon, September 26, October 10, 1996.

32 Harbert, "Remarks Honoring Dixon," 8, and *Harbert Newsletter*, no. 2, 1961, 3.

33 Interview with Fay Ireland, September 12, 1996.

34 Harbert, *The Civil Engineer*, 5.

35 Interview with Wita Harbert, October 17, 1996; interview with Ed Dixon, October 10, 1996; French, "Desire to Survive."

36 Corporation Records, Probate Court, Jefferson County, 73:220.

37 *Harbert Newsletter*, April 1971, 8-9.

38 Interview with Ted and Jane Randolph, March 11, 1997.

39 Interview with Ed Dixon, September 26, 1996.

40 Barrington, Memoir, 1.

41 Corporation Records, Probate Court, Jefferson County, 77:89; *On Site*, January/February 1989, 1.

42 Harbert, *Continuous Beginnings*, 16; interview with Ted and Jane Randolph, March 11, 1997; Barrington, Memoir, 1.

43 John M. Harbert III, "Remarks on the Occasion of Ted's Retirement Dinner," January 29, 1985; Harbert, *Continuous Beginnings*, 16; Barrington, Memoir, 1; interview with Ted and Jane Randolph, March 11, 1997.

44 Harbert, "Remarks on the Occasion of Ted's Retirement," 1.

45 Barrington, Memoir, 4.

46 Harbert, *The Civil Engineer*, 3.

47 *Harbert Newsletter*, April 1971; *On Site*, January/February 1989, 3; interview with Ed Dixon, September 26, 1996; Barrington, Memoir, 1.

48 Harbert, "Remarks on the Occasion of Ted's Retirement"; interview with Ted and Jane Randolph, March 11, 1997.

49 Barrington, Memoir, 4.

50 Interview with Ted and Jane Randolph, March 11, 1997; *Harbert Newsletter*, April 1971, 9-10; Barrington, Memoir, 2.

51 Barrington, Memoir, 2.

52 Wayne Peake to John and Bill Harbert, September 1986, copy courtesy of Wayne and Mildred Noland Peake.

53 Interview with Belton Cooper, November 20, 1996.

54 Marguerite Jones Harbert, *Movers and Doers*, a presentation to the Nineteenth Century Club, November 13, 1985, 7-8.

55 Interview with Wita Harbert, March 18, 1996.

56 Ibid., November 18, 1996; Barrington, Memoir, 12.

57 Interview with Wita Harbert, October 17, 1996; Marguerite Harbert, *Movers and Doers*, 8.

58 Bevelle Comer Nabers, "The Nabers Family in Jefferson County," 3-6, clipping of obituary of Alice Worthington Nabers, August 2, 1952, in Worthington and Nabers Families, Hill Ferguson Collection, Department of Archives and Manuscripts, Birmingham Public Library; Henry Upton Sims, "The Genealogy of the Worthington Family of Alabama, South Carolina, Virginia, and Ohio," 34, Special Collections, Davis Library, Samford University; Florence Hawkins Wood Moss, *Building Birmingham and Jefferson County* (Birmingham: Birmingham Printing Company, 1947), 27-28, 30-31; interview with Wita Harbert and Acky Jones McGriff, August 4, 1996.

59 Henry M. Caldwell, *History of the Elyton Land Company and Birmingham* (1892; reprint, Birmingham: Southern University Press, 1926), 4-5; Leah Rawls Atkins, *The Valley and Hills: An Illustrated History of Birmingham and Jefferson County* (Woodland Hills, California: Windsor Publications, 1981), 50-52.

60 Interview with Wita Harbert, August 4, 1996.

61 *Southern Accent*, 1942, 125; 1943, 72-73, 80, 122-23.

62 Interview with Wita Harbert, November 18, 1996.

63 Ibid., February 12, 1997.

64 Interview with Neville Palmer, October 17, 1996.

65 Interview with Louise Hall, March 24, 1998.

66 Interview with Wita Harbert, August 4, 1996.

67 Interview with Wita Harbert and Acky Jones McGriff, August 5, 1996.

68 Interview with Wita Harbert, November 18, 1996.

69 Ibid., March 18, November 18, 1996.

70 Bill Harbert and Ed Dixon to John M. Harbert III, July 16, 1951, copy in Harbert SB, Personal, 1937-78, and also printed in *Harbert Newsletter*, January 1976, 4-5.

71 John M. Harbert III to Mother, July 31, 1944.

Chapter 5

1 French, "Desire to Survive."
2 Copy of clipping of magazine article, n.id., n.d., but probably 1967, in Harbert SB, Personal, 1937-78.
3 John M. Harbert III, Memorandum Records of Farm Real Estate Purchases, n.d.
4 Clipping, *Birmingham News*, January 2, 1953, and various undated and unidentified clippings, in Harbert SB, Personal, 1937-78.
5 Copy of magazine article, n.id., n.d., but probably 1967, in Harbert SB, Personal, 1937-78.
6 Rebel Chapter, YPO, personal information, 1958, 1964.
7 Barrington, Memoir, 12.
8 Interview with Wita Harbert, October 17, 1996.
9 John M. Harbert III to Wita Harbert, July 24, 1953.
10 Interview with Wita Harbert, February 12, 1997.
11 *Birmingham News*, April 15, 1962. The Harbert home was on the spring and garden tour of the Church of the Advent, April 28-29, 1962.
12 Interview with Wita Harbert, February 12, 1997.
13 Andrew Kilpatrick, "Harbert Corp. founder gets things done," *Birmingham Post-Herald*, January 17, 1989.
14 Interview with Elmer Harris, September 24, 1996.
15 Harbert, *Continuous Beginnings*, 13.
16 Ibid.
17 Ibid.
18 The sewage disposal plant for Tarpon Springs was for $218,467.64 and was to be completed in April 1951. Unidentified clipping, March 1, 1951, in Harbert SB, Jobs, 1971; John M. Harbert III, "Remarks on the Occasion of Ted's Retirement."
19 *The Florida Venture*, Harbert Construction Corporation promotional film.
20 Harbert, "Remarks on the Occasion of Ted's Retirement," 3.
21 Harbert, *A Student's Reflections*, 11.
22 John M. Harbert III, Testimony before the Federal Power Commission, n.d., Florida Gas file.
23 Harbert, *A Student's Reflections*, 11-12.
24 W. J. Bowen to Leah Atkins, June 6, 1997.
25 Harbert, *A Student's Reflections*, 12.
26 Harbert, *Continuous Beginnings*, 12-13.
27 Harbert, *A Student's Reflections*, 13; Gafford, "Harbert Corporation," 24.
28 Harbert, *A Student's Reflections*, 13.
29 John M. Harbert III to Beverly Kees, August 25, 1992.
30 M. F. Pixton to Chester M. Goldman, January 8, 1957, in Harbert SB, Personal, 1937-78.
31 Ibid.
32 W. J. Bowen to Leah Atkins, June 6, 1997.
33 John M. Harbert, "Remarks on the Occasion of Bill Rossman's Retirement Party," May 10, 1985, 2; Gafford, "Harbert Corporation," 25.
34 *Allis-Chalmers Reporter*, May-June 1959, 6-7; interview with Don Cook, June 9, 1997.
35 Interview with Ted and Jane Randolph, March 11, 1997.
36 *Birmingham Post-Herald*, December 27, 1958.
37 *The Florida Venture*, promotional film.
38 Clipping, n.id., December 27, 1958, in Harbert SB, Personal, 1937-78; *The Florida Venture*, promotional film.
39 *Harbert Newsletter*, April 1971, 11.
40 W. J. Bowen to Leah Atkins, June 6, 1997.
41 Interview with George Gambrill, February 11, 1997; *The Florida Venture*, promotional film; *Birmingham News*, September 5, 1957.
42 Barrington, Memoir, 10.
43 Kilpatrick, "Harbert founder gets things done."
44 W. J. Bowen to Leah Atkins, June 6, 1997.
45 Harbert, *A Student's Reflections*, 14.
46 The Columbus, Mississippi, work was Job #307, June 1956, for $94,513.99, and the Brookley work was Job #308 for $1,000,000.
47 John M. Harbert III, *Entrepreneurship: A Game You Can't Play from the Bench*, an address before the Entrepreneurship Forum, Birmingham, May 17, 1986, 2.
48 Ibid., 3.
49 *Sarasota Herald-Tribune*, January 15, 1957.
50 Harbert, *Entrepreneurship*, 3.
51 Interview with George Gambrill, February 11, 1997; Barrington, Memoir, 10.
52 Interview with Wita Harbert, October 17, 1996.
53 Barrington, Memoir, 6; interview with Ted Randolph, February 11, 1997.
54 John M. Harbert III, *The Individual: Industry's Greatest Asset*, 9-10.
55 John M. Harbert III to Margaret Russo, April 2, 1970; interview with Sandi Falkenhagen, August 7, 1997.
56 Gafford, "Harbert Corporation," 21.
57 Harbert, "Risk: Key to Fulfillment," 9.
58 Typed interview with Bill Harbert by Charlotte Gafford, April 22, 1989.
59 Gafford, "Harbert Corporation," 20.
60 Ibid., 31.
61 Interview with Ed Dixon, October 10, 1996.
62 *Harbert Newsletter*, December 1959.

Chapter 6

1 John Gissen, "John Harbert III of Harbert Corporation," *Forbes*, March 26, 1984, 49.
2 Harbert, "Remarks Honoring Dixon," 8.
3 Harbert, *Continuous Beginnings*, 7.
4 Interview with Rex Barrington, June 2, 1997.
5 Harbert, "Risk: Key to Fulfillment," 9.
6 Memo from JMH III, *Harbert Newsletter*, July-August 1960, 1.
7 Deed from M. Lowenstein and Sons, Inc., to John M. Harbert, October 24, 1959, Highlands Property file.
8 Interview with Wita Harbert, August 3, 1996.
9 *Birmingham News*, May 23, 1989.
10 Interview with Wita Harbert, August 4, 1996.
11 *Birmingham News*, December 25, 1960.
12 Ibid., September 14, 1961.
13 *Harbert Newsletter*, Fall 1969, 5-6.
14 *Birmingham News*, December 25, April 24, 1960, April 15, 1962.
15 Interview with Margie Harbert Gray, October 28, 1997.
16 John M. Harbert III, "Remarks to the Samford Business Majors Association and Guests," February 14, 1975, 6-7.
17 *Harbert Newsletter*, April 1960, 2.
18 Gafford, "Harbert Corporation," 37.
19 Typed interview with Bill Rossman by Charlotte Gafford, March 18, 1986, 2.
20 *Harbert Newsletter*, May-June, July-August 1960; typed interview with Bill Rossman by Charlotte Gafford, 2.
21 Jackson [Mississippi] *State Times*, December 9, 1960; typed interview with Bill Rossman by Charlotte Gafford, 2.
22 Typed interview with Bill Rossman by Charlotte Gafford, 2-3; Gafford, "Harbert Corporation," 37.
23 *Harbert Newsletter*, no. 2, 1961, 4-5.
24 Ibid., no. 4, 1961, 4.
25 Typed interview with Bill Rossman by Charlotte Gafford, 3-4.
26 Interview with Wita Harbert, August 3, 1996; Marguerite Harbert, *Movers and Doers*, 8.
27 *Harbert Newsletter*, May-June 1960, 1; Gafford, "Harbert Corporation," 37.
28 Harbert, *Continuous Beginnings*, 14.
29 Typed interview with Bill Rossman by Charlotte Gafford, 5.
30 Harbert, *Continuous Beginnings*, 13.
31 Interview with Ed Dixon, October 10, 1996; Guy McGowan, *Messages: A Selection of Pastoral Essays*, with an introduction by John M. Harbert III (Rutland, Vermont: Academy Books, 1976), i, 13.
32 Harbert, *Continuous Beginnings*, 14; typed interview with Bill Rossman by Charlotte Gafford, 5.
33 Harbert, "Remarks on Rossman's Retirement," 4.
34 Gafford, "Harbert Cooperation," 41.
35 Interview with Evelyn Rossman, February 28, 1996.
36 The clipping with envelope attached are in John's corporate history files.
37 Gafford, "Harbert Corporation," 43.
38 Interview with Evelyn Rossman, February 28, 1996.
39 Jackson *Clarion-Ledger*, November 11, 1962.
40 *Harbert Newsletter*, December 1962, 3-4.
41 Ibid.; typed interview with Bill Rossman by Charlotte Gafford, 5; Gafford, "Harbert Corporation," 44.
42 *Harbert Newsletter*, Fall 1962, 2.
43 Obituary, *Birmingham News*, February 26, 1964; *Birmingham Post-Herald*, February 27, 1964; John M. Harbert, Protective Life Insurance Company form. Mr. Harbert's birth date is incorrectly given in the newspapers. He was born September 14, 1887. John M. Harbert II files.
44 *Harbert Newsletter*, December 1964, 4.
45 *Birmingham Post-Herald*, December 8, 1964; *Birmingham News*, December 8, 1964.
46 Typed interview with Don Cook by Charlotte Gafford, July 11, 1986, 7.
47 Interview with Ed Dixon, October 10, 1996.
48 *Knoxville News-Sentinel*, September 23, 1963.
49 *Harbert Newsletter*, Christmas 1963, 2-3.
50 Gafford, "Harbert Corporation," 63.
51 *Harbert Newsletter*, October 1965, 2-5.
52 *Alabama Roadbuilder*, July 1966, 6-7.
53 "John M. Harbert III," magazine article, n.id., but about 1967, in Harbert SB, Personal, 1937-78.
54 John M. Harbert III, speech, 13-14, Red Mountain Expressway Scrapbook, 1966-76; Mrs. Frank Gafford, "Cut Through the City," *American Road Builder*, April 1971, 10-12.
55 Typed interview with Ted Randolph by Charlotte Gafford, March 18, 1986, 8-9.
56 Ibid., 14-19.
57 *Harbert Newsletter*, April 1966, 6-9; *Birmingham News*, March 12, 1966.
58 *Birmingham Post-Herald*, May 18, 1966; *Alabama Roadbuilder*, July 1966, 9.
59 Harry B. Brock, Jr., to John M. Harbert III, December 13, 1966; *Montreal Star*, December 10, 1966; *Chicago Tribune*, December 10, 1966; *Detroit Free Press*, December 11, 1966.
60 John M. Harbert III to Mother, October 17, 1967;

interview with Wita Harbert, March 17, 1997; interview with Joan Edmonds, May 1, 1997.

61 *Harbert Newsletter*, June 1967, 2-4.

62 Typed interview with Bill Rossman by Charlotte Gafford, 6.

63 *Harbert Newsletter*, February-March 1968, 3; Fall 1969, 2-4; Gafford, "Harbert Corporation," 64-65.

64 Interview with Ed Dixon, October 10, 1996.

65 Harbert, *Continuous Beginnings*, 18; *Harbert Newsletter*, September 1966, February/March 1969; Gafford, "Harbert Corporation," 68-69.

66 Harbert, *Entrepreneurship*, 3-4.

67 Interview with Ed Dixon, September 26, 1996.

68 *Harbert Newsletter*, February-March 1968.

69 John M. Harbert III, banquet address at Harbert management meeting, March 26, 1968, Management Meeting file; *Harbert Newsletter*, April-May, 1968, 3-4.

70 *Harbert Newsletter*, October 1965, 8-9, and YPO certificate in Harbert SB, Personal, 1937-78.

71 Eric T. Webber "John M. Harbert III," *Carnation*, Spring 1994, 6.

72 *Harbert Newsletter*, December 1966, 2.

73 Gissen, "John Harbert III of Harbert Corporation," 49.

74 *Harbert Newsletter*, February-March 1969, 1-2.

Chapter 7

1 Harbert, "Remarks Honoring Dixon," 8-9.

2 Interview with Ed Dixon, June 10, 1997.

3 *Harbert: Diversified Growth Companies*, Harbert promotional booklet, 1974, 5.

4 *Engineering News-Record*, March 20, 1975, 56.

5 Ibid.

6 Gafford, "Harbert Corporation," 72.

7 Harbert, *A Student's Reflections*, 14.

8 Marguerite Harbert, *Movers and Doers*, 9.

9 John M. Harbert III to H. Allen Franklin, December 28, 1993.

10 Typed interview with W. H. Rossman, n.d., by David Jefferson and Associates. Several taped interviews were done during the early 1990s by this firm as preparation for a video presentation on the Harbert Corporation. The final product was never produced.

11 J. A. Hagy, "Report: Coal Reserves Leased to BellCoal, Inc., Bell County, Kentucky," December 20, 1969. There are several reports included, the first one dated January 1, 1968, which analyzed the Gibbs 2,000-acre tract on Cubbage Branch located on the north side of Brushy Mountain; interview with Don Cook, June 2, 1997. BellCoal is spelled in various ways—Bell Coal, Bellcoal, and BellCoal—in Harbert documents; citation follows original spelling.

12 Harry M. Caudill, *My Land Is Dying* (New York: E. P. Dutton, 1971), 31.

13 Paul F. Taylor, *Bloody Harlan: The United Mine Workers of America in Harlan County, Kentucky, 1931-1941* (New York: University Press of America, 1990), 1-11; Harry M. Caudill, *The Watches of the Night* (Boston: Little, Brown, 1976), 58-60. Caudill refers to the fluctuation of the coal market as "The Mad Reign of King Coal."

14 Harry M. Caudill, *Night Comes to the Cumberlands: A Biography of a Depressed Area* (Boston: Little, Brown, 1962), 333.

15 Harbert, *Appalachia*, 2; Gafford, "Harbert Corporation," 74; interview with Don Cook, June 9, 1997.

16 Harbert, *Appalachia*, 3; Mary Jean Bowman and W. Warren Haynes, *Resources and People in Eastern Kentucky: Problems and Potentials of a Lagging Economy* (Baltimore: Johns Hopkins University Press, 1963), 322-23.

17 Harbert, *Appalachia*, 3-4; John M. Harbert III to Alvin Vogtle, January 9, 1971, Coal files.

18 Harbert, *Appalachia*, 3-4.

19 File, "Coal—Mt. Drive Coal Company, Bell Coal Company, Cecil Gibbs, et al."

20 These documents are in John's personal Coal files. The oral agreement between John and the Gibbs family was made on February 9, with a signed closing on April 24, 1970. John Bingham to James C. Helton, April 29, 1970, Coal files.

21 Gafford, "Harbert Corporation," 76.

22 L. L. Stephenson, "Georgia Power Company Coal Prospect, Bellcoal Leases," December 23, 1969, a report for John Harbert.

23 John's Auburn friend wishes to remain anonymous because he recalls that John later sold this section for many times the amount he paid for it.

24 Harbert, *Continuous Beginnings*, 18; interview with Wita Harbert, November 19, 1996.

25 Interview with Wita Harbert, March 18, 1996; Harbert, *A Student's Reflections*, 14.

26 *Birmingham News*, August 12, 1974.

27 Ibid., January 9, 1974.

28 Harbert, *Continuous Beginnings*, 18.

29 John M. Harbert III to R. Denny Schmidt, Chase Manhattan Bank, New York City, December 23, 1970, Coal files.

30 Typed interview with W. H. Rossman by David Jefferson and Associates, n.d., 2; Gafford, "Harbert Corporation," 78.

31 Harbert, *A Student's Reflections*, 15; Harbert, *Continuous Beginnings*, 18.

32 Interview with Don Cook, June 9, 1997; Harbert photograph album, coal mines, 1978.

33 French, "Desire to survive."

34 Nicholas P. Chironis, "Draglines: King of the Strippers," in Nicholas P. Chironis, ed., *Coal Age's New Handbook of Surface Mining* (New York: McGraw-Hill, 1981), 194-98; Harbert, *Appalachia*, 4; interview with Don Cook, June 9, 1997.

35 Harbert, *Appalachia*, 8.

36 Ibid., 10.

37 John M. Harbert III, "My Part in a Coal Miners Strike," speech to the National Conference Board, January 21, 1972, 2-3; interview with John Harbert in *Alabama Construction News*, Winter 1994, 28.

38 John W. Hevener, *Which Side Are You On? The Harlan County Coal Miners, 1931-39* (Urbana: University of Illinois Press, 1978), 21-23, 46-47.

39 Harbert, "My Part in a Coal Miners Strike," 6-7.

40 Gafford, "Harbert Corporation," 117-18; interview with Don Cook, June 2, 1997.

41 John M. Harbert III to Commanding Officer, Kentucky State Highway Patrol, November 30, 1971, and John M. Harbert III to H. E. Grace, Jr., December 17, 1971, Coal files.

42 John M. Harbert III, speech, Winter Southern Conference, the Conference Board, January 21, 1978; interview with Don Cook, June 9, 1997; Ken Mink, "Coal mine battle shapes up in Harlan," Lexington *News-Sentinel*, undated clipping but about November 30, 1973,Coal files; Bryan Woolley, *We Be Here When the Morning Comes* (Lexington: University Press of Kentucky, 1974), 4-5, 52, 58.

43 Gafford, "Harbert Corporation," 119.

44 Interview with Jay Harbert, August 3, 1996.

45 John M. Harbert III, "Remarks: Mountain Drive Christmas Party," December 21, 1979, 1-4.

46 Various documents in Coal files: 1979 picnic.

47 Mrs. Dawn Miracle to Mr. Harbert, October 30, 1974, and John M. Harbert III to Mrs. Dawn Miracle, November 4, 1974. Three weeks later John wrote Mrs. Miracle a thank-you letter for the cake she baked for him. Coal files.

48 See these letters and various others in file "Coal—Mt. Drive Company, Bell Coal Company, Cecil Gibbs, et al."

49 Sandra Falkenhagen, "John M. Harbert III: A Tribute," *View Point*, September 1995, 3.

50 Jack Francisco to John Harbert, n.d., but probably January 1979, Coal files: Eye Foundation Hospital, 1979.

51 Lyndon Davis and Edd Sharpe to John M. Harbert III, November 27, 1979, in ibid.

52 Falkenhagen, "John M. Harbert III," 3.

53 Ibid.

54 Harry M. Caudill, *A Darkness at Dawn: Appalachian Kentucky and the Future* (Lexington: University Press of Kentucky, 1976), 72-73; Harbert, *Appalachia*, 4-5.

55 Harbert, *A Student's Reflections*, 15; Harbert, *Appalachia*, 4; Harbert, *Continuous Beginnings*, 18.

56 Harbert, "Risk: Key to Fulfillment," 10.

57 John M. Harbert III to Durand LeGrand, October 2, 1972, Coal files.

58 Caudill, *My Land Is Dying*, 99.

59 Harbert, *Appalachia*, 4-5.

60 *Middlesboro Daily News*, May 20, 1978.

61 Harbert, "Risk: Key to Fulfillment," 10.

62 Interview with Wita Harbert, June 4, 1997.

63 Ibid.

64 Ibid., March 17, 1997.

65 Interviews with Sandi Falkenhagen, February 12, June 5, 1997.

66 Irving Beiman wrote that John capped a fourteen-year effort by buying into ABC; Beiman, "Fast-moving John Harbert."

67 Frederick G. Koenig, Jr., "The Story of Alabama By-Products Corporation," a presentation to the Kiwanis Club of Birmingham, November 20, 1960, in Harbert ABC file; Childers, *Erskine Ramsay*, 280, 282-85; interview with Ed Dixon, June 10, 1997.

68 Gafford, "Harbert Corporation," 114.

69 Interview with Wita Harbert, February 12, 1997.

70 John M. Harbert III to Catherine Collins, September 9, 1975, Collins correspondence file; *Birmingham News*, October 2, 1974; Gafford, "Harbert Corporation," 116.

71 Irving Beiman, "Mining firm agrees to buy stock in ABC," *Birmingham News*, September 7, 1977.

72 F. G. Koenig, Jr., President ABC, General Bulletin to Employees, October 3, 1974; *Birmingham Post-Herald*, October 3, 1974; *Birmingham News*, October 2, 1974.

73 John M. Harbert III to Catherine Collins, September 9, 1975, Collins correspondence file.

74 *Birmingham News*, March 24, 1975; Alabama By-Products Annual Report for 1974, March 14, 1975; Irving Beiman, "Alabama By-Products exceeds earnings record for seventh year," *Birmingham News*, March 4, 1977.

75 *Birmingham Post-Herald*, October 10, 1974;

Birmingham News, October 2, 1971; Beiman, "Mining firm agrees to buy stock in ABC"; Marjorie Longnecker White, *The Birmingham District: An Industrial History and Guide* (Birmingham: Birmingham Historical Society, 1981), 298. Drummond purchased additional stock in ABC, giving the Jasper coal company controlling interest in the nation's largest producer of foundry coke. Irving Beiman, "Drummond Company buys controlling stock," *Birmingham News*, September 17, 1977; John M. Harbert III to Senator John J. Sparkman, January 27, 1978, ABC file.

76 *First National News*, a publication of the First National Bank of Birmingham, October 1975.

77 *Riverchase*, Harbert pamphlet, n.d.

78 Nancy Campbell, "Ex-gridder studies wildflowers," *Birmingham News*, April 22, 1976.

79 *Harbert Headquarters: An Expression of Commitment*, pamphlet.

80 *Harbert Newsletter*, Fall 1977, 3-4.

81 Susan Hurley, "Working by a Waterfall," *Birmingham Magazine*, October 1978, 39.

82 Ibid.

83 *Harbert Headquarters: An Expression of Commitment.*

84 Robert Hiden to John M. Harbert III, October 8, 15, 23, 25, November 1, 1976; John M. Harbert III to Robert Hiden, November 26, 1976, Robert Hiden correspondence file.

85 *Harbert Newsletter*, Fall 1977, 4.

86 Interview with Sandi Falkenhagen, July 24, 1997.

87 "EPA Proposal to Cause Loss of $220 Million," news release from the Birmingham Area Chamber of Commerce, September 12, 1977.

88 Olivia Barton, "Cahaba fish, James Watt boosted Satterfield into FERC spot," *Birmingham News*, July 21, 1985.

89 William Satterfield, "Conservation: A Realistic Approach," *Constructor*, January 1979, 34, 41-43.

90 James Free, "Stop Overlooking Coal's Use Harbert Tells Congressmen," *Birmingham News*, May 7, 1979.

91 *Harbert Highlights*, Spring 1981, 1-4.

92 Interview with Ed Dixon, June 10, 1997; interview with Don Cook, June 9, 1997; interview with Wita Harbert, May 23, 1996.

93 Typed interview with W. H. Rossman by David Jefferson and Associates, n.d., 8; Gafford, "Harbert Corporation," 112.

94 *Engineering News-Record*, March 20, 1975, 56.

95 Quoted in Robin DeMonia, "Hard times for Harbert," *Birmingham News*, May 24, 1992.

96 Emmett Dedmon, *Challenge and Response: A Modern History of Standard Oil Company (Indiana)* (Chicago: Mobium Press, 1984), 250-52.

97 Marguerite Harbert, *Movers and Doers*, 5.

98 Dedmon, *Challenge and Response*, 68-79; John E. Swearingen, *The Growth of Standard Oil Company (Indiana), (1889-1964)* (New York: Newcomen Society in North America, 1964), i, 5-7.

99 *Harbert Highlights*, Spring 1981, 1-4.

100 Dedmon, *Challenge and Response*, 89, 253; Louisville *Courier-Journal*, August 22, 1981; *Coal Outlook*, August 24, 1981; *Birmingham News*, October 5, 1981; Gafford, "Harbert Corporation," 123.

101 *Birmingham News*, October 5, 1981; *On Site*, September/October 1989, 2.

Chapter 8

1 *Alabama Construction News*, Winter 1994, 26.

2 For instance, the Alabama listings in John's YPO roster for 1968-69 include Fob James, Harry Brock, Red Blount, Prince DeBardeleben, Crawford Johnson III, Billy Rushton, Bill Spencer III, and others. From Georgia, Bo Callaway and Tom Cousins are listed. YPO files.

3 John M. Harbert III to Joseph F. Johnston, March 31, 1969; *Birmingham Post-Herald*, February 22, 1969.

4 Interview with Betty Morrison, September 9, 1997.

5 Interview with Harold Apolinsky, March 26, 1997.

6 Interview with Sandi Falkenhagen, October 1, 1997.

7 *Alabama Construction News*, Winter 1994, 26.

8 John M. Harbert III, "Acceptance Remarks, Alabama Academy of Honor."

9 Interview with Ed Dixon, September 26, 1996.

10 Various letters from William P. Engel to John; John M. Harbert III to Edward M. Friend, Jr., November 11, 1974, William P. Engel file.

11 Interview with Wita Harbert, June 10, 1997; *Birmingham News*, September 17, 1978.

12 Interview with Wita Harbert, June 10, 1997; Leah Rawls Atkins, *Nineteenth Century Club* (Birmingham: Birmingham Publishing Company, 1995), 31, 51, 55.

13 Mrs. Herbert E. Smith, Jr., to John M. Harbert III, January 18, 1963; John M. Harbert III to Mrs. Herbert E. Smith, Jr., January 29, 1963, Harbert YWCA files; Bryding Adams to Leah Atkins, June 6, 1997.

14 The official YWCA records are housed at the Department of Archives and Manuscripts, Birmingham Public Library, but they are rather thin for this period of time.

15 John M. Harbert III to Miss Ethel Gibson, August 15, 1967, and other correspondence in Harbert YWCA files.

16 Bertha Bendall Norton, *Birmingham's First Magic Century: Were You There?* (Birmingham: Lakeshore Press, 1970), 215-16.

17 Donald E. Boomershine to the Family of John M. Harbert III, May 26, 1995.

18 Ibid.; John M. Harbert, YWCA Fund Drive Notebook; *Birmingham News*, January 17, 1973.

19 John M. Harbert III, "Role of the Y.W.C.A. in Changing and Developing Downtown Birmingham," an address to YWCA annual meeting, January 21, 1969.

20 Gail Trechsel to Leah Atkins, June 5, 1997; Minutes of the Board of Directors of the Birmingham Museum of Art, October 21, 1977, book 6, 2057, Museum Library.

21 Interview with Margaret Livingston, August 6, 1997.

22 John M. Harbert III, "The Birmingham Museum of Art," address to the Rotary Club, July 10, 1974.

23 Minutes of the Board of Directors of the Birmingham Museum of Art, February 24, 1978, book 6, 2105, Museum Library.

24 Ibid., October 20, 1978, book 6, 2237; November 25, 1981, book 9, 2933; February 23, 1983, book 11, 3229; December 15, 1984, book 13, 3692, Museum Library.

25 *Harbert Newsletter*, December 1973, 2-4.

26 *Birmingham News*, August 20, 1973. The *News* also ran editorials praising Harbert's cleanup programs in 1976, 1977, and 1979.

27 Copy of WBRC editorial, July 29, 1973; various clippings, in Harbert SB, Clean-Up Program, 1973-82.

28 See the various clippings and letters in Harbert SB, Clean-Up Program, 1973-82.

29 Ibid.; *Harbert Newsletter*, Fall 1978, 23; John M. Harbert III to all Clean-Up Crews, August 15, 1978.

30 *Birmingham News*, June 18, 20, 1979.

31 *Birmingham Post-Herald*, January 30, 1969;John M. Harbert III, *Eagan Memorial Address*, April 22, 1971, 1-2.

32 *First National News*, June 1974, 2.

33 Interview with Wita Harbert, May 5, 1997; *On Site*, March/April 1992, 1.

34 Ralph Holmes, "Harbert given ABC post by Wallace order," *Birmingham News*, February 1, 1973; *Shelby County Reporter*, March 10, 1977; unidentified clipping, Harbert SB, Personal, 1973-78; *On Site*, March/April 1992, 1.

35 Al Fox, "Meeting linked state, business, contractor says," *Birmingham News*, December 7, 1973.

36 William Warren Rogers, Robert David Ward, Leah Rawls Atkins, and Wayne Flynt, *Alabama: The History of a Deep South State* (Tuscaloosa: University of Alabama Press, 1994), 370-74, 499-500; John M. Harbert III, "Address to the Redstone Club," August 8, 1975, 7.

37 See the Minutes of the Alabama Alcoholic Beverage Control Board, especially October 7, 1974, and April 6, 1977, Alabama Department of Archives and History, hereafter ADAH.

38 *Shelby County Reporter*, March 10, 1977.

39 *On Site*, March/April 1992.
40 John M. Harbert III, "Address to Redstone Club," 12-13; John M. Harbert III, "Address to the Birmingham-Jefferson Hotel-Motel Association," April 19, 1979, 3-5.
41 Charles Black, "Don't Let Alabama Folks Kid You—They Buy Booze Elsewhere," *Columbus Enquirer*, October 29, 1975.
42 *Birmingham News*, July 31, 1975; Harbert, "Address to Redstone Club," 1, 17-18.
43 Ralph Holmes, "One-nip bottles on way out, again?" *Birmingham News*, April 11, 1979.
44 John M. Harbert III, "A Businessman's Involvement with Government," The Conference Board, January 26, 1974.
45 *Birmingham News*, editorial, "Liquor Reform Needed," September 10, 1975; Ralph Holmes, "New regulation for liquor by drink," *Birmingham News*, October 17, 1975.
46 Bob Ingram, "The Alabama Scene," *St. Clair News*, July 15, 1976.
47 John M. Harbert III, "Testimony Before Senate Finance and Taxation Committee," April 23, 1980, Harbert ABC file.
48 Alabama Alcoholic Beverage Control Board, 46th Annual Report, October 1, 1981, to September 30, 1982, 3, ADAH.
49 Minutes of the Alabama Energy Advisory Council, March 22, 1973; see also the Energy Advisory Council files, especially John M. Harbert III to Governor George C. Wallace, May 31, 1973, and July 30, 1973, administrative files, Governor George C. Wallace papers, ADAH.
50 John M. Harbert III, "A Positive Look at Stripmining," testimony before the Federal Energy Administration, Atlanta, Georgia, September 25, 1974, 2.
51 *Birmingham News*, January 9, 1974.
52 Falkenhagen, "John M. Harbert III," 1-4.
53 Interview with Wita Harbert, May 18, 1996.
54 John M. Harbert III to Dr. Gene V. Ball, July 12, 1991.
55 Norman R. McMillan, "Remarks on Behalf of the Department of English on the Occasion of the Tenth Anniversary of the Harbert Writing Center, 1979-1989."
56 Ibid.; interview with Wita Harbert, May 18, 1996.
57 Falkenhagen, "John M. Harbert III," 1-4.
58 Alston Callahan, "John M. Harbert III," included in Alston Callahan to Leah Atkins, September 5, 1997; Falkenhagen, "John M. Harbert III," 4.
59 Falkenhagen, "John M. Harbert III," 5.
60 Dr. Buris R. Boshell to John M. Harbert III, February 2, 1968, May 5, 1969, December 24, 1970.
61 John M. Harbert III, "Future Needs the Educated," *Auburn Alumnews*, March 1977, 13.
62 Minutes, Alabama Commission on Higher Education, especially April 9, June 1, 22, 1979, July 17, 1981, February 12, 1982, and March 8, 1983, ADAH.
63 *Birmingham News*, October 26, 1982.
64 Jim Vickrey to Leah Atkins, October 31, 1997.
65 *Auburn Alumnews*, April 1986, 16,
66 Neal R. Berte to Leah Rawls Atkins, September 16, 1997.
67 *Shelby County Reporter*, October 19, 1978; Jim Vickrey to Leah Atkins, October 31, 1997.
68 John M. Harbert III, "Honorary Degree Remarks," Birmingham-Southern College, May 25, 1986.
69 John M. Harbert III, "Introduction of James R. Nelson," Birmingham Rotary, November 9, 1988.
70 James R. Nelson, "John Murdoch Harbert III: A Recollection," in Harbert SB, Personal, 1995.
71 John D. Swanson to John Hanley, April 23, 1979; John M. Harbert III to B. Wayne Peake, July 13, 1989; *Birmingham News*, February 20, 1975.
72 Andrew Kilpatrick, "Civic clubs' dream becomes a 3-story reality," *Birmingham Post-Herald*, June 17, 1986.
73 Interview with Elmer Harris, September 24, 1996.
74 John M. Harbert III, "The History of the Civic Club Foundation, Inc.," March 1, 1985, 1-5.
75 Mitch Mendelson, "The Harbert Center: The building in the gray flannel suit," *Birmingham Post-Herald*, November 24, 1986.
76 Lucille Beeson to John Harbert, May 30, 1986; Lucille Beeson to Civic Club Foundation, Inc., May 30, 1986, Harbert Center Dedication file, 1986.
77 Andrew Kilpatrick, "Harbert Center celebrates fifth birthday," *Birmingham Post-Herald*, June 20, 1991; *Birmingham News*, June 20, 1991.
78 John M. Harbert III, "Acceptance Remarks, Alabama Business Hall of Fame," October 7, 1993.
79 Interview with Eason Balch, March 27, 1997.
80 Interview with Elmer Harris, October 15, 1996.
81 Dave White, "Big contributors in elections mostly are professionals," *Birmingham News*, August 8, 1982.
82 John M. Harbert III, "Greater Birmingham Area Community Service Award Banquet," April 30, 1987, 4.

Chapter 9

1 John M. Harbert III, "Speech to St. Mary's Men's Club: Harbert's Foreign Operations," April 12, 1965.
2 Ibid.
3 Harbert, *A Student's Reflections*, 15.
4 *First National News*, October 1975, 1.
5 *Engineering News-Record*, May 11, 1972, 27.
6 *On Site*, September/October 1991, 1.
7 Ibid.; *Engineering News-Record*, May 11, 1972, 27-28.
8 *On Site*, September/October 1991, 1.
9 *Harbert Diversified Growth Companies*, corporate promotional booklet, n.d., but probably about 1974, 24.
10 *On Site*, May/June 1992, 1.
11 John M. Harbert III, *Abu Dhabi, Angola and Some Thoughts on America*, a speech to the Redstone Club, Birmingham, January 16, 1976, 8.
12 Typed interview with Bill Harbert by David Jefferson and Associates, n.d., but about 1989-90, 6.
13 Harbert, *Abu Dhabi, Angola and Some Thoughts*, 7-10; Gafford, "Harbert Corporation," 128.
14 British Bank of the Middle East, *United Arab Emirates*, September 1989, 3, 10. As John Harbert explained in a speech, "Abu Dhabi is the name of a town, the island the town is on, and the name of the largest Emirate in the group of seven sheikhdoms comprising the United Arab Emirates," which was formed in 1971 after more than a century of British protection. Harbert, *Abu Dhabi, Angola and Some Thoughts*, 1.
15 Harbert, *Abu Dhabi, Angola and Some Thoughts*, 3-4.
16 *Birmingham Post-Herald*, June 18, August 17, 1975; *Birmingham News*, December 18, 1975.
17 John M. Harbert III to Richard T. Howard, April 9, 1976, Abu Dhabi file; Harbert, *Abu Dhabi, Angola and Some Thoughts*, 3-4.
18 *Harbert Highlights*, Winter 1980, 15; Gafford, "Harbert Corporation," 133.
19 Interview with Wita Harbert, November 12, 1997; interview with Joy Harbert, February 25, 1997.
20 Jimmy Carter, *The Blood of Abraham* (Boston: Houghton Mifflin, 1985), 43.
21 Major Karen McKay, "'Operation Ramon': Historic Move to the Negev," *Army* (April 1982): 47; Richard C. Thornton, *The Carter Years: Toward a New Global Order* (New York: Paragon House, 1991), 208-09, 211-13; W. Dale Nelson, *The President Is at Camp David* (Syracuse: Syracuse University Press, 1995), 120-23.
22 Harbert, *The Civil Engineer*, 8-9; Jimmy Carter, *Keeping Faith: Memories of a President* (New York: Bantam Books, 1982), 402.
23 U.S. Army Corps of Engineers, news release, May 17, 1979, in Negev file; *Engineering News-Record*, May 24, 1979, 40; interview with Sandi Falkenhagen, July 15, 1997.
24 Phil H. Shook, "Business as usual for firm's operations in Mideast," *Birmingham News*, December 16, 1979.
25 At a pre-proposal conference in New York, Johnson said that the project was for "top-flight, well-organized companies," not for small businesses, *Engineering News-Record*, April 26, 1997, 10; *Fortune*, July 16, 1979, 62; *Port of Mobile*, September 1979, 11.
26 *Jerusalem Post*, July 10, 1979; *Fortune*, July 16, 1979.
27 Interview with Ted and Jane Randolph, March 11, 1997; Gafford, "Harbert Corporation," 138-39.
28 Interview with Thurlo W. Hooper, July 17, 1997; *New York Times*, November 18, 1979.
29 John M. Harbert III to Thurlo Hooper, October 31, 1979, Negev file.
30 John M. Harbert III to Alfonso Nussbaumer, May 12, 1981, in ibid.
31 Shook, "Business as usual."
32 *Jerusalem Post*, February 5, 1980.
33 Memorandum from John to Bill, June 16, 1981, Negev file.
34 Ellie Copeland to John M. Harbert III, November 16, 1981, in ibid.
35 *Birmingham News*, April 23, 1982.
36 Brigadier General John F. Wall to John M. Harbert III, April 25, 1982, Negev file.
37 Interview with Claude Roberts, July 14, 1997.
38 *Harbert Highlights*, Spring 1985, 24-25.
39 Interview with Wita Harbert, May 21, 1997; W. J. Bowen to Leah Atkins, June 6, 1997.
40 Marguerite J. Harbert, "Trip to China," paper presented to the Nineteenth Century Club, 1980, 1-3.
41 *Harbert Highlights*, Summer 1980, "John Harbert Visits China," 2-3.
42 Ibid., Fall 1980, 15.
43 These were merely two of many close associations between Birmingham and Alabama businesses and the Saudi government. See Steven Emerson, *The American House of Saud: The Secret Petrodollar Connection* (New York: Franklin Watts, 1985), 150-53, 165, and especially chap. 19, entitled "The Arabian South: Birmingham, Saudi Arabia."

44 Ibid., 384-85; Winton M. "Red" Blount, *Doing It My Way* (Lyme, Connecticut: Greenwich Publishing Group, 1996), 150-51.

45 John M. Harbert III, *World Trade: What It Means to Americans*, keynote address, Alabama World Trade Day Celebration, May 25, 1976, 13.

Chapter 10

1 Harbert, Memorandum, Records of Farm Real Estate Purchases, n.d.

2 Interview with Margie Harbert Gray, August 6, 1997.

3 Interview with Neville Palmer, November 29, 1996.

4 Walton Lowry, "No Kidding. There're Kamloopos in Canoe Creek," *Birmingham News*, August 20, 1972; Pell City *Observer*, September 9, 1976; Charles R. Hipp, Jr., to John M. Harbert III, October 13, 1980.

5 Hall W. Thompson to John M. Harbert III, March 28, 1972.

6 Interview with Billy Land, June 9, 1997.

7 Interview with Don Cook, June 9, 1997.

8 Howell Raines, *Fly Fishing Through the Midlife Crisis* (New York: William Morrow, 1993), 111.

9 Lowry, "No Kidding."

10 Ibid.; interview with Bucky Waid, July 10, 1997.

11 E. W. Shell to John M. Harbert III, November 21, 1986, August 31, October 16, December 14, 1987, July 17, 1990, copies courtesy of Dr. Wayne Shell.

12 Interview with Tom Bradford, July 23, 1997.

13 Interview with Wita Harbert, December 20, 1996.

14 *Pinebloom Plantation*, Harbert pamphlet, n.d., 4.

15 *Pinebloom Farms*, U.S. Steel publication, n.d., 1-2.

16 Richard H. Clark, *Memoirs of Judge Richard H. Clark*, ed. Lollie Belle Wylie (Atlanta: Franklin Printing and Publishing, 1898), 342; William J. Northen, *Men of Mark in Georgia* (1911; reprint, Spartanburg, South Carolina: Reprint Company, 1974), 3:68.

17 David King Gleason, *Antebellum Homes of Georgia* (Baton Rouge: Louisiana State University Press, 1987), 119. Unfortunately, the Baker County courthouse at Newton burned about 1872, and floods in 1925 and 1929 destroyed records and rendered some illegible, making it difficult to trace the records associated with Pinebloom. Although the family name is spelled Tarver, the road in front of Pinebloom is spelled Tarva.

18 *Memorial Addresses on the Life and Character of Alfred Holt Colquitt: Delivered in the Senate and House of Representatives, 53rd Congress, 3rd Session* (Washington, D.C.: Government Printing Office, 1895), 20, 22.

19 John R. Swanton, *The Indians of the Southeastern United States* (Washington, D.C.: Smithsonian Institution Press, 1946), 115-16; Charles Hudson, *The Southeastern Indians* (Knoxville: University of Tennessee Press, 1976), 7, 434-36, 443; *Pinebloom Farms*, 1-10; *Pinebloom Plantation*, 1-4.

20 Clark Howell, *History of Georgia* (Chicago: S. J. Clarke, 1926), 1:648, 653; James F. Cook, *The Governors of Georgia, 1754-1995* (Macon: Mercer University Press, 1995), 159, 161-62.

21 *Pinebloom Plantation*, 3-4.

22 Everett Skehan, "Larry Moon: Preparing a Dog to Win," *Pointing Dog Journal* 5 (March/April 1997): 30; interview with Larry Moon, December 21, 1996.

23 Interview with Wita Harbert and Acky Jones McGriff, August 4, 1996.

24 John M. Harbert III to Dr. William B. Muse, June 17, 1993, copy courtesy of Dr. Wayne Shell.

25 Memorandum from Dr. Lowell T. Frobish to Dr. Wayne Shell et al., June 28, 1993, and draft of letter to John M. Harbert III, Office of Director of Alabama Agricultural Experiment Station, July 22, 1993, copies courtesy of Wayne Shell and James Marion, dean of the Auburn College of Agriculture.

26 Interview with Wita Harbert, October 17, 1996.

27 Ibid., December 21, 1996.

28 *Pinebloom Plantation*, 5-6.

29 Interview with Deanna Paisley, March 25, 1996.

30 Interview with Larry Moon, March 25, 1996.

31 Interview with Wendell Hines, December 21, 1996.

32 Interview with Wita Harbert, December 21, 1996.

33 Interview with Deanna Paisley, March 25, 1996.

34 Deanna Paisley to Leah Atkins, November 7, 1997.

35 Interview with Wita Harbert, June 11, 1997.

36 John M. Harbert III to Dr. E. W. Shell, May 29, 1984, April 10, October 29, 1986; John M. Harbert III to Dr. William D. Davies, February 6, 1994, copies courtesy of Dr. Wayne Shell.

37 John M. Harbert III to Jack Bowen, January 29, 1986, Pinebloom file, 1985-87.

38 W. J. Bowen to Leah Atkins, June 6, 1997.

39 Interview with Sam Gray, October 28, 1997.

40 Interview with Jack Biddle, January 25, 1996.

41 Interview with Wita Harbert, December 21, 1996.

42 William V. Muse, Recollections of John M. Harbert III, 1.
43 Interview with Wita Harbert, December 21, 1996; interview with Larry Moon, December 21, 1996.
44 Interview with Wita Harbert, June 10, 1997.
45 Hunting Guide, Pinebloom Plantation.
46 Interview with Wita Harbert, December 21, 1996.
47 Ibid.; interview with Larry Moon, December 21, 1996.
48 Interview with Wita Harbert, December 21, 1996.
49 Ibid.
50 Wita Harbert, Journal, book 1, May 12, 19, 20, 1983.
51 Ibid., May 2, 1983.
52 W. J. Bowen to Leah Atkins, June 6, 1997.
53 John M. Harbert III to Mr. and Mrs. Richard Walgate, Cuxwald Hall, January 24, 1986, Pinebloom file, 1985-87.

Chapter 11

1 John M. Harbert III to B. W. Peake, June 3, 1986, copy courtesy of Wayne Peake.
2 John M. Harbert III, "Presentation to the Redstone Club on the AmSouth/Harbert Plaza," October 13, 1989, 9.
3 Interview with Kathryn Harbert, November 11, 1997; interview with John Heilman, September 15, 1997.
4 Interview with Margie Harbert Gray, August 6, 1997.
5 Raymond J. Harbert, *The Unproven Path*, remarks to the Rotary Club of Birmingham, September 26, 1990.
6 Harbert, "Remarks on the Occasion of Ted's Retirement," 1-4.
7 Harbert, "Remarks on Rossman's Retirement," 5.
8 Edwin M. Dixon, "Remarks at the Memorial Service for William H. Rossman," January 27, 1996.
9 Harbert, "Remarks Honoring Dixon," 9.
10 Hill Ferguson, "Interview with John M. Harbert III," August 2, 1977, Hill Ferguson Papers.
11 Charlotte Gafford to John M. Harbert III, July 7, 1981.
12 John M. Harbert III to Charlotte Gafford, July 15, 1981.
13 Interview with Hall Thompson, February 26, 1997.
14 Interview with Wita Harbert, October 1, 1997.
15 The information is from interviews with Wita Harbert, November 18, 1996, February 12, 1997, and October 1, 1997, from an unpublished manuscript by Sandra W. Falkenhagen, "The Man at the Medical Forum," from Enzo Plazzotta, *Flashes of Memory* (London: Plazzotta, 1987), and from Bill Hutto, "Medical Forum," in *Over the Mountain Journal*, February 25, 1993.
16 Wita Harbert Journal, book 1, May 21-26, 1983; Marguerite Harbert, *Movers and Doers*, 4.
17 Wita Harbert Journal, book 1, May 24-31, 1983.
18 *Birmingham News*, September 18, 1984.
19 Wita Harbert Journal, book 2, August 21, 1983.
20 Ibid., August 18-23, 1983.
21 Ibid., book 6, August 23, 1984. Wita was referring to John's stock purchases with Boone Pickens, deals that are discussed later in this chapter.
22 Ibid., August 24, 1984.
23 Ibid., August 25-26, 1984; interviews with Wita Harbert, August 22, October 1, 1997.
24 Interview with Wita Harbert, August 6, 1997.
25 Ibid., September 12, 1996.
26 Wita Harbert Journal, book 4, May 5-12, 1984; interviews with Wita Harbert, November 19, 1996, October 1, 1997.
27 Wita Harbert Journal, book 10, June 23-30, 1985; interview with Wita Harbert, October 17, 1996.
28 Wita Harbert Journal, book 10, July 1-14, 1985.
29 Margaret M. Blair, ed., *The Deal Decade: What Takeovers and Leveraged Buyouts Mean for Corporate Governance* (Washington, D.C.: Brookings Institution, 1993), 1, 57-58, 270-71.
30 Isadore Barmash, *A Not-So-Tender Offer: An Insider's Look at Mergers and Their Consequences* (Englewood Cliffs, New Jersey: Prentice Hall, 1995), 153.
31 Marguerite Harbert, *Movers and Doers*, 1.
32 T. Boone Pickens, Jr., *Boone* (Boston: Houghton Mifflin, 1987), 149-69; interview with Wita Harbert, March 17, 1997.
33 Sidney A. Swensrud, *"Gulf Oil": The First Fifty Years, 1901-1951* (New York: Newcomen Society in North America, 1951), 8-14.
34 Patrick A. Gaughan, *Mergers and Acquisitions* (New York: HarperCollins, 1991), 189-90.
35 Moira Johnston, *Takeover: The New Wall Street Warriors* (New York: Penguin Books, 1987), 147.
36 Pickens, *Boone*, 181-83, 187.
37 Dorin P. Levin, "Gulf Oil Seeks Increase to Add Defense," *Wall Street Journal*, October 17, 1983.
38 Pickens, *Boone*, 190-91.
39 *Wall Street Journal*, October 18, 1983; *Pittsburgh Post-Gazette*, October 18, 1983; Pickens, *Boone*, 191-92.

40 Bill Koenig and Thomas Hargrove, "Harbert in group seeking Gulf Oil stake," *Birmingham Post-Herald*, October 18, 1983.
41 William Allan, "Pickens' partners shun the limelight," *Pittsburgh Press*, December 12, 1983.
42 Hilary Rosenberg, "Pickens vs. Lee: The Battle over Gulf," *Financial World*, December 31, 1983, 10.
43 Marguerite Harbert, *Movers and Doers*, 2.
44 Interview with Boone Pickens, June 12, 1997.
45 Milton L. Rock, *The Mergers and Acquisitions Handbook* (New York: McGraw-Hill, 1987), 442.
46 Pickens, *Boone*, 208-09.
47 Marguerite Harbert, *Movers and Doers*, 3; interview with Wita Harbert, March 17, 1997.
48 Pickens, *Boone*, 211-15; Rosenberg, "Pickens vs. Lee," 9-11.
49 S. Y. Yana Davis, "A Business Briefing with John Harbert," *Birmingham Business Journal*, October 16, 1987, 32; Pickens, *Boone*, 214-15.
50 Dean Burgess, "Diamond Shamrock deal could prove lucrative for Harbert," *Birmingham News*, December 4, 1986; *New York Times*, December 8, 1986; Patrick A. Gaughan, *Mergers, Acquisitions, and Corporate Restructuring* (New York: John Wiley and Sons, 1996), 378.
51 *Birmingham Post-Herald*, December 20, 1986; *Wall Street Journal*, January 8, 1987; Harihar Krishnan, "Pickens drops try to take over Shamrock," *Houston Chronicle*, February 10, 1987; Johnston, *Takeover*, 388, 399-400.
52 *Wall Street Journal*, August 14, 1987; *Birmingham News*, November 19, 1987; Pickens, *Boone*, 216.
53 *Time*, March 4, 1985, 64.
54 Davis, "Business Briefing with Harbert," 32.
55 White, *Downtown Birmingham*, 121.
56 Harbert, "Presentation to the Redstone Club," 2.
57 Ibid., 5-6.
58 John M. Harbert III, "Remarks," in *In Commemoration of AmSouth/Harbert Plaza Groundbreaking Ceremonies*, March 2, 1987, 11-12.
59 John M. Harbert III, "Remarks, Workers' Topping-Out Celebration," August 19, 1988.
60 Mitch Mendelson, "Different styles help make tower distinct," *Birmingham Post-Herald*, September 4, 1989.
61 Harbert, "Presentation to the Redstone Club," 8.
62 Mendelson, "Different styles."
63 Paul Goldberger, *Buildings Against Cities: The Struggle to Make Plans* (Birmingham: Birmingham Historical Society, 1989), 5-6, 14.
64 *Business First*, August 14, 1989, 1.
65 John M. Harbert III, "Topping Out Speech for AmSouth/Harbert Plaza," October 13, 1988, 6.
66 *On Site*, November/December 1988, 2.
67 *Birmingham News*, November 2, 1989.
68 Michaelle Chapman, "Harbert has plaza all for itself," *Birmingham Post-Herald*, October 6, 1989.
69 Andrew Kilpatrick, *A Legacy of Leadership: The History of AmSouth Bank* (Birmingham: AmSouth Bancorporation, 1996), 82.
70 "Alabama-based Harbert Corporation Saw Its Future in Diversification," *Alabama Quarterly*, Winter 1990, 6-9.
71 *Birmingham Business Journal*, November 1988, 8.
72 John M. Harbert III, Remarks to Harbert Project Services (a division of Harbert Corporation) business strategy meeting, August 1, 1988, 3.
73 Interview with Raymond Harbert, August 7, 1996.
74 John M. Harbert III to Sir Joseph Nickerson, September 8, 1989.
75 "Birmingham Steel, Harbert Affiliate Merge" [This headline is misleading.], *Business Alabama Monthly*, November 1989, 54; Patrick Rupinski, "Buy-out by Harbert endorsed," *Birmingham Post-Herald*, November 29, 1989.
76 Charlie Ingram, "Market's reaction since Harbert bid raising questions," *Birmingham News*, January 9, 1990; *Wall Street Journal*, January 24, 1990; *American Banker*, January 25, 1990, 18.
77 Charlie Ingram, "Young Harbert to `stand back right now' as CEO," *Birmingham News*, August 5, 1990.
78 John to my dearest sweet wife, Christmas Day 1989.
79 John M. Harbert III, "Introduction of Raymond J. Harbert," in Raymond Harbert, *Unproven Path*, i.
80 John M. Harbert III, "Presentation to Management Conference," July 25, 1990, 7-8; *On Site*, September/October 1990, 2-3, 5.

Chapter 12

1 Interview with Hall Thompson, February 26, 1997.
2 Interview with Raymond Harbert, July 9, 1997.
3 Interview with Sandi Falkenhagen, August 27, 1997.
4 *Alabama Construction News*, Winter 1994, 23.
5 Chris Roberts, "Alabama business giant Harbert retires as CEO," *Birmingham News*, July 27, 1990.
6 Patrick Rupinski, "Harbert Corporation changes leadership," *Birmingham News/Birmingham Post-Herald*, combined Saturday edition, July 28, 1990.
7 Raymond Harbert, *Unproven Path*, 5; Andrew Kilpatrick, "Harbert looks forward to challenges," *Birmingham Post-Herald*, September 27, 1990.
8 Harbert, "Risk: Key to Fulfillment," 11.
9 Interview with Raymond Harbert, October 29, 1997.
10 Charlie Ingram, "Harbert's own building boom alive and well," *Birmingham News*, September 9, 1990.
11 Charlie Ingram, "Harbert layoffs rise to 40," *Birmingham News*, November 3, 1990; Blount, *Doing It My Way*, 206-07.
12 Blount, *Doing It My Way*, 208.
13 *Alabama Roadbuilder*, March/April 1990, 6-7, 31; Bob Paul, "Mobile's Cochrane Bridge," *Dixie Contractor*, July 22, 1991; *Mobile Register*, April 12, 1990.
14 Lender meeting outline, October 10, 1991.
15 DeMonia, "Hard times for Harbert"; news release, Harbert Corporation, May 14, 1992.
16 John M. Harbert III to Raymond Harbert, November 1990.
17 John to my dearest Wita, Christmas Day 1990.
18 John M. Harbert III to Beverly Kees, January 24, 1991.
19 Interviews with Wita Harbert, November 19, 1996, March 17, 1997.
20 John M. Harbert III, "Remarks to Employees," Holiday celebration, December 20, 1991, 3-5.
21 Interview with Wita Harbert, November 19, 1996.
22 Ibid.
23 John M. Harbert III to Beverly Kees, April 30, 1992,
24 Interview with Wita Harbert, March 17, 1997; interview with Sandi Falkenhagen, October 22, 1997.
25 John M. Harbert III to Beverly Kees, August 25, 1992.
26 Wita Harbert, Journal, [no book number], June 8, 1992.
27 Ibid., June 11, 1992.
28 John M. Harbert III to Beverly Kees, August 25, 1992.
29 Ibid.; interview with Wita Harbert, November 18, 1996.
30 "Contractor John Harbert diversifies to thrive," *Engineering News-Record*, March 20, 1975, 56.
31 Jeff B. Hansen, "Changes at Harbert Corp.," *Birmingham News*, December 3, 1992.
32 John M. Harbert III, *Acceptance Remarks, The Moles' Outstanding Achievement in Construction Award*, January 27, 1993, 6-9.
33 News release, Harbert Corporation, June 17, 1993; *Birmingham Post-Herald*, June 18, 1993; *Montgomery Advertiser*, June 19, 1993.
34 *Birmingham News/Birmingham Post-Herald*, combined Saturday edition, June 19, 1993; *Engineering News-Record*, June 28, 1993, 12.
35 Interview with Harold Apolinsky, March 26, 1997; Harold I. Apolinsky to Mrs. John M. Harbert III, March 21, 1997.
36 Harbert, *Acceptance Remarks: The Cornerstone Award*, 8-10.
37 Interview with Sandi Falkenhagen, October 27, 1997.
38 W. J. Bowen to Leah Atkins, June 6, 1997.
39 Interview with Wita Harbert, May 21, 1997.
40 Interview with Margie Harbert Gray, August 6, 1997.

Chapter 13

1 John M. Harbert III, "Remarks at Birmingham-Southern College Commencement," May 25, 1986.
2 Interview with Wita Harbert, June 10, 1997.
3 Interview with Margie Harbert Gray, August 6, 1997.
4 Hall Thompson, "Remarks at the unveiling of the statue of John M. Harbert III," AmSouth/Harbert Plaza, February 24, 1997.
5 Interview with Raymond Harbert, October 22, 1997.
6 Interview with Margie Harbert Gray, August 6, 1997.
7 Interviews with Wita Harbert, March 18, 1996, December 15, 1997.
8 Harbert, *Continuous Beginnings*, 7.
9 Interview with Raymond Harbert, October 22, 1997.
10 John M. Harbert III, "The Last Word," *On Site*, January/February 1989, 22.
11 Thompson, "Remarks at the unveiling."
12 James R. Nelson, "John Harbert was, in fact, an artist," *Birmingham News*, April 8, 1995.
13 Neal R. Berte to Leah Rawls Atkins, September 16, 1997.
14 Harbert, *Acceptance Remarks, The Moles' Award*, 9.

INDEX

PHOTOGRAPHIC CREDITS

Jacket/Front Portrait photographed by Billy Brown. Printed with permission.
Jacket/Back Birmingham Skyline photographed by C. Brent Falkenhagen. Printed with permission.
Page ii Portrait photographed by Billy Brown. Printed with permission.
Page x Portrait photographed by Billy Brown. Printed with permission.
Page xix Photograph by Heritage Photography, Albany, Georgia. Printed with permission.
Page 12 Courtesy of Wayne Peake.
Page 25 Courtesy of Fay Belt Ireland.
Page 37 (right) Courtesy of Fay Belt Ireland.
Page 48 Courtesy of Ed Dixon. Photograph by Jimmy Wilson. Printed with permission.
Page 55 Photograph by Charlie Preston. Printed with permission.
Page 61 Photograph by Lester Kierstead Henderson. Printed with permission.
Page 65 Photograph by Ed Dixon. Printed with permission.
Page 66 Courtesy of Ed Dixon. Allis-Chalmers photograph printed with permission.
Page 76 Photograph by Lester Kierstead Henderson. Printed with permission.
Page 91 Photograph by Billy Brown. Printed with permission.
Page 95 Photograph by George C. Schaeffer, Schaeffer Studio. Printed with permission.
Page 96 Photograph by Curtis Frizzell. Printed with permission.
Page 99 Photographs by Bruce Davidson, Magnum Photos. Printed with permission.
Page 104 Photograph by Ron Council. Printed with permission.
Page 105 Photographs by Charles Beck. Printed with permission.
Page 106 Photograph by Charles Beck. Printed with permission.
Page 108 Courtesy of Ed Dixon and Cypress Amax Minerals Company. Printed with permission.
Page 112 (lower) Photograph by Lewis Arnold, Samford University. Printed with permission.
Page 113 March 31, 1974. © Photo by the *Birmingham News*, 1998. All rights reserved. Reprinted with permission.
Page 116 Photograph by Charles Beck. Printed with permission.
Page 123 Courtesy of Auburn University. Printed with permission.
Page 124 Courtesy of Birmingham-Southern College. Printed with permission.
Page 125 (top) Courtesy of Birmingham-Southern College. Printed with permission.
(bottom) Courtesy of the University of Montevallo. Printed with permission.
Page 133 Photograph by Bruce Davidson, Magnum Photos. Printed with permission.
Page 151 Photograph by Larry Moon. Printed with permission.
Page 160 Photographs by Dicki Boykin Arn. Printed with permission.
Page 161 (top) Photograph by Dicki Boykin Arn. Printed with permission.
(bottom left) Photograph by Ernest Rawlins, Rawlins Photography. Printed with permission.
(bottom right) Photograph by Dicki Boykin Arn. Printed with permission.
Page 164 Photograph by Hugh Hunter. © Printed with permission.
Page 169 Courtesy of Lady Eugenie Nickerson. Photograph by John Winter. Printed with permission.
Page 172 Courtesy of Miles Pollard.
Page 178 Photograph by M. Lewis Kennedy, Jr., Kennedy Studios. All rights reserved. © Printed with permission.
Page 181 Photograph by Crosby Thomley. Printed with permission.
Page 198 Photograph by M. Lewis Kennedy, Jr., Kennedy Studios. All rights reserved. © Printed with permission.
Page 200 Courtesy of CAMS (the Center for Advanced Medical Studies), the University of Alabama in Birmingham. Printed with permission.
Page 201 Photograph by Heritage Photographers, Albany, Georgia. Printed with permission.
Page 204 Photograph by T. McCrea, © Smithsonian Institution. #97-25052/36. Printed with permission.

All other photographs are courtesy of The Harbert Corporation Archives, Marguerite Jones Harbert, or the Harbert family.

John M. Harbert III

Marching to the Beat of a Different Drummer

DESIGN AND PRODUCTION
Bob and Faith Nance
Auburn, Alabama

TYPEFACES
Palatino and Centaur

BINDING MATERIALS
Odyssey and Rainbow
Ecological Fibers

PRINTING PAPER
Meade Moistrite Matte

PRINTING AND BINDING
Walsworth Publishing Company